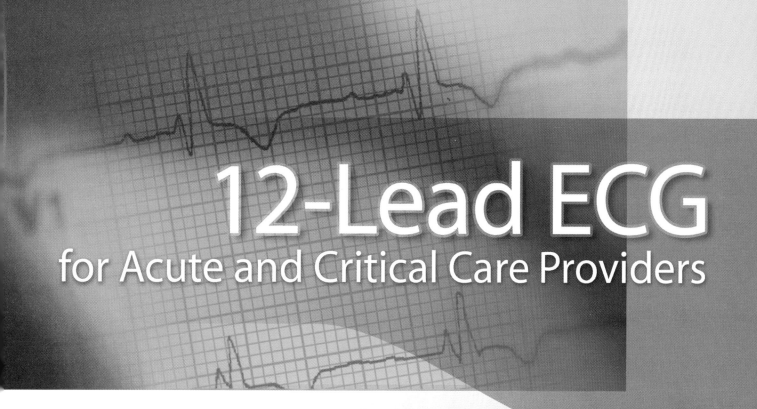

12-Lead ECG
for Acute and Critical Care Providers

Bob Page
AAS, NREMT-P, CCEMT-P, I/C

PEARSON

Prentice
Hall

Upper Saddle River, NJ 07458

Library of Congress Cataloging-in-Publication Data

Page, Robert, (date)
  12-lead ECG for acute and critical care providers / Robert Page.
    p. ; cm.
  Includes index.
  ISBN 0-13-022460-X
  1. Electrocardiography.
    [DNLM: 1. Electrocardiography--methods. 2. Critical Care. 3. Heart
  Diseases--diagnosis. WG 140 P133z 2005] I. Title: Twelve-lead ECG for
  acute and critical care providers. II. Title.

  RC683.5.E5P265 2005
  616.1'207547--dc22   2004025876

Publisher: Julie Levin Alexander
Publisher's Assistant: Regina Bruno
Executive Editor: Marlene McHugh Pratt
Senior Managing Editor for Development: Lois Berlowitz
Project Manager: Josephine Cepeda
Editorial Assistant: Matthew Sirinides
Director of Marketing: Karen Allman
Senior Marketing Manager: Katrin Beacom
Channel Marketing Manager: Rachele Strober
Marketing Coordinator: Michael Sirinides
Director, Image Resource Center: Melinda Reo
Manager, Rights and Permissions: Zina Arabia
Manager, Visual Research: Beth Brenzel
Manager, Cover Visual Research & Permissions: Karen Sanatar
Image Permission Coordinator: Fran Toepfer
Director of Production and Manufacturing: Bruce Johnson
Managing Editor for Production: Patrick Walsh
Production Liaison: Faye Gemmellaro
Production Editor: Mark Corsey/nSight, Inc.
Manufacturing Manager: Ilene Sanford
Manufacturing Buyer: Pat Brown
Creative Director: Cheryl Asherman
Senior Design Coordinator: Christopher Weigand
Composition and Interior Design: Laserwords
Cover Design: Solid State Graphics
Printing and Binding: Banta Menasha
Cover Printer: Phoenix Color

Pearson Education Ltd.
Pearson Education Singapore, Pte. Ltd.
Pearson Education Canada, Ltd.
Pearson Education—Japan
Pearson Education Australia Pty., Limited
Pearson Education North Asia Ltd.
Pearson Educación de Mexico, S.A. de C.V.
Pearson Education Malaysia, Pte. Ltd.
Pearson Education Upper Saddle River, NJ

Notice: The author and the publisher of this book have taken care to make certain that the information given is correct and compatible with the standards generally accepted at the time of publication. Nevertheless, as new information becomes available, changes in treatment and in the use of equipment and procedures become necessary. The reader is advised to carefully consult the instruction and information material included in each piece of equipment or device before administration. Students are warned that the use of any techniques must be authorized by their medical advisor, where appropriate, in accordance with local laws and regulations. The publisher disclaims any liability, loss, injury, or damage incurred as a consequence, directly or indirectly, of the use and application of any of the contents of this book.

Studentaid.ed.gov, the U.S. Department of Education's website on college planning assistance, is a valuable tool for anyone intending to pursue higher education. Designed to help students at all stages of schooling, including international students, returning students, and parents, it is a guide to the financial aid process. The website presents information on applying to and attending college as well as on funding your education and repaying loans. It also provides links to useful resources, such as state education agency contact information, assistance in filling out financial aid forms, and an introduction to various forms of student aid.

10 9 8 7 6 5 4 3 2

0-13-022460-X

Dedication

I would like to dedicate this book to the memory of my mother, Mary Francis Page, RN. She was a caring and compassionate nurse and instructor and a hard worker. She raised our family as a single mom after my father died of heart disease when I was only seven years old. Perhaps it was destiny that I became so interested in cardiology. Although she never pushed me to go into the medical field, she encouraged me to be what I wanted to be and supported my decisions unconditionally. Although she is not here to see this book released, I hope she is smiling with pride from Heaven.

I would also like to dedicate this book to the thousands of participants worldwide of my Multi-Lead Medics™ 12-Lead ECG Interpretation Workshops. It is because of your dedication and inspiration that I have written this book. May it help you in your field of practice always and help you make a difference in the life and lifestyle of others. Remember, in Lead II, You Got No Clue!

R.P.

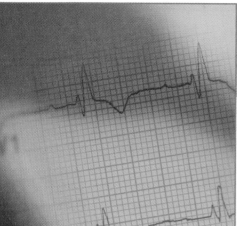

Contents

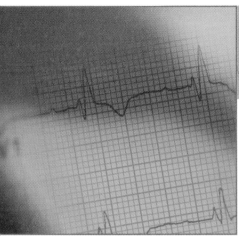
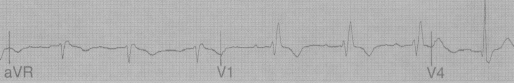

Preface

It doesn't have to be difficult. I have always believed in the ability of people. When I began my career in acute medicine, "upper-level" knowledge always had a mystique. Medicine is cluttered with paradigms on how things should always be done. I can recall boundaries to learning. Skills were assigned to the level of licensure. For example, a paramedic could do this, a registered nurse could do that, and only the doctor could perform certain procedures and tasks. Reading the 12-lead ECG was one of those things reserved for the doctor.

I recall sitting in on a few classes with physicians and some experienced cardiac care nurses to learn this advanced knowledge. Armed with an above-average skill at recognizing basic cardiac rhythms, I set out to learn. It was after the first slide that I learned that I was in way over my head. Sure, I could recognize a P wave, but I could not spell or pronounce some of the information. One thing I did remember, however, was ST segment elevation. I saw a picture of that on the first slide. For the next 7 hours and 55 minutes, I did not understand why all the technical measuring and laborious tasks required for recognizing this elevation were necessary.

I remember an occasion when my paramedic instructor pointed out ST segment elevation on a Lead II rhythm strip. It really didn't faze me because, on the basis of the patient's history and complaint and the current assessment findings, I was convinced that it was a heart attack, even without the ECG. The ECG monitor was there to help me look for ectopic beats and arrhythmias.

After the class, I started to ask questions and pose analogies to the emergency physicians and cardiologists who had presented the seminars. I have spent many hours in seminars and in reading almost every book I can find on the subject of 12-lead ECGs and have found that it really doesn't have to be difficult. It's all in how you learn it.

One analogy I use in my seminars is that of the German chocolate cake. My sister Janie made a wonderful German chocolate cake. She made it from scratch, gathering all the ingredients and even grating the coconut and pecans for the icing. It took a long time, but it was a great cake. Now, people can buy German chocolate cake mix in a store and just add water and spread the frosting. The two cakes taste the same, look the same—they *are* the same. As with the German chocolate cake, I realize that there are many different ways to read a 12-lead ECG. This book presents the "just-add-water" type.

Life is about change. Human beings are not programmed to stay the same. This book is based on the Multi-Lead Medics™ 12-Lead ECG Interpretation Workshops I have presented to thousands of paramedics, nurses, respiratory therapists, doctors, and other acute-care providers.

This book recognizes the roots and pathophysiology of more complex methods of electrocardiography. Many books are available on 12-lead ECG interpretation. However, this book is greatly simplified for the acute-care provider. It is simplified without compromising accuracy. All examples and 12-lead ECGs used in this book have been over-read by cardiologists for accuracy. Compared with more traditional methods of interpretation, these methods have demonstrated comparable accuracy and increased speed of diagnosis.

For simplicity, only the rapid methods of recognition are presented. Therefore, this book is comprehensive in topics, yet it is focused on a few easy-to-use methods for practical acute-care use. The book provides plenty of examples for you to practice your skills. I believe in the ability of the acute-care provider. This book is for you. Happy learning, and remember, it doesn't have to be difficult.

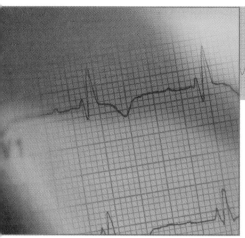

Acknowledgments

I would like to thank the outstanding men and women of the St. John's EMS of St. John's Regional Health System in Missouri. Since 1993, your cooperation and the courage you have shown in trying something new have made my job as your educator the most wonderful and fulfilling job I have ever had in my life. I am proud to wear the uniform with you.

In the same breath, I want to thank the St. John's EMS administrators past and present (Chip Woyner, Steve Bassett, Bob Patterson, and Chuck Wollard) for their support of my speaking endeavors and allowing me the time off for the scores of seminars I present annually.

I also want to thank Dr. Phillip Carr, retired cardiologist at St. John's, and Dr. Janet Jordan, Medical Director of St. John's EMS, for their support and encouragement of my 12-lead programs and for the vision, leadership, and trust that have made our EMS what it is today.

I would like to acknowledge the efforts of the cardiovascular services at St. John's Regional Health Center in Springfield, Missouri, for saving thousands of 12-lead ECGs for me to read. I also thank the many acute-care providers from across the country who have sent material for use in this book.

I want to recognize the efforts of Mike Taigman, an early mentor who sparked my interest in ECGs. I also want to thank Dr. H.J.L. Marriott for his lifelong work in the field of electrocardiography and for believing in his students' abilities. Thanks also for their contributions and outstanding publications on the subject. These two men have inspired my "call to arms" to present this information whenever I can.

I want to recognize and thank the University of Maryland, Baltimore County, for allowing me to present this material as part of the CCEMTP course.

I also want to thank the staff at Brady/Prentice Hall: in particular, Judy Streger and Katrin Beacom for their help in this project and Marlene Pratt for encouraging my progress. Additionally, I want to thank Jo Cepeda for her positive attitude and helpful suggestions in seeing the project through. I couldn't have done it without you. And to the reviewers of this project, thank you for your kind, and unkind, comments. They all helped to make this book possible.

Finally, I want to express my love, admiration, and devotion to my soul mate and beautiful wife, Angela. I thank you for your countless hours of help and understanding during the long nights at home and when I was away from home on seminars. Words cannot express my appreciation for the love and encouragement you give to me. I also want to thank my three children, Robert Baden Page, Ashley Ann Page, and Aaron Michael Page, for bearing with me while I was working. I love you all.

REVIEWERS

I wish to thank the following reviewers for providing invaluable feedback and suggestions during the development of this text.

Leigh Ann Bedrich, BFA, LP
Assistant Professor, Health Sciences
Tarrant County College
Hurst, TX

Carl S. Cramer
Program Director
Our Lady of the Lake College—EMS Department
Baton Rouge, LA

Merlin Curry, EMT-P
Clackamas Community College
Oregon City, OR

Tom Ezell, NREMT-P
Captain
James City County Fire Department
Yorktown, VA

Scott Garrett
Director of Education
Upstate EMS Council
Greenville, SC

Jeff Gould
Paramedic, Retired. Educator
Long Beach, CA

Dr. Craig Jacobus
Lifelink Medical Center
Orland Park, IL

Diana J. Jansen, RN, CCRN
Paramedic Instructor
University of Wisconsin Hospital & Clinics
Madison, WI

Chad E. Jarvis, NREMT-P, CCEMT-P
Randolph Community College, Ashboro, NC

Jeff Jarvis, MS, EMT-P
Department Chair, EMS Technology
Temple College
Temple, TX

Deborah J. McCoy, RN, NREMT-P
Regional EMS Coordinator
Altru Health System
Grand Forks, ND

Scott Phelps, JD, MPH, NREMT-P
Assistant Professor of Emergency Medicine
The George Washington University
Washington, DC

William S. Proctor, NREMT-P, CCEMT-P
Advisory Committee
School of EMS
Cleveland Clinic Health Systems
Euclid, OH

John A. Rasmussen
Greenville County EMS
Greenville, SC

Mark Register, EMT-PI
Warrenville, SC

Valarie Rumbley, RN, BSN, CEN, EMT-P
Springhill Medical Center
Mobile, AL

Shannon Stevens, NREMT-P, CCEMT-P
Department of Emergency Medicine/EMS Education
University of Alabama at Birmingham
Birmingham, AL

Beth L. Torres, RN, BSN
Chippenham Medical Center/Johnston-Willis
    Hospital,
Richmond, VA
Education Coordinator
Medical & Wellness Services, Inc.
Consultant/Education Coordinator
Midlothian, VA

Jim Williams
Training Officer
Medical Center EMS
Bowling Green, KY

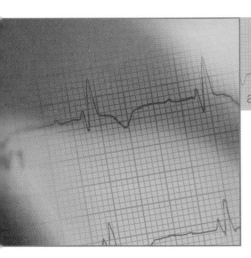

About the Author

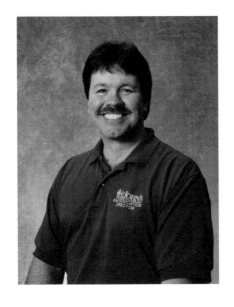

Multi-Lead Medics™ is the trademarked 12-Lead ECG interpretation workshop developed by **Bob Page, AAS, NREMT-P, CCEMT-P, I/C.** His mission is to develop and present high-quality, innovative, informative, and entertaining educational programs for personnel involved in the emergency and critical care of patients.

Bob Page is an internationally known speaker, instructor, author, and paramedic. He has presented seminars across the United States, Canada, and in Europe. He is recognized for his energetic, humorous, and motivational style. Bob takes ordinarily dry and hard-to-teach topics and transforms them into a fun, learning experience. Bob calls it "Edutainment."

Bob's presentations are accompanied by exciting AV support from the PowerPoint® and Keynote programs with graphics, animation, audio, and video clips. Bob has authored dozens of articles on cardiology and other emergency and critical care topics and more recently has developed the cardiology section of the Critical Care Emergency Medical Transport Course from the University of Maryland, Baltimore County.

Bob has been an instructor since 1975, teaching a variety of adult education courses from customer service to advanced medical care. He has an Associate degree in Paramedical Technology from Southwest Baptist University. He is a nationally registered and critical care paramedic. He has been involved in EMS since 1978, when he became a CPR instructor. Bob is Director of Emergency Care Education at St. John's Regional Health Center in Springfield, Missouri. He is the lead instructor for the paramedic program and has taught at all levels of EMS and nursing. He has earned an adjunct faculty appointment at the University of Maryland, Baltimore County, and is also a guest instructor at Southwest Baptist University's College of Nursing.

chapter 1

Lead Placement and Acquisition of the 12-Lead Electrocardiogram

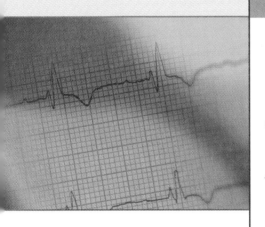

objectives

After reading this chapter, you should be able to:

1. Differentiate bipolar and unipolar limb leads, and precordial leads.

2. Describe the lead placement for a 12-lead electrocardiogram.

3. Describe the procedure for 12-lead ECG acquisition.

4. Describe the procedure for multi-lead ECG acquisition using a 3-lead bipolar machine.

INTRODUCTION

Electrocardiogram (ECG) monitors were first used in coronary care units to monitor patients for arrhythmias. But some nurses soon found that even when the **electrodes** were correctly placed, patients who were brushing their teeth or moving their arms and legs developed artifact resembling ventricular arrhythmias (namely, ventricular fibrillation, or VF). To eliminate this problem, the nurses experimented by moving the leads from the arms onto the chest.

The result was dramatic: a marked reduction in artifact caused by patient movement. The accuracy of monitoring for ventricular fibrillation (VF), or asystole, did not change. Thus, the nurses discovered that for simple monitoring or looking for change, placement of the limb lead was irrelevant. Electrodes on the chest quickly became the enduring paradigm for lead placement.

Correct lead placement is important for ECG interpretation and for diagnosis. This chapter focuses on proper lead placement for a 12-lead electrocardiogram, which provides a "surface map" of the body.

ELECTRODES

The **12-lead ECG** uses 10 electrodes. On most ECG machines, the lead designation is on the electrode wire. The electrodes are of two types: limb and precordial.

LIMB LEAD ELECTRODES

The four limb lead electrodes have letter codes that designate their placement:

- RA—designates the right arm.
- LA—designates the left arm.
- LL—designates the left leg.
- RL—designates the right leg.

Some 3-lead monitors also use color coding, as follows:

- White—designates the right arm.
- Black—designates the left arm.
- Red—designates the left leg.
- Green—designates the right leg, if a fourth electrode wire is available.

In addition, providers may use mnemonics (memory aids) such as these:

- White to right, and red to bed.
- Salt, pepper, and catsup.
- Smoke over fire (black and white over red).

Limb leads are designed to go on the arms and legs for accurate diagnosis of axis deviation and myocardial infarction (MI) location. Upper or lower limb placement is patient dependent; that is, the upper limb shows less artifact than lower in some. However, the leads can be placed on the chest for other purposes. In other words, determining whether to place limb leads on the limbs or on the chest depends on the purpose of the ECG. For example, a physician looking for the presence rather than the site of ischemic changes during a stress test will put the limb leads on the chest. For a patient who is

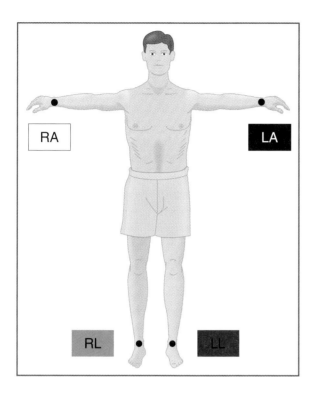

Figure 1–1. Placement of the four standard limb leads.

awake and swinging his arms, the artifact would be unacceptable and would render almost half of the 12 leads unreadable. But if the purpose of the ECG is diagnostic for all conditions and complications, all the leads need to be placed and the patient asked to remain still for a few seconds while the ECG is being acquired. The designated positions for the limb leads are shown in Figure 1–1.

BIPOLAR LIMB LEADS

Limb leads are either bipolar or unipolar. **Bipolar limb leads** are identified by the Roman numerals I, II, and III. Each bipolar lead uses both a positive and a negative electrode. Because an ECG machine is unable to pick up and accurately read the voltage from a single positive electrode, a small unreadable QRS complex results. Therefore, the negative electrode is used to enhance the voltage. The negative electrode also provides a reference point for the positive electrode. That is, the positive electrode "sees" where this point intersects the heart. Leads I, II, and III and their respective views of the heart comprise Einthoven's triangle (Figure 1–2) and are used to determine axis deviation, discussed in a later chapter.

- With the positive electrode on the left arm and the negative electrode on the right arm, Lead I provides a view of the left side of the heart, looking toward the right.
- With the positive electrode on the left leg and the negative electrode on the right arm, Lead II provides a view of the bottom (inferior aspect) of the heart, looking toward the right arm.
- With the positive electrode on the left leg and the negative electrode on the left arm, Lead III provides another inferior aspect of the heart, looking toward the left arm.

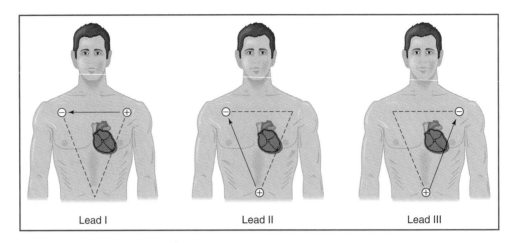

Figure 1–2. Leads I, II, and III form Einthoven's triangle.

UNIPOLAR LIMB LEADS

The **unipolar limb leads** are identified by three letters. The first two are aV (augmented voltage). The third letter—R (right arm), L (left arm), or F (left leg)—refers to the lead placement of the positive electrode. The unipolar limb leads, like the bipolar leads, must be augmented. Augmentation is achieved by taking an average of the other three leads that are not positive. The result places a point—the center terminal (CT)—in the center (Figure 1–3).

The positive electrodes look at the CT, which is their reference point. The **aV leads** are so called because they use an average rather than a single identifiable negative lead. They are unipolar in that only the positive electrode is identified.

PRECORDIAL LEAD ELECTRODES

The **precordial lead electrodes** are the second type of electrode and true chest leads. The six precordial, or voltage, leads are designated V1 through V6. Each precordial lead has a specified location. Thus, for every individual, each precordial lead is in the same relative position (Figure 1–4).

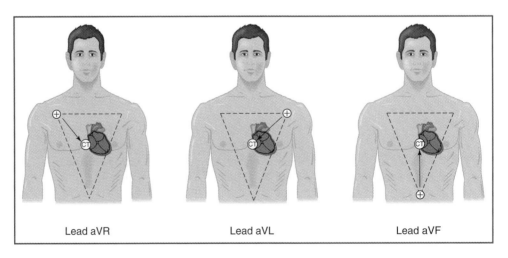

Figure 1–3. The augmented-voltage leads and the center terminal point.

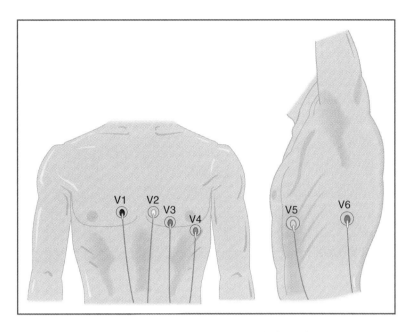

Figure 1–4. The six precordial leads.

Precordial leads are unipolar, using only one positive electrode. Because these leads are so close to the heart, no voltage augmentation is necessary (Figure 1–5).

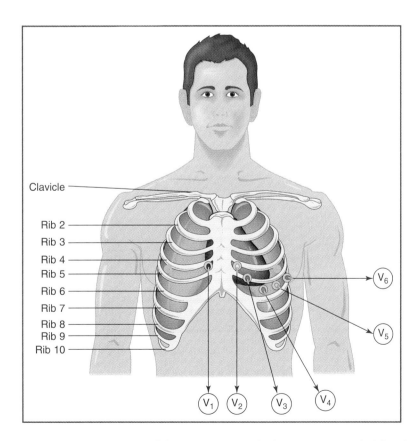

Figure 1–5. Schematic of the six horizontal-plane, or precordial, leads.

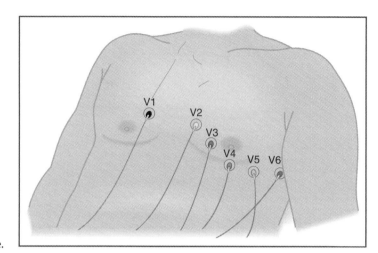

Figure 1–6. Leads V4, V5, and V6 correctly placed in a straight line.

- V1 and V2 are placed in the fourth intercostal space (ICS) just to the right and left, respectively, of the sternum. This location can be found by counting the ribs from the clavicle. The first rib felt below is rib 2, then rib 3, followed by rib 4. Between ribs 4 and 5 is the fourth intercostal space. Another method of finding the fourth intercostal space is to locate the angle of Louis at the bottom of the manubrium, where the corresponding rib is rib 2. On most adult male patients, this space is at or just above the nipple; rarely is this interspace below the nipple line. Note that the **septum** of the heart lies in this area and so is examined by Leads V1 and V2.
- V3 is placed between V2 and V4, either on the fifth rib or in the fifth interspace.
- V4 is usually next. It is in the fifth intercostal space in the midclavicular line. This easy-to-find landmark is about halfway down the clavicle, between the sternum and the shoulder, just below the nipple. You may have to lift a woman's breast for placement.
- V5 is positioned in the fifth intercostal space at the anterior axillary line. This line can be found by placing the patient's arm by his side and following the crease line from the armpit, down the front of the patient's chest. Lead V5 is positioned where this line intersects the fifth interspace.
- V6 is placed at the fifth interspace mid-axillary line.

Note that because they are positioned over the front (anterior) of the left ventricle, Leads V3 and V4 are commonly referred to as the **anterior leads**. Leads V5 and V6 look at the heart from the lower aspect of the left side and so are known as **lateral leads**. By contrast, Leads I and aVL, with the positive electrode on the left arm, look at the upper lateral wall of the left ventricle. Leads V4, V5, and V6, correctly placed, are all in a straight line in the fifth intercostal space (Figure 1–6).

ACQUIRING THE ELECTROCARDIOGRAM

POSITIONING AND PREPARING THE PATIENT

Ideally, the patient should be lying down (supine). Often, however, this is not possible. A patient with acute onset of chest pain, for example, may not feel comfortable lying down. Therefore, the Fowler's position (sitting up) is generally used for acute patients.

For male patients, another aspect of preparation involves possibly clipping or shaving the chest hair so that the electrodes will stick to the skin. For both men and women, it is also helpful to prep the skin by lightly abrading the area where the electrodes will be placed with skin-prep tape. Doing so removes some of the dead epidermal cells, thus facilitating better electrode contact and adhesion.

Finally, it is important to dry diaphoretic (sweaty) skin. Some providers use skin-prep solutions to aid in drying the skin.

USING A 12-LEAD MONITOR

The 12-lead ECG is a standard assessment tool in the hospital setting and is becoming increasingly important to the overall care of cardiac patients. In out-of-hospital settings, the ECG has been used mainly in focusing on life-threatening arrythmics and for supportive care. Recently, however, the focus has shifted to the early recognition and treatment of cardiac conditions.

On most 12-lead machines, acquiring the ECG is as simple as pushing a button. Many machines allow the clinician to enter other data to be printed out, such as the patient's age, which may be relevant as a criterion for machine analysis. Of course, such information, along with the patient's name, must be entered before printing the ECG.

To ensure a clean tracing, the patient needs to remain still for about 10 seconds before the button is pushed to print the ECG, as many machines continue to monitor during those last seconds. In some cases, the machine may return a "Waiting for Good Data" message. If so, the machine will wait until it can get 10 seconds of reasonably good data. This feature can be overridden on some machines, printing whatever data is being obtained. The override feature will disengage the machine analysis and print an "ECG Override" message.

Sometimes, the ECG complexes are so large as to be unprintable and so are abbreviated, or cut off. In hospitals, many ECG machines allow the operator to cut the size by half to allow for morphology interpretation. In such cases, the machine will print a message, such as "1/2 Standard Voltage," to alert the reader to the fact that the voltage has been altered. Doing so affects the size of the ST segment elevation or hypertrophy measurements.

USING A STANDARD 3-LEAD MONITOR

Before the advent of 12-lead machines, physicians acquired ECGs simply by moving the electrodes to various positions on the heart, using the positive electrode to see the various locations. Advances in technology have made the need to move electrodes unnecessary. However, the concept still applies. Because not all hospital services have 12-lead capabilities or because they use 3-lead monitors for backup, the old ways can be adapted to obtain a multi-lead ECG.

Lead II monitoring alone is inadequate. For example, common anti-arrhythmic drugs are contraindicated in severe degrees of intraventricular block. But Lead II alone would show only a normal sinus rhythm. In short, the complete information provided by a 12-lead ECG is needed.

The 3-lead ECG monitor can be adapted to provide multi-lead quality information. The following procedure uses only nine electrode pads, as the RL lead is omitted:

1. Place the electrodes in the same locations as for the 12-lead process.
2. Turn on the machine, select Lead I, and print a 6-second strip of the reading.
3. Switch the machine to Lead II and record the reading.
4. Switch the machine to Lead III, using the lead-select switch, and record the reading.

These four steps provide three of the six limb leads. Although the three augmented leads cannot be performed on a standard 3-lead machine, Leads II and III cover the area seen by aVF, and Lead I corresponds to Lead aVL. Lead aVR has very limited benefit.

When acquired with a 3-lead monitor, the precordial voltage leads are called **modified chest left (MCL)** leads. The modification refers to the fact that a bipolar machine is being used to record standard unipolar leads. The negative electrode is placed on the left arm. With this modification, the 3-lead monitor MCL leads and the 12-lead monitor V leads see the same view. Thus, MCL-1 is equivalent to V1; MCL-2 is equivalent to V2, and so on.

The next two steps continue the procedure, running the precordial MCL leads. With the machine's lead-select switch still in Lead III:

5. Move the red electrode wire—or the LL lead—up to the V1 position (to the fourth intercostal space, to the right of the sternum) and record the tracing.
6. Move the electrode to positions V2, V3, V4, V5, and V6, in order, recording a tracing at each position.

When you complete this six-step process, you will have a 9-lead ECG: Leads I, II, III and MCL-1, MCL-2, MCL-3, MCL-4, MCL-5, and MCL-6. The resulting ECG provides almost all the information available on a standard 12-lead ECG, including the ability to diagnose dangerous conditions that cannot be diagnosed using Lead II alone.

To make the 9-lead strips easier to read and compare to 12-leads, the leads should be mounted in a manner consistent with the sequence of a 12-lead machine (Figure 1–7). This process can be summarized as follows:

1. Record Leads I, II, and III, using the lead-select switch on the ECG monitor.
2. Leave the monitor lead-select switch set to Lead III.
3. Detach the LL (red) electrode wire from the left leg, place the electrode on the V1 electrode position, and record the tracing.

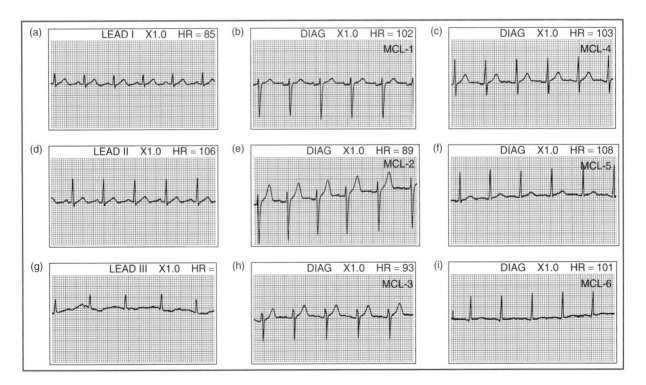

Figure 1–7. Out-of-hospital 9-lead ECG.

4. Move the LL electrode to the remaining five positions, recording the tracing at each position.
5. Trim the resulting strip to a three-second strip, labeling and mounting it as in Figure 1–7.
6. Return the LL electrode wire to the V1/MCL-1 position for monitoring.

With some 3-lead monitors, the operator can reset the machine's frequency response. Increasing the frequency response—the diagnostic quality—enables the machine to more accurately pick up subtle changes in the ECG, such as minimal ST segment elevation and pacer spikes.

However, 3-lead monitors also have filters limiting the frequency response, so as to enhance a clear, noise-free ECG for monitoring the patient. Thus, monitor quality can result in less accurate assessment of the ST segment. Indeed, when operating in monitor-quality mode, the machine tends to exaggerate ST segment elevation, especially in the precordial leads. No elevation may in fact exist (Figure 1–8). Note, however, that in instances of obvious elevation, the monitor-quality mode, too, may pick it up.

Monitor-quality mode has no effect on all other aspects of the ECG, including diagnosing axis deviation and heart chamber enlargement, determining bundle-branch blocks, and interpreting arrhythmias. In short, the multi-lead ECG does have diagnostic quality and should be used to record the ECG. The machine manufacturer or your biomedical department can provide more information.

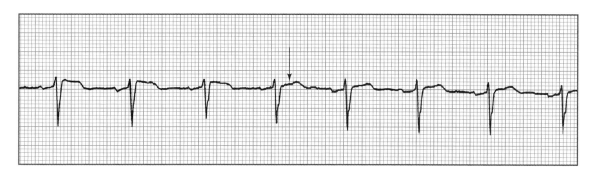

Figure 1–8. Exaggeration of ST segment elevation in monitor-quality mode.

SUMMARY

Lead placement generally depends on the purpose of the ECG. If the patient is being monitored only for general information, such as ventricular fibrillation or asystole changes, lead placement is irrelevant. But proper lead placement is imperative when the ECG is being used to gain maximal information about the patient's condition.

Following are the key points of this chapter:

- The 12-lead ECG uses 10 electrodes: one on each limb and six on the chest.
- Limb leads should be placed on the arms and legs.
- Precordial leads are placed in specified positions on the chest.
- A multi-lead ECG uses only nine electrode pads.
- A multi-lead ECG can be run by using a standard 3-lead monitor, moving the LL electrode to each of the precordial lead placement positions.

- Precordial leads acquired with a 3-lead monitor are called modified chest left (MCL) leads.
- MCL leads provide the same view as 12-lead V leads.
- An increased frequency response is more accurate in assessing the ST segment but is not necessary for assessing various other conditions.

GLOSSARY

12-lead ECG a standard assessment tool that uses 10 electrodes—one on each limb and six on the chest.

anterior leads Leads V3 and V4, which are positioned over the front (anterior) of the left ventricle.

aV leads augmented voltage leads; they use an average rather than a single identifiable negative lead.

bipolar limb leads Leads I, II, and III.

electrocardiogram (ECG) graphic representation of the electrical activity of the heart.

electrode an adhesive pad that contains conductive gel and is designed to be attached to the patient's skin.

lateral leads Leads V5, V6, I, and aVL, which look at the heart from the lower and upper aspect of the left side.

leads electrodes connected to the monitor or ECG machine by wires, which relay the electrical impulse from the generator to the myocardium.

modified chest left (MCL) precordial voltage leads, when acquired with a 3- or 4-lead monitor.

precordial lead electrodes the six precordial or voltage leads, which are designated V1 through V6; second type of electrode and true chest leads.

septum a dividing wall or membrane, especially between bodily spaces or masses of soft tissue. The septum of the heart is examined by Leads V1 and V2.

unipolar limb leads Leads aVR, aVL, and aVF.

chapter 2

Understanding the 12-Lead ECG Printout

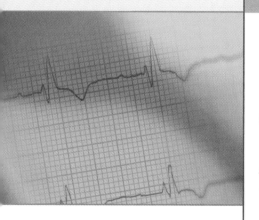

objectives

After reading this chapter, you should be able to:

1. Locate bipolar and unipolar limb leads and precordial limb leads on a 12-lead ECG printout.

2. Find information about PR, QRS, and QT intervals; heart rate; and axis angles on the printout.

3. Discuss the benefits and limitations of machine analysis.

4. Explain how to use R wave progression and Lead I negativity to check lead placement in precordial and limb leads.

5. Convert measurement readings from seconds to milliseconds.

6. Describe the measurement relating to vertical deflections in millivolts.

7. Locate the isoelectric line, using the calibration spike as a reference.

INTRODUCTION

A 12-lead ECG contains a great deal of information. In order to maximize use of one, the acute-care provider needs to understand what the printout is showing.

FORMAT OF THE 12-LEAD ECG PRINTOUT

Most hospital-based 12-lead machines print out on an 8-1/2" x 11" sheet of paper, showing six rows of ECG data (Figure 2–1). The top three rows represent the 12-ECG leads. The lower three rows are the recorded rhythm strips in three leads: a limb lead and two precordial leads showing different ends of the heart. In Figure 2–1, the lower three rows show data for Lead II, along with data for V2 and V5. Alternatively, data for Leads V1 and V6 could have been given. Data from the lower three rows offer the best view of the heart to aid in rhythm interpretation and ectopy.

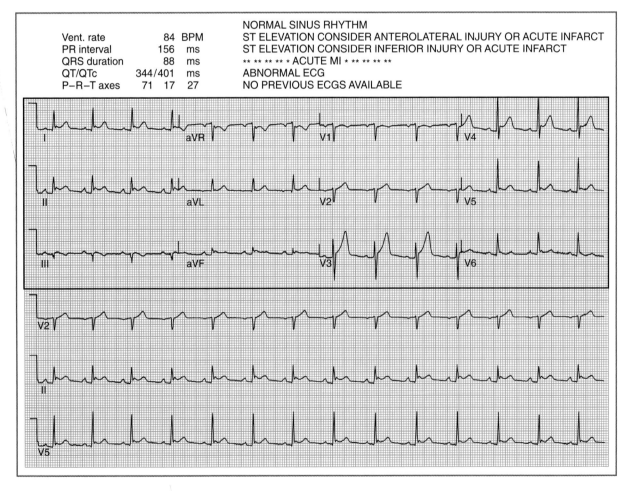

Figure 2–1. Sample hospital-based ECG printout.

Out-of-hospital ECG machines provide printouts of various methods and printout sizes. Most out-of-hospital printouts are on smaller paper—90 mm or 100 mm—and show only the top three rows of the 12-lead ECG data (Figure 2–2). These rows are divided into four columns:

- Column 1 shows data for Leads I, II, and III, which are the bipolar limb leads.
- Column 2 shows data for Leads aVR, aVL, and aVF, which are the unipolar augmented limb leads.
- Column 3 contains data for Leads V1, V2, and V3.
- Column 4 contains data for Leads V4, V5, and V6.

Some machines acquire the electrocardiogram sequentially; that is, one channel, or one column, at a time. Thus, for example, all the leads in channel 1—Leads I, II, and III—are acquired for 2.5 seconds. Next, all the leads in channel 2—Leads aVR, aVL, and aVF—are acquired for 2.5 seconds, and so on. In contrast, other machines acquire the data for all leads simultaneously (Figure 2–3).

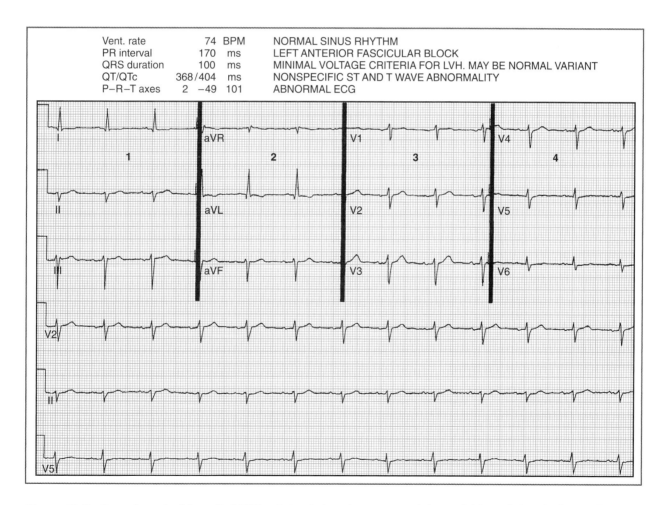

Figure 2–2. Sample out-of-hospital ECG printout showing sequential acquisition of data in four columns.

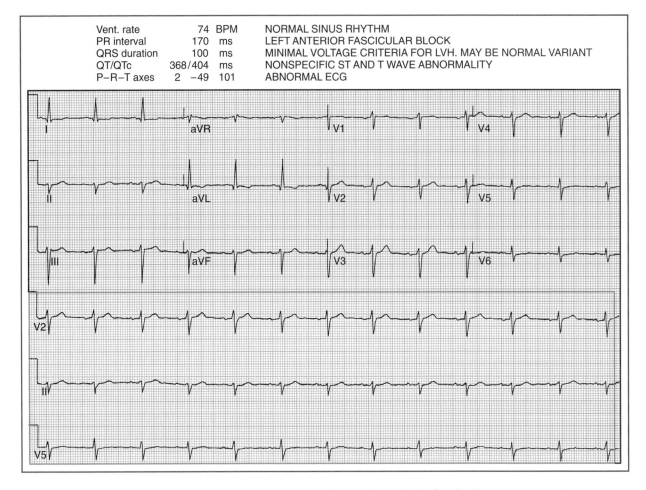

Vent. rate	74 BPM	NORMAL SINUS RHYTHM
PR interval	170 ms	LEFT ANTERIOR FASCICULAR BLOCK
QRS duration	100 ms	MINIMAL VOLTAGE CRITERIA FOR LVH. MAY BE NORMAL VARIANT
QT/QTc	368/404 ms	NONSPECIFIC ST AND T WAVE ABNORMALITY
P–R–T axes	2 –49 101	ABNORMAL ECG

Figure 2–3. Continuous simultaneous recording at three leads for rhythm interpretation.

CONTENT OF ECG MACHINE ANALYSIS

The ECG machine provides data on intervals, voltage, and axis angle. A computer-generated analysis is based on a logical algorithm that relies solely on numbers and other measurements.

INTERVALS

The ECG machine accurately measures heart rate, PR interval, **QRS duration**, and **QT interval**. All these measurements relate to time, the horizontal measurement on the ECG. The machine can also provide the QT interval, which is used in determining certain drug and electrolyte imbalances and other conditions of delayed repolarization. These conditions are discussed later in this text.

VOLTAGE

The ECG machine also provides information on the height, or vertical measurements of P, QRS, and T waves (Figure 2–4). These measurements are sensed as voltage. Some

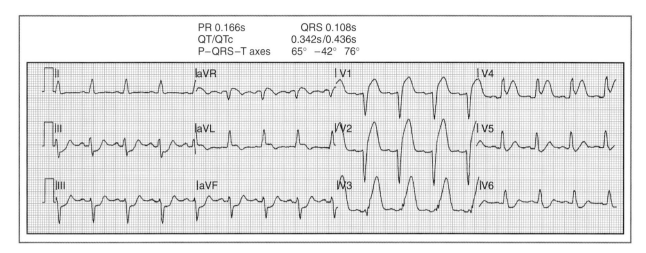

PR 0.166s   QRS 0.108s
QT/QTc   0.342s/0.436s
P–QRS–T axes   65° −42° 76°

Figure 2–4. Information on P waves, QRS complex, and T waves.

clinicians refer to this measure as the **QRS-size measurement**, which is useful in determining such conditions as the presence of an enlarged heart, ST segment elevation, or pulmonary conditions stemming from the lack of voltage.

The voltage changes associated with the waves make the interval measurements accurate. These measurements may be more accurate than the machine-drawn lines, which may be thick and therefore add to the measurement or make it difficult to determine the precise point to measure to or from. In short, the lead measurements may be misleading, unlike the interval measurements. Because they are based on voltage readings, the interval measurements are accurate and should be used as an aid to determine whether any abnormal conditions exist or not.

AXIS ANGLE

The ECG machine can also measure the electrical axis of the heart. These measurements include the axis of the **P wave**, the axis of the **QRS complex**, and the axis of the **T wave**. Each of these measurements has certain normal parameters. The QRS axis is discussed at length in a later chapter. The axis measurements are very accurate and should be used in conjunction with a chart or a guide to help the clinician rapidly determine any possible deviation.

The machines generally list three numbers in a row after the heading of P-R-T axes:

• Angle of the P wave axis.
• Angle of the QRS axis.
• Angle of the T wave axis.

In some circumstances, an axis may have a negative number.

UNITS OF MEASURE

Some machines express measurements in seconds (sec); others, in milliseconds (ms). Conversion between the two units of measurement is easy. For example, to convert a reading from milliseconds to seconds, move the decimal point three places to the left. Thus, a machine reading of 160 ms is the same as 0.16 sec:

$$160 \text{ ms} = 0.16 \text{ sec}$$

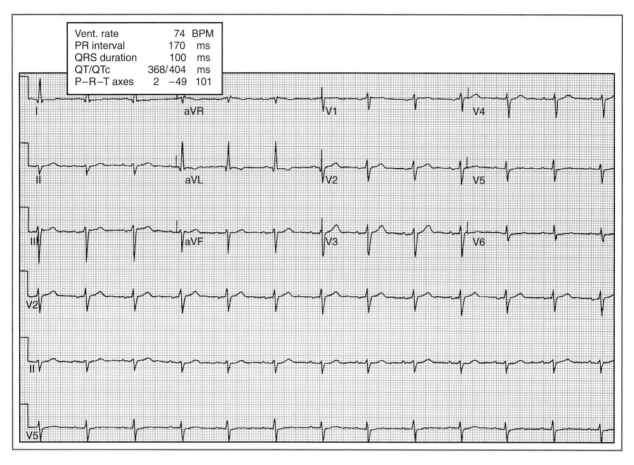

Vent. rate	74	BPM
PR interval	170	ms
QRS duration	100	ms
QT/QTc	368/404	ms
P–R–T axes	2 –49 101	

Figure 2–5. Example of a machine-sensed negative complex below the isoelectric line and a parenthetical: (Leads II and III).

Conversely, to convert seconds to milliseconds, move the decimal point three places to the right. Thus, a machine reading of 0.136 sec is the same as 136 ms:

$$0.136 \text{ sec} = 136 \text{ ms}$$

The vertical measurement is usually expressed in millimeters (mm), which the machine senses as voltage. On standard ECG paper, one small square is one millimeter (1 mm). The translation is as follows: 10 mm is one millivolt (1 mv) on the machine. Therefore, a 0.3 mv P wave would have a height of 3 mm. A positive number indicates the height of the complex above the **isoelectric line**. A negative number indicates the depth of the complex below the isoelectric line. Thus, a machine-sensed QRS complex of −1.0 mv is a negative complex 10 mm below the isoelectric line (Figure 2–5).

FROM MACHINE ANALYSIS TO HUMAN INTERPRETATION

Machines can analyze the data obtained, but only people can interpret that data. Many 12-lead machines offer an analysis of the conditions present by ECG criteria. Machine algorithms have become increasingly accurate but are not without errors and flaws.

ECG computerized analysis is based on interval and voltage measurements. However, the application of this criterion in the "conclusion or analysis" may be questionable.

One area of difficulty for machine interpretation has been rhythm analysis, particularly heart blocks and wide complex tachycardia (Figure 2–6). Because of these difficulties, the machine will print "Unconfirmed" or "MD must review" on the 12-lead ECG. This area is also a reason for the acute-care provider to be able to interpret the findings of an ECG.

The first step in interpreting the ECG is to find the isoelectric line. At times, the isoelectric line may be difficult to locate in complexes. The easiest way to locate this line is to look at the start of the 12-lead printout. As shown in Figure 2–7, the printout begins with a calibration spike (one mv, or two large squares) for each lead. The bottom of this spike is the isoelectric line. Some cardiac monitors allow the operator to use the calibration spike to adjust the size of the QRS to standard size: 1 mv = 10 mm high.

The next step is to ensure that the leads are in the correct place. One potential area of lead misplacement is Lead I, which should have the P wave, QRS, and T wave positively deflected. If all three are negative, limb lead misplacement is likely (Figure 2–8).

A second potential area of lead misplacement is the V lead, which on a normal electrocardiogram should demonstrate **R wave progression**. R wave progression refers to the size of the positively deflected R wave in the precordial V leads. As the views change from Leads V1 to V6, the R waves should get progressively taller. In other words, Lead V1 should have a small R wave, Lead V2 should have a bit larger one, and so on.

The **transition zone** usually occurs between Leads V3 and V4. It is the point at which the overall R wave should go from predominately negative to positive. This transition occurs normally in the heart as the lead view "turns the corner" (Figure 2–9). Poor R wave progression and early or late transition can be caused by a number of factors, including lead misplacement, old and new myocardial infarction, or certain arrhythmias (Figure 2–10).

```
NORMAL SINUS RHYTHM
LEFT ANTERIOR FASCICULAR BLOCK
MINIMAL VOLTAGE CRITERIA FOR LVH. MAY BE NORMAL VARIANT
NONSPECIFIC ST AND T WAVE ABNORMALITY
ABNORMAL ECG
```

Figure 2–6. Sample machine conclusion.

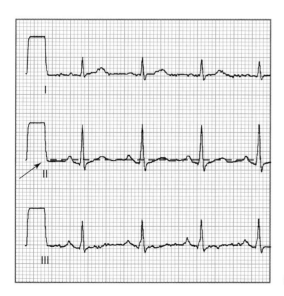

Figure 2–7. Locating the isoelectric line.

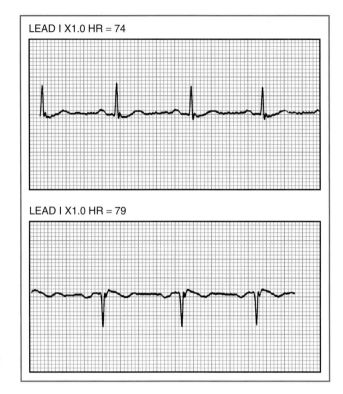

LEAD I X1.0 HR = 74

LEAD I X1.0 HR = 79

Figure 2–8. Misplacement of Lead I on ECG printout.

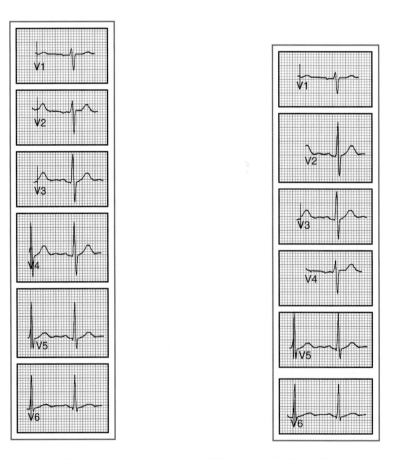

Figure 2–9. Normal R wave progression.

Figure 2–10. Poor R wave progression.

SUMMARY

The bottom line on machine-generated analysis is that machines provide analysis, but people make interpretations. Only someone trained to read ECGs can interpret what the printout shows, taking into account the many coexisting conditions that may have a bearing on the analysis.

Following are the key points of this chapter:

- Computerized interpretation has benefits and limitations.
- Computerized measurements and intervals can be useful in the rapid interpretation of serious conditions.
- Computerized analysis may be inaccurate, and the acute-care provider must be able to recognize the limitations of machine analysis.
- Machine analysis may be erroneous. Therefore, the clinician must be able to read, understand, and interpret the 12-lead ECG.
- Limb-lead misplacements are recognized by global negativity of Lead I.
- Poor R wave progression could indicate lead misplacement or other more serious problems, especially in the symptomatic patient.

GLOSSARY

isoelectric line the bottom of the calibration spike (one millivolt or two large squares), found at the start of the 12-lead printout.

mm millimeters.

ms milliseconds.

mv millivolts.

P wave represents depolarization of the left and right atria.

QRS complex represents the conduction of the electrical impulse from the bundle of His throughout the ventricular muscle, or ventricular depolarization.

QRS duration refers to the width of the QRS complex; used to determine wide vs. narrow complexes. In adults >120 milliseconds is considered wide.

QRS-size measurement determines conditions such as the presence of an enlarged heart, ST segment elevation, or pulmonary conditions stemming from the lack of voltage.

QT interval determines certain drug and electrolyte imbalances and other conditions of delayed repolarization; it is measured from the start of the QRS complex to the end of the T wave.

R wave progression refers to the size of the positively deflected R wave in the precordial V leads as they progressively increase in size from Leads V1 to V4.

sec seconds.

T wave represents ventricular repolarization and follows the ST segment.

transition zone occurs between Leads V3 and V4; it is the point at which the overall R wave should go from predominately negative to positive.

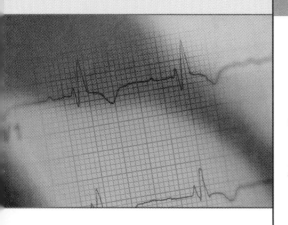

chapter 3

Determining Axis and Hemiblock

objectives

After reading this chapter, you should be able to:

1. Describe the anatomy of the intraventricular conduction system.

2. Define *axis* and *axis deviation*.

3. Explain how axis is determined, based on positive electrode lead placement.

4. Use a simple chart to determine the mean axis, using Leads I, II, and III.

5. Describe the significance of axis deviation in fascicular blocks.

6. Use the Rapid Axis and Hemiblock Chart to determine the presence of anterior and posterior fascicular block.

7. Describe the clinical significance of fascicular block in the acute-care setting.

HEXAXIAL SYSTEM

Axis can be defined as the general direction of electrical impulses as they travel through the heart. As they travel, they are carried in different directions. Ninety percent of the impulses cancel one another out. The remaining 10 percent travel in one primary direction. Assessing the direction, or axis, of these impulses provides clues about the severity of a patient's condition and helps to guide treatment.

Traditionally, the hexaxial system has been used to determine axis. The **hexaxial system** includes limb Leads I, II, and III and the augmented Leads aVL, aVR, and aVF (Figure 3–1). The result is like a pie of six equal pieces and lines to which you add in the degrees.

To determine the axis, run Leads I, II, and III. Normally, electrical impulses start from the SA node in the upper right chest and travel downward to the lower left side of the heart. Conducted impulses usually travel toward the positive electrodes in Leads I, II, and III. When an impulse travels toward a positive electrode, it creates an upward QRS complex deflection on the ECG paper. Therefore, impulses in a normal axis show an upward deflection in Leads I, II, and III (Figure 3–2).

LEFT-AXIS DEVIATION

In some cases, such as obesity, the axis may be rotated slightly more to the left, showing as an upward deflection in Lead I and either an upward or an isoelectric deflection in Lead II. Because the impulses are traveling away from Lead III, a negative deflection is seen. This **physiological left-axis deviation** is usually a normal variant (Figure 3–3) and is no cause for alarm.

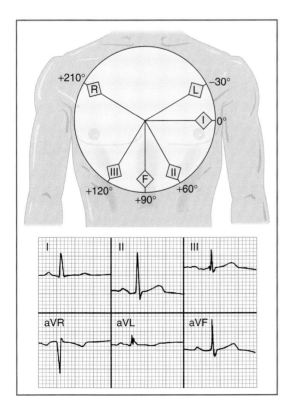

Figure 3–1. The hexaxial system.

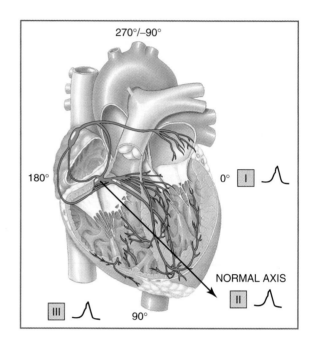

Figure 3–2. A normal axis.

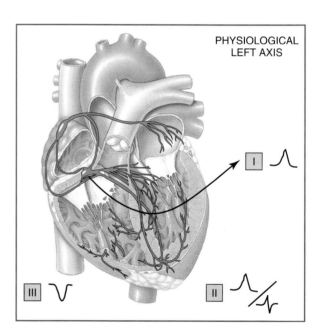

Figure 3–3. Physiological left-axis deviation.

To determine whether the deflection is up or down, count the number of small squares that the QRS goes above the baseline on the ECG, and subtract the number of small squares that the QRS goes below the baseline. If the number is positive, the complex is predominately upright. If the number is at or close to dead center, the complex is considered equiphasic, or equally up and down. If the axis deviates farther to the left (generally greater than –40 degrees), something is wrong. This pathological left-axis deviation is distinguished by an upright complex in Lead I and negative complexes in Leads II and III (Figure 3–4).

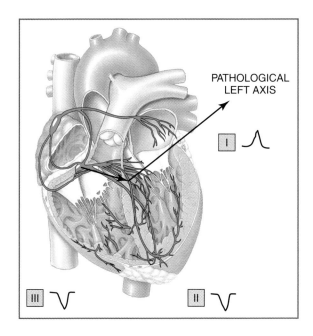

Figure 3–4. Pathological left-axis deviation.

All left-axis deviations have positive complexes in Lead I and negative complexes in Lead III. Therefore, Lead II is helpful in determining whether the deviation is pathological or physiological. A positive or isoelectric complex means physiological axis deviation, whereas a negative complex in Lead II indicates pathological left axis.

RIGHT-AXIS DEVIATION

In some patients, the axis may be deviated to the right side. In children, this variant is normal. But in adults, a right-axis deviation has a negative deflection in Lead I and a positive deflection in Lead III. Lead II could be positive, negative, or isoelectric (Figure 3–5).

Right-axis deviation is considered pathological in adults and can indicate many things:

- Posterior hemiblock.
- Right ventricular hypertrophy, or enlargement.
- Cor pulmonale, or right heart failure.
- Pulmonary embolism.
- Arrhythmias.

But ECG criterion is only one piece of the puzzle and is premature for diagnosing a single condition.

If the axis is deviated toward the right shoulder, the direction of the impulse is predominantly backward and is called an **extreme right-axis deviation (ERAD)**. Leads I, II, and III would have a negative complex (Figure 3–6).

The impulse is originating in the ventricles. A wide, fast complex is most likely to be ventricular tachycardia.

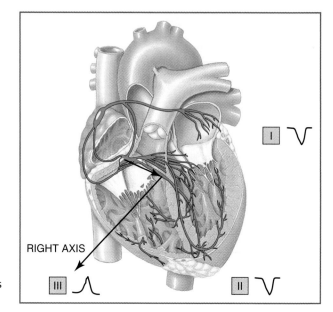

Figure 3–5. Right-axis deviation in an adult.

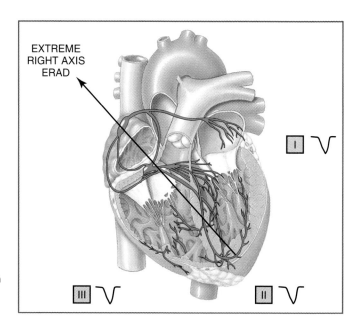

Figure 3–6. Extreme right-axis deviation, with a negative complex in Leads I, II, and III.

HEMIBLOCK

Axis deviations indicate hemiblock. A **hemiblock** is best defined as a block of one of the two fascicles of the left bundle branch system (Figure 3–7).

Note that there is a right bundle branch and a left bundle branch that divides into two separate **fascicles**, or what this book refers to as **hemifascicles.** These hemifascicles—known as the left anterior and the left posterior—and the right bundle branch make up a trifascicular system.

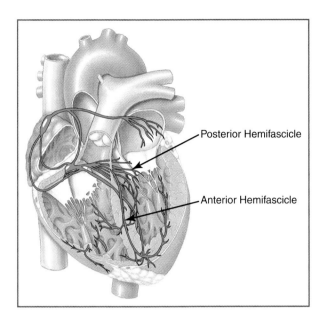

Figure 3–7. A hemiblock.

Impulses can travel in three ways to the ventricles:

* Right bundle branch.
* Left posterior hemifascicle.
* Left anterior hemifascicle.

Blocks in this system can be a precursor to heart block. Information on the presence of hemiblock can help the clinician determine which patients are at risk for developing complete heart block. Determining axis is about 98 percent of detecting hemiblock. Hemiblock can also indicate something about the severity of the patient's acute problem.

LEFT ANTERIOR HEMIBLOCK

A **left anterior hemiblock** occurs when the anterior hemifascicle of the left bundle branch system becomes blocked, thereby causing, in effect, a pathological left-axis deviation. Other clues to a left-anterior hemiblock are a small Q wave in Lead I and a small R wave in Lead III. A hemiblock can have a narrow QRS complex; a wide complex (>0.12 sec) is not the only indicator of an intraventricular conduction deficit.

The left anterior hemifascicle is made up of living, breathing cardiac conduction system (CCS) cells. In other words, they need a blood supply. The left anterior descending (LAD) branch of the left coronary artery provides blood supply for the anterior hemifascicle. Note that the left anterior hemifascicle is long and thin (Figure 3–7) and is the more common of the hemiblock.

An anterior hemiblock alone is usually well tolerated by an asymptomatic patient and generally requires no treatment. However, in the setting of an acute myocardial infarction (AMI), an anterior hemiblock indicates a more serious condition. Normally, impulses travel via three paths to the ventricles; with an anterior hemiblock, only two are available. This difference has been attributed to an occlusion of a feeder artery that branches off the coronary artery proximally. Furthermore, studies have suggested that a person with a conduction-system problem, such as a hemiblock in the setting of an AMI, has a mortality rate four times higher than someone without such a problem.

LEFT POSTERIOR HEMIBLOCK

A **left posterior hemiblock** occurs when the posterior fascicle of the left bundle branch system is blocked. For field purposes, a right-axis deviation indicatives a left posterior hemiblock. Other clues are small R waves in Lead I and small Q waves in Lead III. The clinician could also inspect for the presence of right ventricular hypertrophy: jugular vein distention (JVD), pedal edema, and patient history. However, because the clinician is targeting the worst condition, posterior hemiblock should be assumed in the patient with signs and symptoms of a myocardial infarction.

The posterior hemiblock is worse than the anterior hemiblock. Note in Figure 3–7 that the posterior hemifascicle is thicker than the anterior hemifascicle, having more cells and needing a supply of blood. Dead cells do not conduct impulses. A redundant blood supply is required from two different coronary arteries: the right coronary artery and the circumflex. If both coronary arteries are blocked, extensive coronary occlusion occurred. In one study of 3,160 patients with acute MIs, only 70 had posterior hemi-blocks. Of those, 14 percent died before they left the hospital. Of the remaining patients who were followed, 63 percent had persistent cardiac problems, 22 percent got congestive heart failure (CHF), 13 percent had another MI, and the last 2 percent died within 20 days to 24 months. In other words, a posterior hemiblock with an MI is a serious sign. In such circumstances, it may be necessary to combat both conduction problems and, possibly, hypotension/cardiogenic shock.

CLINICAL SIGNIFICANCE OF HEMIBLOCK

The clinical significance of hemiblock can be summarized as follows:

- Four times higher mortality rate for patients having an AMI with a hemiblock than those without hemiblock.
- Risk factor for complete heart block; if another block is present with a hemiblock, the patient is at high risk for complete heart block.
- In the setting of an AMI, can indicate proximal artery occlusion.

RAPID AXIS AND HEMIBLOCK CHART

It has been said that one should never commit to memory what can be written down. The Rapid Axis and Hemiblock Chart (Figure 3–8) is designed to quickly allow the clinician to determine the presence of axis deviation and hemiblock.

The chart can be used in two ways. If a 3-lead monitor or other machine that does not provide axis information is being used, the following method applies. Look at Leads I, II, and III. Determine whether the QRS complex is more positively or negatively deflected in each lead. Compare your findings to the Rapid Axis and Hemiblock Chart to identify the axis and hemiblock.

If a 12-lead machine is being used and provides the numerical angle, use this information.

CALCULATED AXIS ANGLE

Recall that the 12-lead machine can calculate the axis information accurately. The number to look for is the R axis or QRS axis. With this information available, the Rapid Axis and Hemiblock Chart can be used to identify the axis deviation. For example, suppose that the

Rapid Axis and Hemiblock Chart

Axis	Lead I	Lead II	Lead III	Notes
Normal Axis 0° to 90°				
Physiological Left Axis 0° to –40°				
Pathological Left Axis –40° to –90°				Anterior Hemiblock
Right Axis 90° to 180°				Posterior Hemiblock
Extreme Right Axis >180°				Ventricular in origin

Figure 3–8. Rapid Axis and Hemiblock Chart.

Vent. rate	64	BPM
PR interval	192	ms
QRS duration	82	ms
QT/QTc	398/404	ms
P–R–T axes	46 –53 63	

Figure 3–9. The 12-lead machine can calculate axis information accurately.

machine shows an R axis of –53; the chart shows that –53 is in the range –40 to –90: a pathological left-axis deviation and an anterior hemiblock. This number represents the exact geometrical axis angle, based on the hexaxial system. (See Figure 3–9.)

SIGNIFICANCE OF AXIS NUMBERS

The practice exercises (see below) use two rapid ways of determining axis. Notice that the calculated angle seems exact, whereas the range it fits into is broad. Thus, the question remains: Is it important to get an exact angle—a number—of the axis? In the emergency setting, with a patient having a myocardial infarction, the acute-care provider is concerned about the presence of a pathological condition, not necessarily the exact angle. In other words, whether the axis calculates to –51 or –76 would be irrelevant. Both numbers are in the pathological range, and one is no worse than the other.

PRACTICE: DETERMINING AXIS AND HEMIBLOCK

Use the Rapid Axis and Hemiblock Chart and determine the axis of the following 12-lead ECGs (Figures 3–10 through 3–20). In each case, use both the QRS deflection and the calculated axis angle to determine the axis. All answers are provided in the Answer Key at the back of the book. Example:

Lead I: _____Up_____   Lead II: _Down_   Lead III: _Down_

R axis: _____   Axis: _Pathological Left-Axis Deviation_

Hemiblock: _____

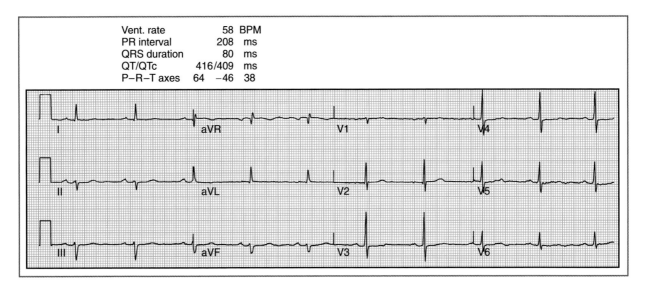

Vent. rate	58	BPM
PR interval	208	ms
QRS duration	80	ms
QT/QTc	416/409	ms
P–R–T axes	64 –46	38

Figure 3–10.

Lead I: _____   Lead II: _____   Lead III: _____

R axis: _____   Axis: _____   Hemiblock: _____

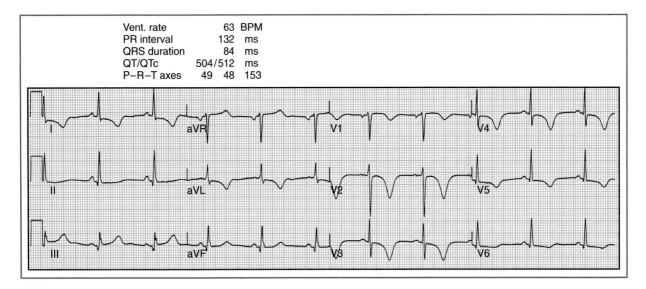

Vent. rate	63	BPM
PR interval	132	ms
QRS duration	84	ms
QT/QTc	504/512	ms
P–R–T axes	49 48	153

Figure 3–11.

Lead I: _____   Lead II: _____   Lead III: _____

R axis: _____   Axis: _____   Hemiblock: _____

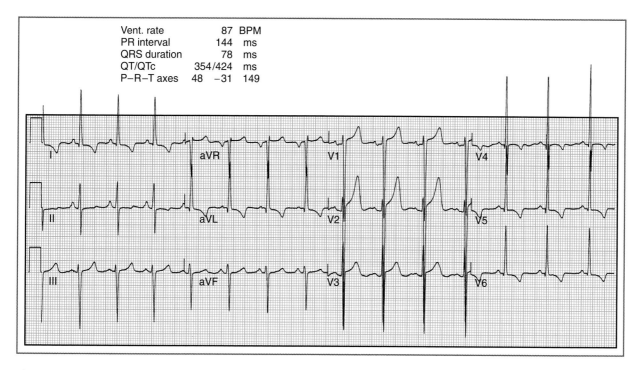

Figure 3–12.

Lead I: _____   Lead II: _____   Lead III: _____

R axis: _____   Axis: _____   Hemiblock: _____

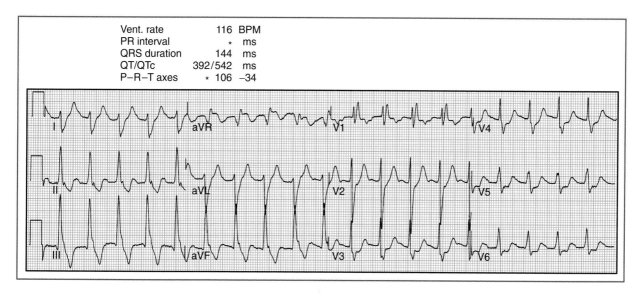

Figure 3–13.

Lead I: _____   Lead II: _____   Lead III: _____

R axis: _____   Axis: _____   Hemiblock: _____

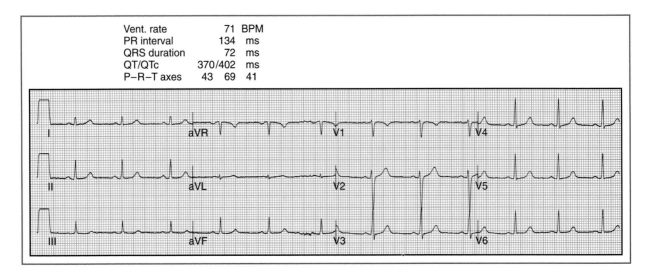

Vent. rate   71 BPM
PR interval   134 ms
QRS duration   72 ms
QT/QTc   370/402 ms
P–R–T axes   43 69 41

Figure 3–14.

Lead I: _____   Lead II: _____   Lead III: _____

R axis: _____   Axis: _____   Hemiblock: _____

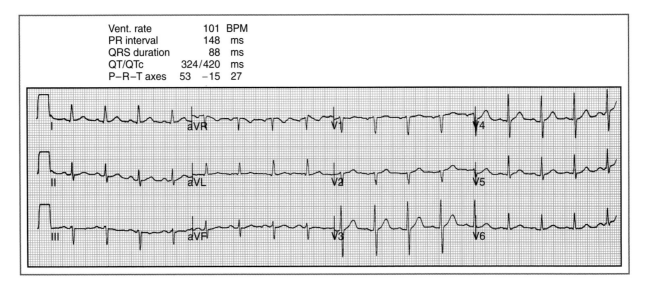

Vent. rate   101 BPM
PR interval   148 ms
QRS duration   88 ms
QT/QTc   324/420 ms
P–R–T axes   53 –15 27

Figure 3–15.

Lead I: _____   Lead II: _____   Lead III: _____

R axis: _____   Axis: _____   Hemiblock: _____

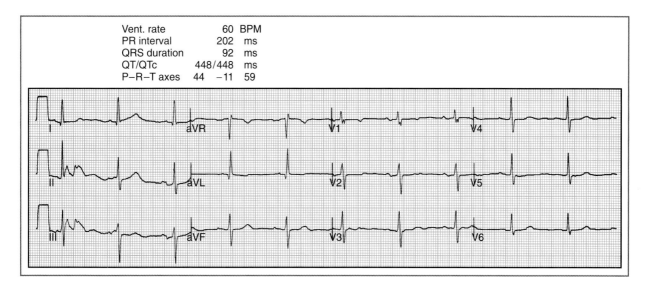

Vent. rate	60	BPM
PR interval	202	ms
QRS duration	92	ms
QT/QTc	448/448	ms
P–R–T axes	44 −11 59	

Figure 3–16.

Lead I: _____

R axis: _____

Lead II: _____

Axis: _____

Lead III: _____

Hemiblock: _____

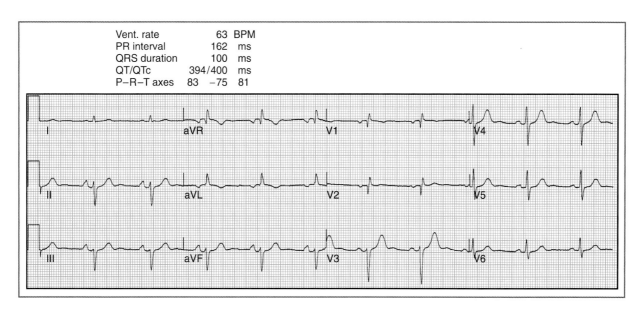

Vent. rate	63	BPM
PR interval	162	ms
QRS duration	100	ms
QT/QTc	394/400	ms
P–R–T axes	83 −75 81	

Figure 3–17.

Lead I: _____

R axis: _____

Lead II: _____

Axis: _____

Lead III: _____

Hemiblock: _____

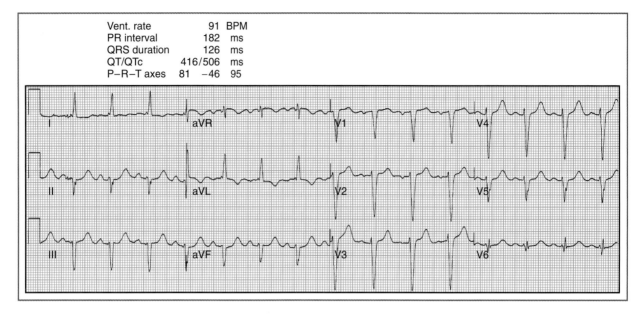

Vent. rate	91	BPM
PR interval	182	ms
QRS duration	126	ms
QT/QTc	416/506	ms
P–R–T axes	81 –46	95

Figure 3–18.

Lead I: _____   Lead II: _____   Lead III: _____

R axis: _____   Axis: _____   Hemiblock: _____

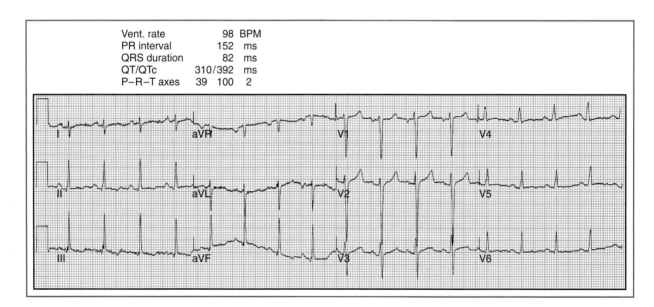

Vent. rate	98	BPM
PR interval	152	ms
QRS duration	82	ms
QT/QTc	310/392	ms
P–R–T axes	39 100	2

Figure 3–19.

Lead I: _____   Lead II: _____   Lead III: _____

R axis: _____   Axis: _____   Hemiblock: _____

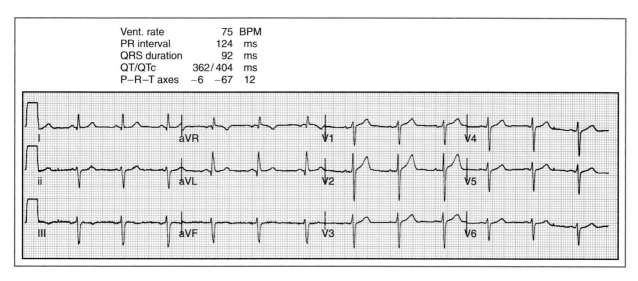

Vent. rate   75 BPM
PR interval   124 ms
QRS duration   92 ms
QT/QTc   362/ 404 ms
P–R–T axes   −6   −67 12

Figure 3–20.

Lead I: _____   Lead II: _____   Lead III: _____

R axis: _____   Axis: _____   Hemiblock: _____

SUMMARY

Following are the key points of this chapter:

- The term *axis* refers to the mean direction of travel of electrical impulses through the ventricles of the heart.
- As an electrical impulse travels in the direction of a positive electrode, it will make a positive deflection on the ECG tracing.
- Leads I, II, and III alone can be used to determine axis, based on the net deflection of the QRS complex. The Rapid Axis and Hemiblock Chart can be used for this purpose.
- The calculated axis angle can also be used in conjunction with the Rapid Axis and Hemiblock Chart.
- An axis deviation can be significant when caused by a hemiblock and other pathological conditions.

GLOSSARY

axis the general direction of electrical impulses as they travel through the heart.

extreme right-axis deviation (ERAD) a condition in which the direction of the impulse is predominantly backward due to the axis being deviated toward the right shoulder.

fascicles the two main divisions of the left bundle branch.

hemiblock a block of one of the two fascicles of the left bundle branch system.

hemifascicles two separate fascicles formed by the division of a right bundle branch and a left bundle branch.

hexaxial system a system that includes limb Leads I, II, and III and the augmented Leads aVL, aVR, and aVF.

left anterior hemiblock occurs when the anterior hemifascicle of the left bundle branch system becomes blocked, causing a pathological left-axis deviation (–40 to –90 degrees).

left posterior hemiblock occurs when the posterior fascicle of the left bundle branch system is blocked, causing a right-axis deviation (90 to 180 degrees).

physiological left-axis deviation the rotation of the axis slightly more to the left, showing an upward deflection in Lead I and either an upward or an isoelectric deflection in Lead II; range is from 0 to –40 degrees.

chapter 4

Understanding Bundle Branch Blocks

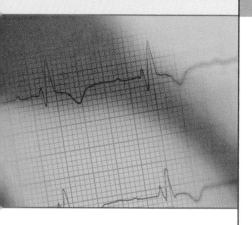

objectives

After reading this chapter, you should be able to:

1. Locate the J point on the electrocardiogram.

2. Describe the benefits of Lead MCL-1 (V1).

3. Describe the properties of the ventricular conduction system.

4. Use Lead MCL-1 (V1) and a simple criterion to determine the presence and location of bundle branch block.

5. Describe the hemodynamic implications of a bundle branch block.

6. Describe the conduction system problems associated with a bundle branch block.

INTRODUCTION

A **bundle branch block (BBB)** is an electrical phenomenon characterized by a widened QRS complex of at least 0.12 sec (120 ms) or greater and, in most cases, a definitive QRS morphology pattern. A BBB is diagnosed from an ECG. Differential diagnosis is most easily made in Lead MCL-1 (V1).

BUNDLE BRANCH SYSTEM

ANATOMY AND PHYSIOLOGY

The right bundle branch (RBB) is a single branch, whereas the left bundle branch (LBB) divides into anterior and posterior hemifascicles. These three fascicles make up a trifascicular system (Figure 4–1). The blood supply for the bundle branches usually comes from the left anterior descending coronary artery but can also be from the AV nodal artery of the right coronary artery.

The bundle branch system is an important part of the ventricular depolarization **syncytium**, the feature of the ventricles or the atrium that produces simultaneous depolarization. The result of simultaneous depolarization is an organized contraction.

Bundle branches are made up of cardiac conduction system cells that conduct electrical impulses many times faster than regular myocardial cells. This speed advantage allows the ventricles to depolarize at once rather than slowly. The result is a more effective contraction and better cardiac output.

PATHOPHYSIOLOGY

The cardiac conduction system cells that comprise the bundle branches need a constant oxygenated blood supply that, if reduced or cut off, slows or even stops the conduction of impulses. If no impulses are conducted, depolarization must occur through the working myocardial cells. Such depolarization can happen but is very slow. If the

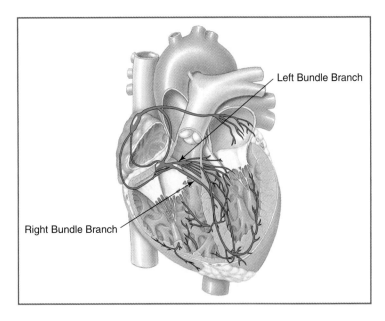

Figure 4–1. The trifascicular system.

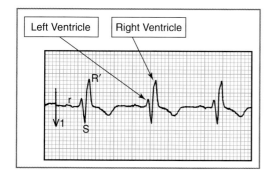

Figure 4–2. A right bundle branch block.

patient has no history of ischemia, a bundle branch block can also develop secondary to hypertension or as primary or degenerative myocardial disease.

Bundle branch blocks produce some classic patterns, which are predictable and explainable, based on the mechanism of syncytium, which allows both ventricles to contract at the same time. This simultaneous contraction causes the QRS complex to be narrow and crisp in a normal beat. But if the right bundle branch is blocked, for example, the impulses going to the right ventricle are slowed. Because the impulses going to the left side are not slowed, two complexes are produced: the left ventricle depolarizes first and then the right ventricle, resulting in a wide QRS (<0.12 sec). Figure 4–2 shows what happens in a right bundle branch block (RBBB): the ventricles are out of sync.

DIAGNOSING BUNDLE BRANCH BLOCKS

MCL-1 (V1) is the lead to use to call bundle branch blocks. This lead looks across the ventricles and can see both bundle branches, thereby acting as an eyewitness to an accident. To run MCL-1 (V1), leave your lead select in Lead III, and place the red electrode in the fourth intercostal space to the right of the sternum.

To diagnose bundle branch blocks, use the **turn signal criteria** (Figure 4–3). Note, however, that this method works only in Lead MCL-1 (V1) and that the QRS must be >0.12 sec (120 ms), or three small squares on the ECG paper.

First, find a supraventricular complex, one having a P wave associated with it; that is, >0.12 sec. Next, find the J point, the point at which the QRS complex turns into

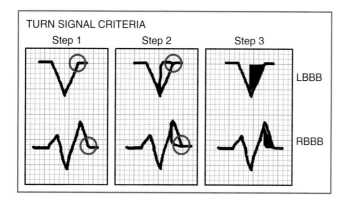

Figure 4–3. Turn signal criteria. (1) Find and circle the J point. (2) Draw a line back toward the complex in the direction of the terminal deflection. (3) Shade in the triangle, or arrowhead. If the arrowhead points up, it is a right bundle branch block (RBBB). If it points down, it is a left bundle branch block (LBBB).

the ST segment. Then, look at the direction from which the QRS complex terminates. In other words, right before the J point, did the complex come from above or below the isoelectric line? Draw a line back toward the complex. Go up or down in the direction of the terminal deflection. This line makes a triangle with the terminal part of the complex. Shade in the triangle. If the triangle points up, you have a right bundle branch block (RBBB). (Similarly, a driver pushes the turn signal up to indicate a right turn.) If the triangle points down, you have a left bundle branch block (LBBB).

Figure 4–4 shows a right bundle branch block. Note the rsR' complex and the positive terminal deflection in Lead MCL-1 (V1). The QRS duration is 144 ms. In Figure 4–5, which shows a left bundle branch block, note the negative terminal deflection in Lead V1 (MCL-1). The QRS complex is 144 ms. Also note that Lead I shows a notched R wave, another indicator of a left bundle branch block.

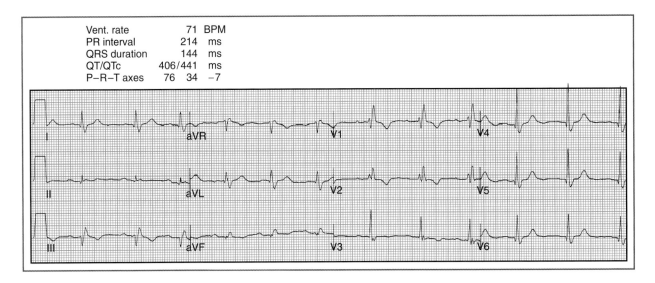

Vent. rate		71	BPM
PR interval		214	ms
QRS duration		144	ms
QT/QTc	406/441		ms
P–R–T axes	76	34	–7

Figure 4–4. A right bundle branch block.

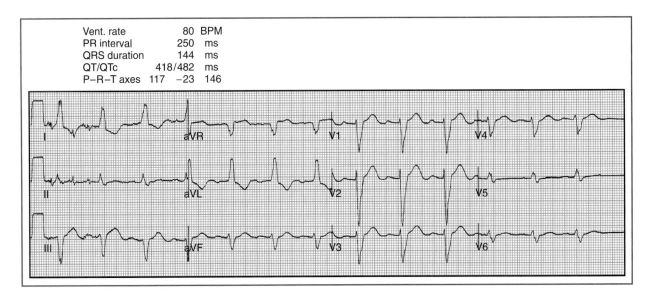

Vent. rate		80	BPM
PR interval		250	ms
QRS duration		144	ms
QT/QTc	418/482		ms
P–R–T axes	117	–23	146

Figure 4–5. A left bundle branch block.

SIGNIFICANCE OF BUNDLE BRANCH BLOCKS

Bundle branch blocks can be permanent or temporary, depending on the presence of dead or ischemic tissue. Because a bundle branch block is an electrical conduction problem, many asymptomatic patients may be able to tolerate it. For example, someone may complain about chest pain and dizziness after getting up but later be asymptomatic with no complaints. But running multi-leads would reveal conduction problems, such as BBBs. Although a weak conduction system may be able to support a person at rest, symptoms of hypoperfusion may present when the person gets up to do something, placing greater demand on the heart than the compromised conduction system can handle.

In the setting of an acute myocardial infarction, a bundle branch block is a serious complication that usually indicates extensive coronary artery occlusion and anterior wall damage. Patients with a BBB complication of an MI have a mortality rate four times greater than those without BBB. Symptomatic BBBs may entail complete heart blocks. Patients with occlusions to the left anterior descending coronary artery, producing an anterior wall MI, frequently develop complete heart blocks. Another possible complication is ventricular fibrillation.

The presence of an LBBB obscures the ST segment, making ECG diagnosis of an AMI very difficult. In fact, most cardiologists do not even try. However, in the setting of an RBBB, the ST segment is intact, and MI determination is easier. Two classic RBBB patterns demonstrate those that were caused and not caused by an MI.

The risk of complete heart block accompanies bundle branch blocks. For example, when combined with a hemiblock, an RBBB is called a **bifascicular block**, with two of the three fascicles blocked, as shown in Figure 4–1. An LBBB is also a bifascicular block.

When a bifascicular block exists, such drugs as lidocaine, procainamide, and sometimes even morphine will further slow conduction through the ventricles, resulting in a drug-induced complete heart block or, possibly, ventricular asystole. So important is a bifascicular block that 12-lead machines use bold print and asterisks to draw attention to this information (Figure 4–6). This is the machine's way of alerting the provider to information that may change the approach to the patient's treatment.

NORMAL SINUS RHYTHM
RIGHT BUNDLE BRANCH BLOCK
LEFT ANTERIOR FASCICULAR BLOCK
*** **BIFASCICULAR BLOCK** ***

Figure 4–6. 12-lead machines use bold print and asterisks to draw attention to a bifascicular block.

HEMODYNAMIC EFFECTS OF BUNDLE BRANCH BLOCKS

In some cases, a bundle branch block can have significant hemodynamic effects. In a bundle branch block, the ventricles are firing out of sync, which may result in a reduction of preload. Furthermore, a bundle branch block means delayed conduction and depolarization time. Patients with a bundle branch block and a QRS complex that is wider than 170 ms (0.17 sec) usually have an ejection fraction of less than 50 percent.

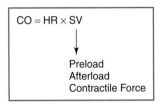

Figure 4–7. Cardiac output. A BBB compromises preload and if the QRS duration exceeds 170 ms, the contractility is also compromised.

Ejection fraction is one measure of left ventricular effectiveness; the normal range is between 60 percent and 75 percent. This fact represents a compromise to contractility. Therefore, if a BBB is wider than 170 ms, the patient is a risk for hemodynamic compromise, and the acute-care provider should be aware that a precipitous drop in blood pressure may occur if vasodilator medication, such as nitroglycerin, is used. The reason is that, most likely, the patient is perfusing with this condition because of increased afterload secondary to peripheral vasoconstriction compensating for the other conditions (Figure 4–7).

PRACTICE: DIAGNOSING BUNDLE BRANCH BLOCKS

See Figures 4–8 to 4–19. Work the practice examples for the presence and type of bundle branch blocks. All answers are provided in the Answer Key at the back of the book.

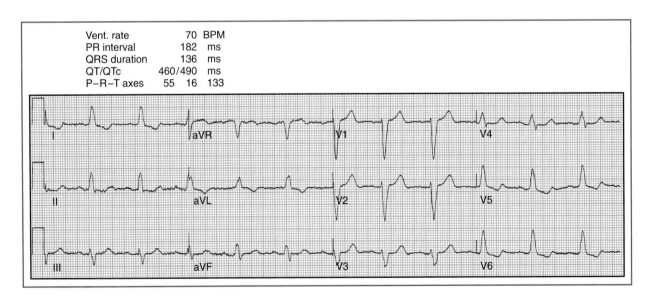

Figure 4–8.

QRS duration: _____

Bundle branch block: _____

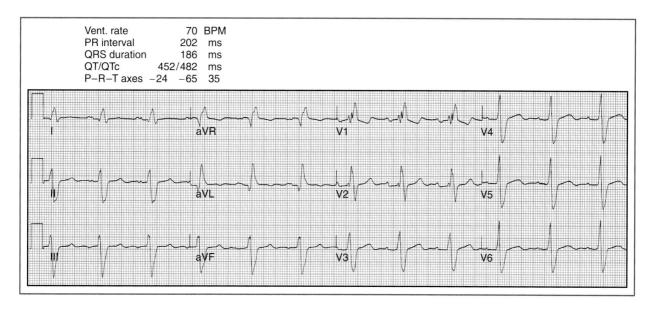

Figure 4–9.

QRS duration: _____

Bundle branch block: _____

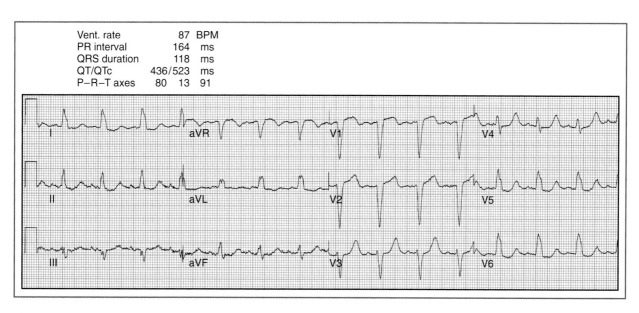

Figure 4–10.

QRS duration: _____

Bundle branch block: _____

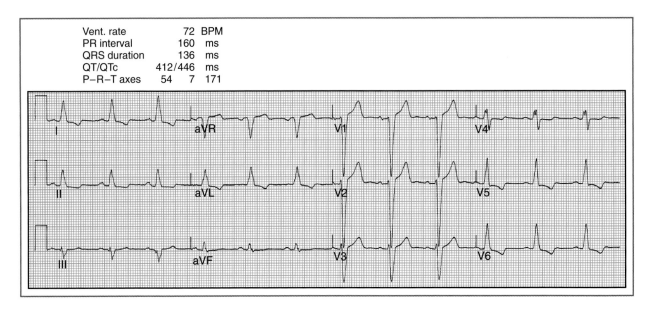

Vent. rate   72 BPM
PR interval   160 ms
QRS duration   136 ms
QT/QTc   412/446 ms
P–R–T axes   54 7 171

Figure 4–11.

QRS duration: _____

Bundle branch block: _____

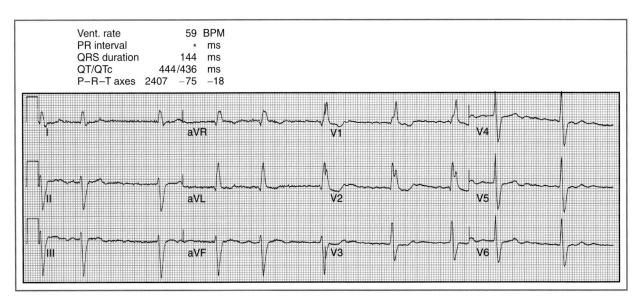

Vent. rate   59 BPM
PR interval   * ms
QRS duration   144 ms
QT/QTc   444/436 ms
P–R–T axes 2407 −75 −18

Figure 4–12.

QRS duration: _____

Bundle branch block: _____

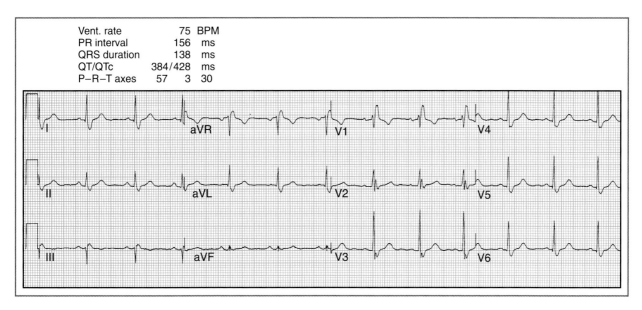

Figure 4–13.

QRS duration: _____

Bundle branch block: _____

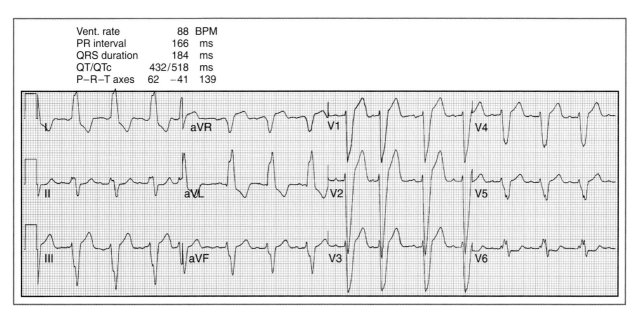

Figure 4–14.

QRS duration: _____

Bundle branch block: _____

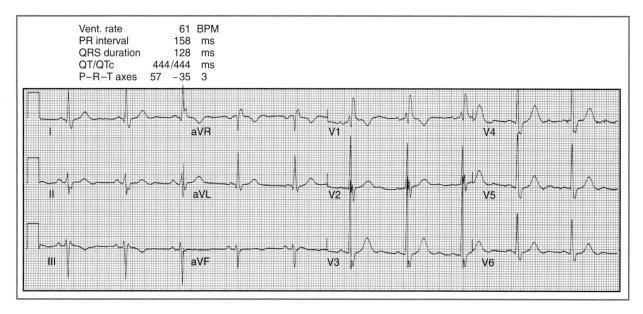

Figure 4–15.

QRS duration: _____

Bundle branch block: _____

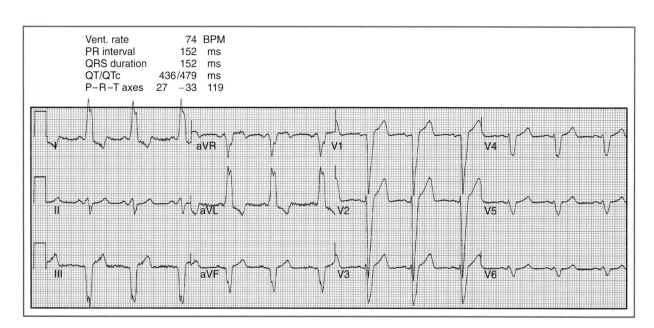

Figure 4–16.

QRS duration: _____

Bundle branch block: _____

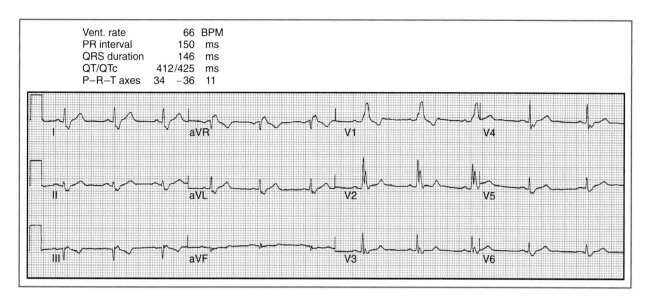

Figure 4–17.

QRS duration: _____

Bundle branch block: _____

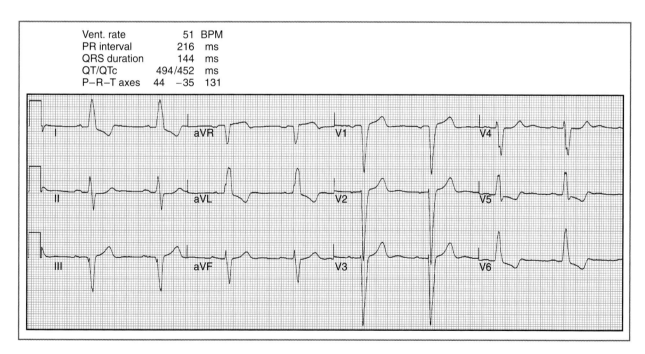

Figure 4–18.

QRS duration: _____

Bundle branch block: _____

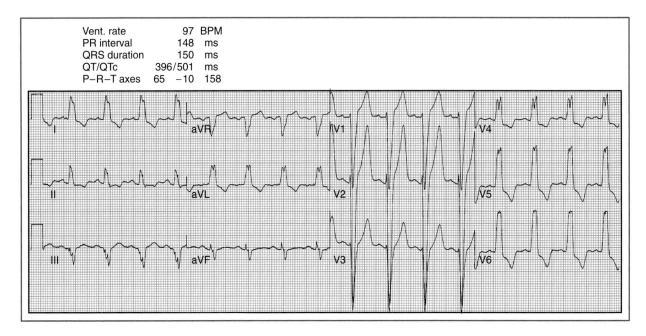

Vent. rate	97	BPM
PR interval	148	ms
QRS duration	150	ms
QT/QTc	396/501	ms
P–R–T axes	65 –10	158

Figure 4–19.

QRS duration: _____

Bundle branch block: _____

SUMMARY

Following are the key points of this chapter:

- If damaged, the bundle branches will not work properly.
- Syncytium is necessary for crisp contractions and good cardiac output.
- BBB can cause a reduction in preload and contractility.
- Wide QRS (>170 ms) means reduced ejection fraction to below 50 percent.
- Use the turn signal criteria to aid in calling left and right BBBs.
- You cannot accurately or consistently call an LBBB or an RBBB from a Lead II strip.
- BBB means at least 25 percent greater mortality.
- As with hemiblocks, people can live asymptomatically with BBBs. A BBB usually has greater effect on a person's lifestyle, however. Because of hemodynamic effects, a patient with BBB will not be able to undertake much strenuous activity before having to lie down.
- As always, pay attention to your patient. Keep all this information in mind as you consider the possible problems and treatment options.

GLOSSARY

bifascicular block a right bundle branch block combined with a hemiblock or a left bundle branch block.

bundle branch block (BBB) an electrical phenomenon characterized by a widened QRS complex of at least 0.12 seconds (120 milliseconds) or greater and, in most cases, a definitive QRS morphology pattern.

ejection fraction the volume percent of blood ejected in one contraction; one measure of left ventricular effectiveness; the normal range is between 60 and 75 percent.

J point the point at which the QRS complex turns into the ST segment.

syncytium cardiac muscle cell groups that are connected together and function collectively as a unit; the feature of the ventricles or the atrium that produces simultaneous depolarization.

turn signal criteria used to diagnose bundle branch blocks and works only in Lead MCL-1 (V1) when the QRS is 0.12 seconds (120 milliseconds) or three small squares on the ECG paper.

chapter 5

Determining Patient Risk for Complete Heart Block

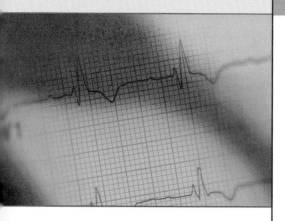

objectives

After reading this chapter, you should be able to:

1. Define the three types of bifascicular block.

2. Describe the clinical implications of a bifascicular block.

3. Identify drugs that could be contraindicated in the setting of a bifascicular block.

4. List examples of severe degrees and high risk for complete heart block.

5. Identify steps that can be taken to prepare for the patient at high risk for complete heart block.

6. Given a 12-lead ECG, discover which patients are at high risk for complete heart block.

HEART BLOCK AND DRUG CONTRAINDICATION

Heart block occurs along a continuum of severity (Table 5–1). The degree of severity is closely related to the use or contraindication of various drugs.

All the information needed to determine which patients are at risk of complete heart block is available with a 12-lead or by running the 4-lead baseline (I, II, III, and MCL-1). This information is important to know, as some commonly used drugs can be contraindicated in the presence of **intraventricular heart block** (either a hemiblock or a bundle branch block) (Figure 5–1). In short, whenever a block appears or is implied twice in the ECG interpretation, such as "1st degree block + hemiblock," the patient is at high risk for complete heart block. In such cases, both lidocaine and procainamide are contraindicated, and morphine should be used with caution.

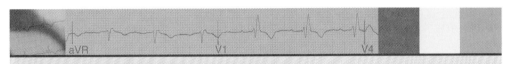

TABLE 5–1. *Severe Degrees of Block*

- Second-degree type 2
- Third-degree CHB
- Bifascicular block
- First-degree block plus hemiblock
- First-degree block plus BBB
- Any time you say or imply block twice in the interpretation, the patient is a high risk for complete heart block. Antiarrhythmics such as lidocaine and procainamide are contraindicated.

CONTRAINDICATIONS
Lidocaine is contraindicated in patients with a known hypersensitivity to local anesthetics of the amide type.
Intravenous injection is contraindicated in patients with Adams-Stokes syndrome or with severe degrees of sinoatrial, atrioventricular, or intraventricular heart block.

WARNINGS
Constant monitoring with an electrocardiograph is essential for proper intravenous administration of lidocaine. Signs of excessive depression cardiac conductivity, such as prolongation of PR interval and Q complex and appearance or aggravation of arrhythmias, should followed by prompt cessation of intravenous injection or infusion of agent. It is mandatory to have emergency equipment immediately available to manage possible adver the cardiovascular, respiratory, or central n prop

Figure 5–1. Part of the information included on a drug insert for lidocaine.

BIFASCICULAR BLOCK

A bifascicular block is a blockage of two of the three pathways to contract the ventricles in an organized fashion. This condition can also compromise myocardial contractility. In previous chapters, we explained how to locate hemiblock and bundle branch blocks individually. This chapter combines them and describes the preparation for managing this serious condition.

The three types of bifascicular block are:

- Anterior hemiblock and a right bundle branch block (Figure 5–2).
- Posterior hemiblock and a right bundle branch block (Figure 5–3).
- Left bundle branch block (Figure 5–4).

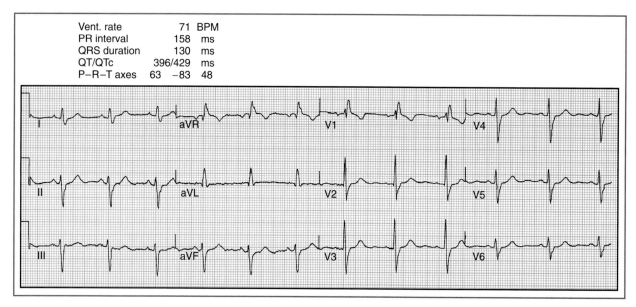

Figure 5–2. Anterior hemiblock and right bundle branch block.

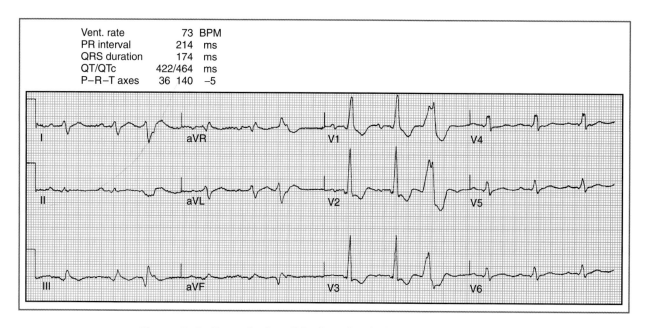

Figure 5–3. Posterior hemiblock and right bundle branch block.

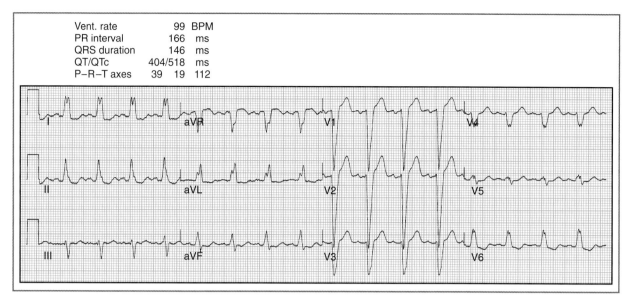

Figure 5–4. Left bundle branch block.

PRACTICE: WHO IS AT RISK FOR COMPLETE HEART BLOCK

Work through Figures 5–5 through 5–19 to discover who is at risk for complete heart block, hemodynamic compromise, and sudden cardiac death. Figure 5–5 is done for you as an example. All answers are provided in the Answer Key at the back of the book.

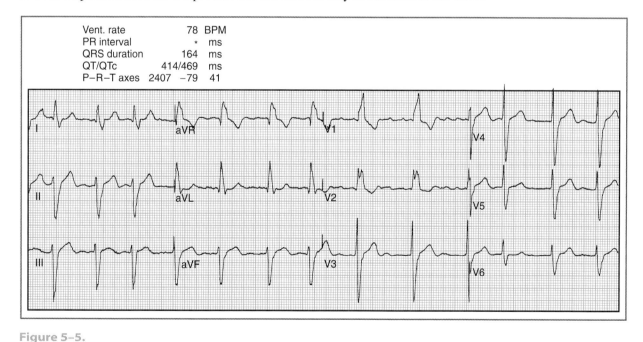

Figure 5–5.

Lead I: ___↑___   Lead II: ___↓___   Lead III: ___↓___   R Axis: ___–79___

Axis: _Path left_____   Hemiblock: _Anterior_____

QRS width? _____164_____   BBB? _____Right_____   BFB? _____Yes_____

Risk for: Complete heart block? ___Yes___   Sudden cardiac death? ___Yes___

       Hemodynamic compromise? ___No___

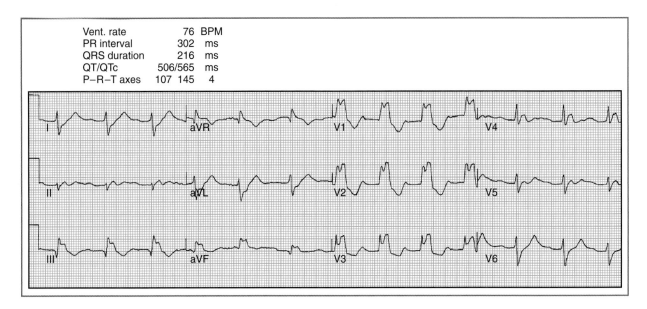

Vent. rate	76	BPM
PR interval	302	ms
QRS duration	216	ms
QT/QTc	506/565	ms
P–R–T axes	107 145	4

Figure 5–6.

Lead I: _____   Lead II: _____   Lead III: _____   R Axis: _____

Axis: _____   Hemiblock: _____

QRS width? _____   BBB? _____   BFB? _____

Risk for: Complete heart block? _____   Sudden cardiac death? _____

      Hemodynamic compromise? _____

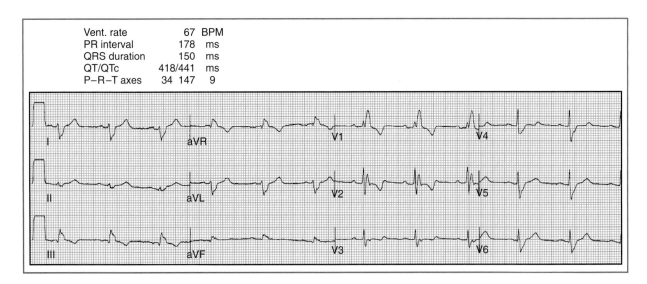

Vent. rate	67	BPM
PR interval	178	ms
QRS duration	150	ms
QT/QTc	418/441	ms
P–R–T axes	34 147	9

Figure 5–7.

Lead I: _____   Lead II: _____   Lead III: _____   R Axis: _____

Axis: _____   Hemiblock: _____

QRS width? _____   BBB? _____   BFB? _____

Risk for: Complete heart block? _____   Sudden cardiac death? _____

      Hemodynamic compromise? _____

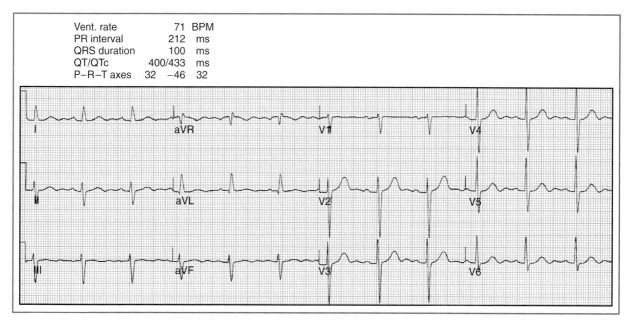

Vent. rate   71 BPM
PR interval   212 ms
QRS duration   100 ms
QT/QTc   400/433 ms
P–R–T axes   32   −46   32

Figure 5–8.

Lead I: _____   Lead II: _____   Lead III: _____   R Axis: _____

Axis: _____   Hemiblock: _____

QRS width? _____   BBB? _____   BFB? _____

Risk for: Complete heart block? _____   Sudden cardiac death? _____

            Hemodynamic compromise? _____

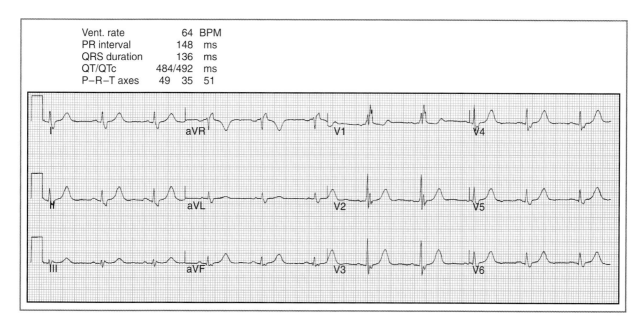

Vent. rate   64 BPM
PR interval   148 ms
QRS duration   136 ms
QT/QTc   484/492 ms
P–R–T axes   49   35   51

Figure 5–9.

Lead I: _____   Lead II: _____   Lead III: _____   R Axis: _____

Axis: _____   Hemiblock: _____

QRS width? _____   BBB? _____   BFB? _____

Risk for: Complete heart block? _____   Sudden cardiac death? _____

            Hemodynamic compromise? _____

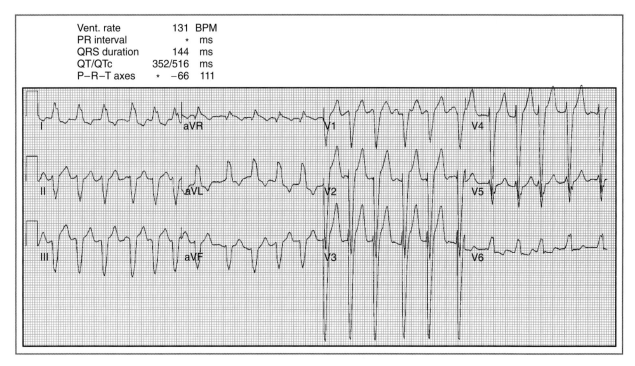

```
Vent. rate          131  BPM
PR interval           *  ms
QRS duration        144  ms
QT/QTc          352/516  ms
P–R–T axes       *  –66  111
```

Figure 5–10.

Lead I: _____   Lead II: _____   Lead III: _____   R Axis: _____

Axis: _____   Hemiblock: _____

QRS width? _____   BBB? _____   BFB? _____

Risk for: Complete heart block? _____   Sudden cardiac death? _____

       Hemodynamic compromise? _____

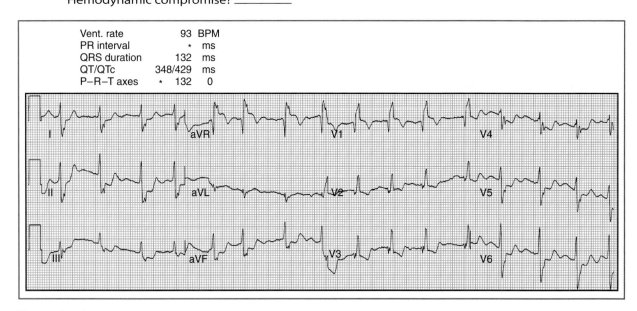

```
Vent. rate           93  BPM
PR interval           *  ms
QRS duration        132  ms
QT/QTc          348/429  ms
P–R–T axes       *  132    0
```

Figure 5–11.

Lead I: _____   Lead II: _____   Lead III: _____   R Axis: _____

Axis: _____   Hemiblock: _____

QRS width? _____   BBB? _____   BFB? _____

Risk for: Complete heart block? _____   Sudden cardiac death? _____

       Hemodynamic compromise? _____

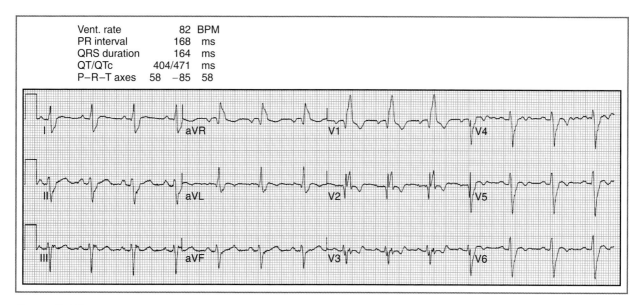

```
Vent. rate          82   BPM
PR interval        168   ms
QRS duration       164   ms
QT/QTc         404/471   ms
P–R–T axes      58  –85  58
```

Figure 5–12.

Lead I: _____   Lead II: _____   Lead III: _____   R Axis: _____

Axis: _____   Hemiblock: _____

QRS width? _____   BBB? _____   BFB? _____

Risk for: Complete heart block? _____   Sudden cardiac death? _____

　　　　　Hemodynamic compromise? _____

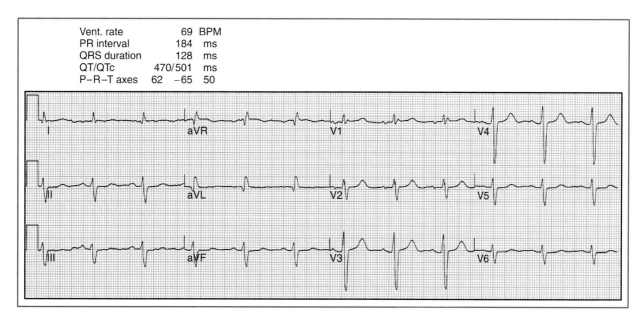

```
Vent. rate          69   BPM
PR interval        184   ms
QRS duration       128   ms
QT/QTc         470/501   ms
P–R–T axes      62  –65  50
```

Figure 5–13.

Lead I: _____   Lead II: _____   Lead III: _____   R Axis: _____

Axis: _____   Hemiblock: _____

QRS width? _____   BBB? _____   BFB? _____

Risk for: Complete heart block? _____   Sudden cardiac death? _____

　　　　　Hemodynamic compromise? _____

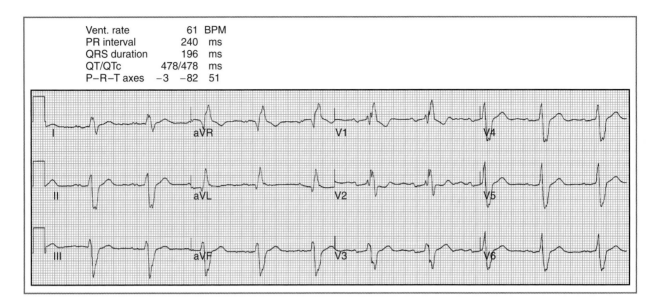

Vent. rate   61 BPM
PR interval   240 ms
QRS duration   196 ms
QT/QTc   478/478 ms
P–R–T axes   −3 −82 51

Figure 5–14.

Lead I: _____   Lead II: _____   Lead III: _____   R Axis: _____

Axis: _____   Hemiblock: _____

QRS width? _____   BBB? _____   BFB? _____

Risk for: Complete heart block? _____   Sudden cardiac death? _____

            Hemodynamic compromise? _____

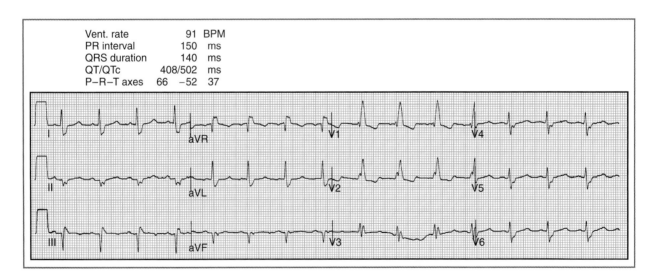

Vent. rate   91 BPM
PR interval   150 ms
QRS duration   140 ms
QT/QTc   408/502 ms
P–R–T axes   66 −52 37

Figure 5–15.

Lead I: _____   Lead II: _____   Lead III: _____   R Axis: _____

Axis: _____   Hemiblock: _____

QRS width? _____   BBB? _____   BFB? _____

Risk for: Complete heart block? _____   Sudden cardiac death? _____

            Hemodynamic compromise? _____

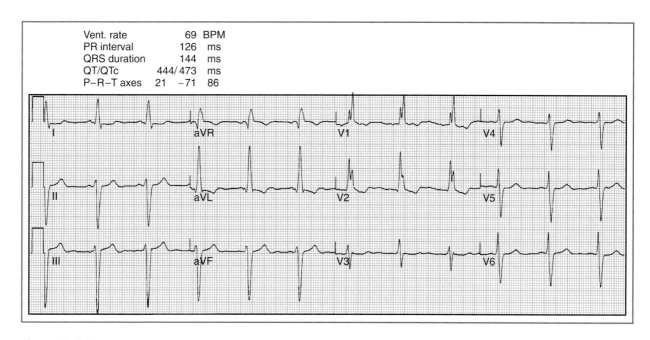

Vent. rate   69 BPM
PR interval   126 ms
QRS duration   144 ms
QT/QTc   444/ 473 ms
P–R–T axes 21 −71 86

Figure 5–16.

Lead I: _____ Lead II: _____ Lead III: _____ R Axis: _____

Axis: _____ Hemiblock: _____

QRS width? _____ BBB? _____ BFB? _____

Risk for: Complete heart block? _____ Sudden cardiac death? _____

       Hemodynamic compromise? _____

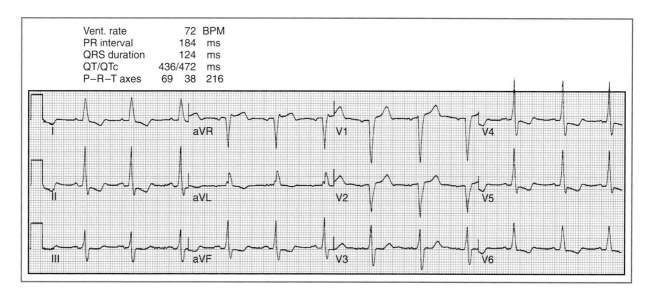

Vent. rate   72 BPM
PR interval   184 ms
QRS duration   124 ms
QT/QTc   436/472 ms
P–R–T axes 69 38 216

Figure 5–17.

Lead I: _____ Lead II: _____ Lead III: _____ R Axis: _____

Axis: _____ Hemiblock: _____

QRS width? _____ BBB? _____ BFB? _____

Risk for: Complete heart block? _____ Sudden cardiac death? _____

       Hemodynamic compromise? _____

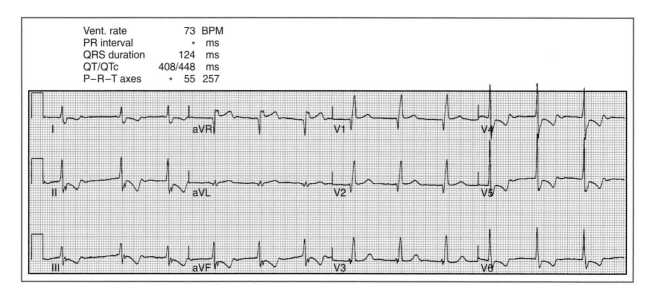

Figure 5–18.

Lead I:_____ Lead II:_____ Lead III:_____ R Axis:_____

Axis:_____ Hemiblock:_____

QRS width?_____ BBB?_____ BFB?_____

Risk for: Complete heart block?_____ Sudden cardiac death?_____

Hemodynamic compromise?_____

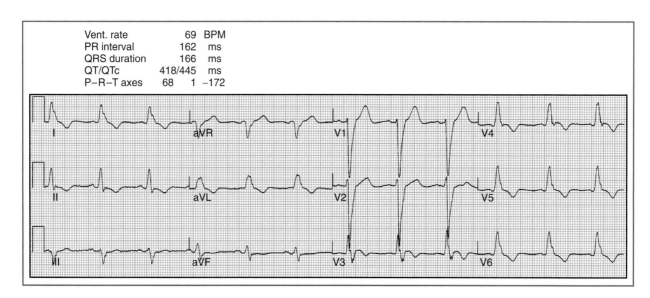

Figure 5–19.

Lead I:_____ Lead II:_____ Lead III:_____ R Axis:_____

Axis:_____ Hemiblock:_____

QRS width?_____ BBB?_____ BFB?_____

Risk for: Complete heart block?_____ Sudden cardiac death?_____

Hemodynamic compromise?_____

SUMMARY

A bifascicular block is a serious conduction system problem. Some patients may be asymptomatic with an old condition. However, patients who present with signs and symptoms of an acute myocardial infarction and have a bifascicular block should be aggressively managed. The clinician should prepare for possible cardiac arrest, bradycardia, and/or heart block. In other words, be prepared for the worst. Realize the patient is much sicker than someone with an uncomplicated MI. He may go into complete heart block suddenly and without warning. Blood pressure may drop precipitously. He may go into V-fib or VT without warning.

- Lidocaine, procainamide, and like antiarrhythmia medications are contraindicated unless the patient is in VT or VF.
- Place pacer/defibrillator pads or multifunction pads on an unstable patient.
- Be prepared to pace the patient.
- Be prepared to defibrillate the patient.

As noted earlier, some patients may tolerate this condition well as long as they are at rest. But because of the compromised conduction system, the heart cannot fill the request for extra output when those patients try to get up.

GLOSSARY

intraventricular heart block a block within the ventricular conduction system.

chapter 6

Wide Complex Tachycardia

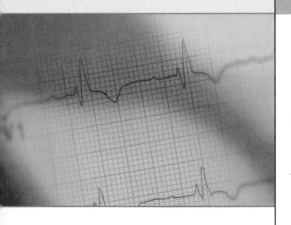

objectives

After reading this chapter, you should be able to:

1. Describe possible pitfalls in diagnosing wide complex tachycardia.

2. Describe the potential complications that can result from misdiagnosing a wide complex tachycardia.

3. Describe four simple criteria for differentiating VT from SVT with a wide QRS complex.

4. Given a 12-lead ECG and the VT chart, identify the origin of various wide complex arrhythmias.

INTRODUCTION

A familiar algorithm addresses a wide complex tachycardia of uncertain origin. This algorithm, based partly on the QRS width being greater than 140 ms, is only about 70 percent specific overall, as it does not identify the complex in which the measurement should be taken. It has been demonstrated that in using Lead MCL-1 (V1), the criterion for QRS width is altered between positively and negatively deflected complexes. Recent guidelines now suggest getting a 12-lead ECG to attempt to diagnose the rhythm. This information is usually not presented to most students in an ACLS course.

MISDIAGNOSIS OF VENTRICULAR TACHYCARDIA

Misdiagnosis of ventricular tachycardia in the clinical setting can lead to immediate collapse of the patient's blood pressure in the acute stage of therapy. Furthermore, if the patient survives and the condition is still misdiagnosed, improper treatment can result in the patient's death. One group studied 150 patients with a wide complex tachycardia and found that 122 had ventricular tachycardia (VT), 21 had supraventricular tachycardia (SVT), and 7 had something that looked like Wolf-Parkinson-White syndrome (WPW). But only 39 of the 122 patients with VT were diagnosed correctly in the acute setting.

Although the study did not give the reasons for this misdiagnosis, the following two factors were probably involved:

- Patients probably had good blood pressure and no bad signs or symptoms. This situation could lead to the assumption that because the patients appeared to be so stable, the diagnosis could not be VT. In fact, some patients can tolerate VT and others cannot. Allowing vital signs to cloud diagnostic judgment on VT is one of many pitfalls encountered.
- VT gets providers excited. This rhythm is a known lethal one, and many acute-care providers treat it without first analyzing a 12-lead ECG, completing a history, or performing a physical exam. Despite the perception that SVT occurs more often than VT, the reverse is true. Unfortunately, VT occurs more often.

Another problem that occurs with misdiagnosis is that some drugs given, such as procainamide, could terminate both SVT and VT. Therefore, if SVT was assumed, the VT could be recurrent and deadly later. In the acute setting, you may be the only one to see that arrhythmia. A 12-lead ECG can be a useful diagnostic for the hospital cardiologist and can greatly increase the chances of finding the location and mechanism of the tachycardia, whether VT, SVT, or WPW. If the location and the mechanisms are known, the patient can get a safe and effective cure for the condition. Therefore, with just a little extra investigation, the clinician can identify the arrhythmia, provide immediate treatment, and help facilitate a beneficial end to the patient's problem later at the hospital.

Most clinicians use four protocols to treat tachycardia. Three of the protocols are specific to rhythm diagnosis and one is a guess. Are you asking: If the uncertain origin is that valuable, why not just treat all tachycardia with that fourth protocol? The answer is simple. Knowing for sure provides more benefit and less risk. In other words, diagnose and treat the problem in the most effective manner according to medical research and practice. Dependence on a single lead—specifically, Lead II—has tied the hands of many acute-care providers in the past.

DIFFERENTIATING VT FROM SVT

It is tempting to allow technology to work its magic. Clinicians have come to welcome it in and out of the hospital setting, as thousands of pulse oximetry, capnometry units, monitors, and other pieces of equipment are used on a daily basis. ECG machines offer a computer analysis of the ECG, but this diagnosis may be grossly inaccurate and misleading (Figure 6–1). Therefore, the acute-care provider needs to learn how to use a multi-lead approach to differentiate VT from SVT.

THE PRIMARY SURVEY

The differentiation of a wide complex tachycardia should be done when you see the 12-lead. If you find a life threat during the primary survey, you should treat that threat immediately. Ventricular tachycardia is a life-threatening condition and should be correctly identified, recorded, and terminated before you continue assessing the 12-lead for other problems. To do so, follow these steps:

1. Measure the QRS width.
2. Determine the axis.
3. Look at morphology changes.
4. Look at concordance criteria.
5. Look for signs of AV dissociation.
6. Get a good patient history.
7. Do a physical exam.

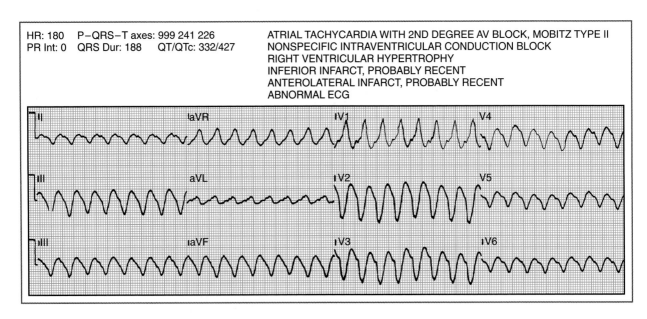

Figure 6–1. Example of an inaccurate, misleading ECG analysis.

ECG axis criteria   If the ECG shows extreme right-axis deviation—negative deflections in Leads I, II, and III, with Lead MCL-1 (V1) positive—the rhythm is VT (Figure 6–2). Recall from Chapter 3 that this type of axis originates in the ventricles; the impulse is going away from Leads I, II, and III. Moreover, Lead MCL-1 (V1) shows an upright complex, solidifying the diagnosis (Figure 6–3). This extreme right-axis deviation (ERAD), also known as indeterminate axis, northwest axis, or "no man's land," does not occur in SVT.

This criterion is one of the most accurate for calling VT and should be the first one you look for. It can also be found by using a 4-lead baseline—Leads I, II, III, and MCL-1 (V1).

Not all VT can be classified as ERAD, however. VT can have other axis deviations. Another useful axis criterion for VT—in this case, a wide complex tachycardia—is having a right-axis deviation and a negative MCL-1 (V1) (Figures 6–4 and 6–5).

In a patient with a previous MI, VT usually has either a pathological left- or an extreme right-axis deviation, especially when Lead MCL-1 (V1) is positive. If MCL-1 (V1) is negative, a left-axis deviation is not helpful in calling VT. Finally, in a patient with a preexisting BBB, SVT can also have an abnormal axis.

QRS morphology   QRS morphology reflects the route impulses travel through the ventricles. Ventricular beats are usually wide and bizarre, reflecting the erratic pattern caused by the impulses as they travel through the ventricles outside the bundle branches. The beats are wide because it takes time for the impulse to travel throughout

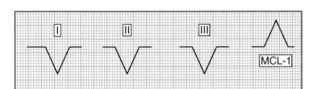

Figure 6–2. Extreme right-axis deviation and a positive MCL-1 (V1).

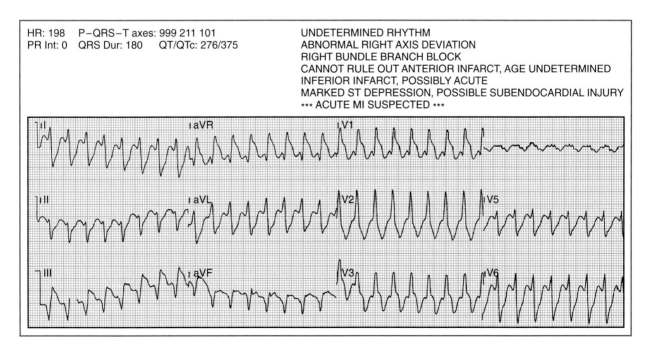

HR: 198   P–QRS–T axes: 999 211 101
PR Int: 0   QRS Dur: 180   QT/QTc: 276/375

UNDETERMINED RHYTHM
ABNORMAL RIGHT AXIS DEVIATION
RIGHT BUNDLE BRANCH BLOCK
CANNOT RULE OUT ANTERIOR INFARCT, AGE UNDETERMINED
INFERIOR INFARCT, POSSIBLY ACUTE
MARKED ST DEPRESSION, POSSIBLE SUBENDOCARDIAL INJURY
*** ACUTE MI SUSPECTED ***

Figure 6–3. Ventricular tachycardia: extreme right-axis deviation and a positive MCL-1 (V1).

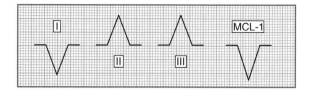

Figure 6–4. Right-axis deviation plus a negative MCL-1 (V1).

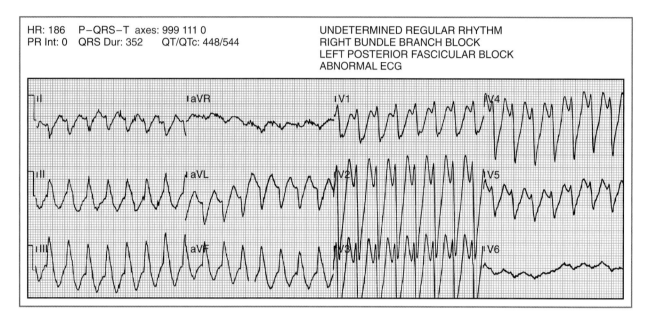

Figure 6–5. Ventricular tachycardia: right-axis deviation and a negative MCL-1 (V1).

both ventricles. Even using only one Lead MCL-1 (V1) or MCL-6 (V6), accurate criteria have been established strongly suggestive of VT.

With a QRS positive in Lead MCL-1 (V1), three criteria suggest VT (Figure 6–6). In Figure 6–6, the tracing marked "a" shows the left peak is taller than the right peak. One nurse suggests that "big mountain/little mountain" means "big problem," or VT. Other people use the analogy of big rabbit ear/little rabbit ear, with the latter a bad rabbit, or VT. The tracing marked "b" shows another clue for VT: a single upright peak, especially when the axis is ERAD. The tracing marked "c" shows a single peak with a slur, or lopped-off ear.

Figure 6–7 shows another morphology pattern, this one with the QRS complex negative in Lead MCL-1 (V1). In Figure 6–7, the tracing marked "a" shows the R wave is fat (>40 ms). In the tracings marked "b" and "c," the initial downstroke shows a notch and a slur, respectively.

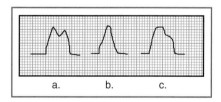

Figure 6–6. Ventricular tachycardia: QRS positive in MCL-1 (V1), with three variables.

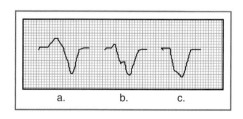

Figure 6–7. Ventricular tachycardia: QRS negative in MCL-1 (V1).

In some circumstances, it may be unclear whether the complex goes up or down in Lead MCL-1 (V1), owing to artifact or other abnormality or because no clues are to be found in Lead MCL-1 (V1). In these cases, because Lead MCL-1 (V1) is not helpful, Lead V6 (MCL-6) should be looked at for morphology criteria (Figure 6–8).

Any predominately negative complex in Lead V6 (MCL-6) suggests VT. The reason is that the positive electrode in V6 is at the lower left part of the heart. Impulses originating in the ventricles will more than likely go away from this electrode, thus producing a negative complex (Figure 6–9).

Concordance criteria Simply put, **concordance** means all the same. In other words, all the precordial leads (MCL-1, V1 through V6) will be up or down, and both conditions suggest VT (Figure 6–10). However, it is important in these circumstances to rule out a couple of conditions that could mimic VT and therefore lead to the wrong diagnosis and management.

- Although negative concordance suggests VT (Figure 6–11), the acute-care provider must look carefully to determine whether the rhythm is atrial in origin. An LBBB can be negatively concordant and in the circumstance could be a tragic misdiagnosis.
- Positive concordance may indicate either VT or WPW (Figure 6–12). Therefore, the acute-care provider must rule out WPW before making the call. Typically, WPW can be identified by the characteristic delta wave that slurs on the initial upstroke toward the P wave.

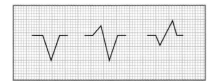

Figure 6–8. Lead V6 (MCL-6) morphology criteria.

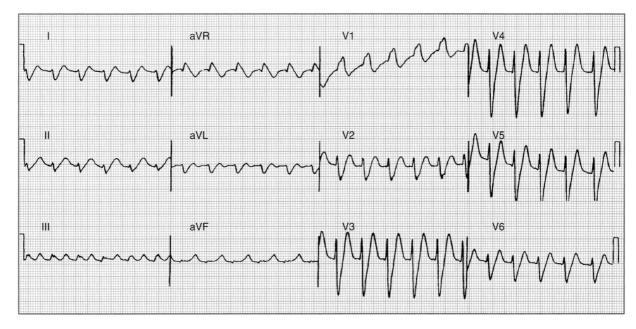

Figure 6–9. Ventricular tachycardia: V6 with a negative deflection.

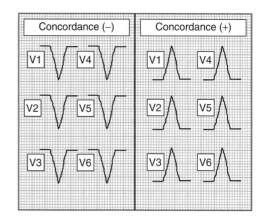

Figure 6–10. Concordance criteria can be positive or negative deflecting.

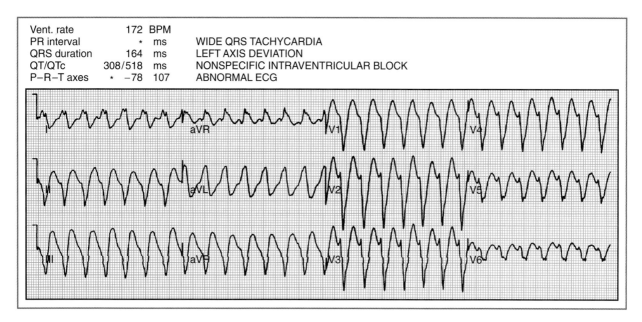

Vent. rate	172	BPM	
PR interval	*	ms	WIDE QRS TACHYCARDIA
QRS duration	164	ms	LEFT AXIS DEVIATION
QT/QTc	308/518	ms	NONSPECIFIC INTRAVENTRICULAR BLOCK
P–R–T axes	*	−78 107	ABNORMAL ECG

Figure 6–11. Ventricular tachycardia: negative concordance in V1–V6.

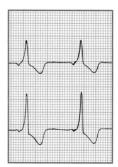

Figure 6–12. Delta waves characteristic of WPW.

Measurements The acute-care provider's ability to measure accurately can be an important asset in differentiating VT from SVT. For example, a positive QRS complex >140 ms in MCL-1 (V1) suggests VT. In a negative MCL-1 (V1), a QRS >160 ms points to VT.

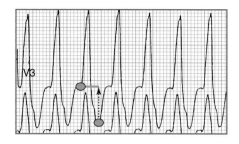

Figure 6–13. The nadir point, found at the end of ventricular activation at the peak of the S wave.

One highly reliable measurement criterion is the **RS interval**, frequently cited in the literature because of its accuracy in describing VT. The RS interval is measured from the start of the R wave to the tip, or nadir point, of the S wave (Figure 6–13). This interval measures the ventricular activation time. If this interval is more than 100 ms, the diagnosis is VT.

AV dissociation **AV dissociation**, another tool for diagnosing VT, can be discovered both clinically and on the ECG. Clues to AV dissociation include:

- Cannon A waves.
- P waves out of place and isolated.
- Different S1 (first heart sound).

Cannon A waves are pressure waves that shoot up through the jugular veins at irregular intervals because the atria occasionally contract when the ventricles are not prepared, sending the pressure waves into the jugular veins. This action proves AV dissociation. If the beat were normal, the left heart would fill with the atrial contraction.

Some other conditions also can produce cannon waves, or pulsating jugular veins. Right-heart failure, for whatever reason, also causes this but for every beat. VT, by contrast, is erratic, with no pattern to the cannon A waves.

Some acute-care providers maintain that if P waves are present, the rhythm cannot be VT. In fact, the reverse is true. The presence of P waves usually indicates VT. When looking for P waves as a clue to VT, one must look at all 12 leads and try to find a P wave that is unique to one or perhaps two leads. But this pattern is not repeating. In other words, you may see it after one complex in a strip but not in the others.

Patient history Obtaining a patient history is an integral part of acute-care practice. An accurate one from a patient who may be experiencing VT is crucial and makes diagnosis easier.

One clue involves asking two questions that have probably already been asked or discovered in some way:

- Have you ever had a heart attack before?
- Did you have tachycardia—fast heart rates—starting after your heart attack?

If the answer to both questions is yes, the likelihood is high that the rhythm is VT, especially if the axis deviation is extreme right or pathological left.

Other useful information Ventricular tachycardia, with the exception of some forms of polymorphic ventricular tachycardia (torsades de pointes), is usually very regular. One common misdiagnosis in wide complex tachycardia is incorrectly interpreting an irregular rhythm as VT. Atrial fibrillation, characterized by irregular rhythm and fast ventricular response, is about the only arrhythmia that meets that criterion (Figure 6–14). Misdiagnosing and improper treatment of this rhythm can have bad outcomes.

Figure 6–14. Atrial fibrillation with rapid ventricular response.

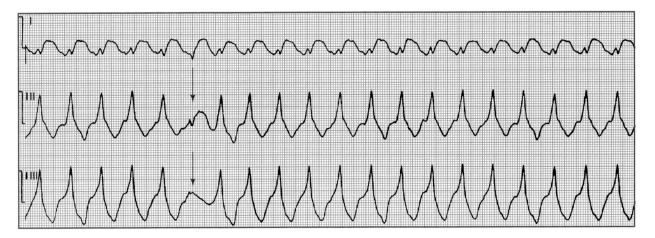

Figure 6–15. Capture, or fusion, beats.

Although not seen frequently, another bit of useful information indicative of VT is the presence of capture, or fusion, beats (Figure 6–15). These beats are narrow complex beats occurring within a sustained VT rhythm. The atria are "sneaking one in" on the ventricles. According to basic ECG interpretation, the fastest pacemaker usually drives the heart. If the ventricles are firing impulses at 160 beats per minute and the atria are firing at 120 beats per minute, the ventricles will be leading the heart. Occasionally, a normally conducted beat catches the ventricles at just the right time, and the beat goes through. This sign demonstrates AV dissociation, which is diagnostic for VT. This phenomenon is visible only about 25 percent of the time.

PUTTING IT ALL TOGETHER

This chapter has introduced criteria that can be used to differentiate VT from SVT. But no discussion or examples of diagnosing SVT were given. No criteria are specific to SVT. Rather, it is much more important to find and to treat VT than it is to look for SVT.

Because of the difficulty of memorizing all the criteria for VT, the system described in Table 6–1 was developed for assessing the 12-lead for VT. This easy-to-use list for identifying wide complex tachycardia >150 is simple to learn and apply quickly in the field. The criteria are listed in order of ease of use, most often seen, and specificity (accuracy).

To use this systematic approach, first run a 12- or 9-lead. Start at the top with the first criterion. If it is satisfied, no more looking is needed. If this criterion is not satisfied, go to the next one in the list. Continue down the list if the diagnosis is not made by earlier criteria. If you get to the bottom and still have no clear-cut diagnosis, the measurement criterion becomes your only option.

PRACTICE: DIAGNOSING WIDE COMPLEX TACHYCARDIA

Practice diagnosing wide complex tachycardia on the ECGs in Figures 6–16 through 6–22. Use the system outlined in Table 6–1 for your diagnosis. List the criteria you find as positive for VT. All answers are provided in the Answer Key at the back of the book.

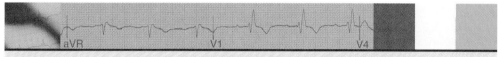

TABLE 6–1. *Wide Complex Tachycardia >150*

The criteria herein are listed in order of ease of use, most often seen, and specificity (accuracy) for assessing the 12-lead for VT.

1. ERAD and positive V1 (MCL-1).
2. QRS morphology in V1 (MCL-1).
3. QRS morphology in V6 (MCL-6).
4. ERAD and negative V1 (MCL-1).

5. Concordance in V1 through V6 (up or down).
6. RS interval >100 ms any V lead.
7. QRS >140 ms if up or >160 if down in V1 (MCL-1).

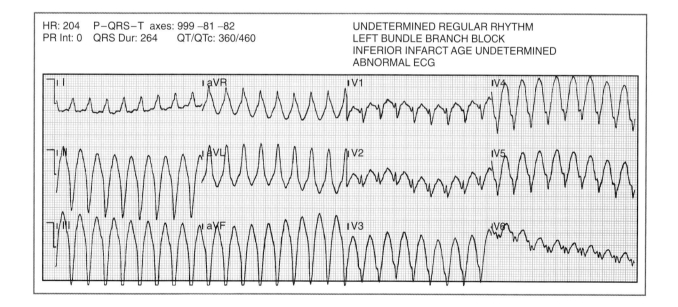

HR: 204   P–QRS–T axes: 999 –81 –82
PR Int: 0   QRS Dur: 264   QT/QTc: 360/460

UNDETERMINED REGULAR RHYTHM
LEFT BUNDLE BRANCH BLOCK
INFERIOR INFARCT AGE UNDETERMINED
ABNORMAL ECG

Figure 6–16.

1. _____
2. _____
3. _____
4. _____
5. _____

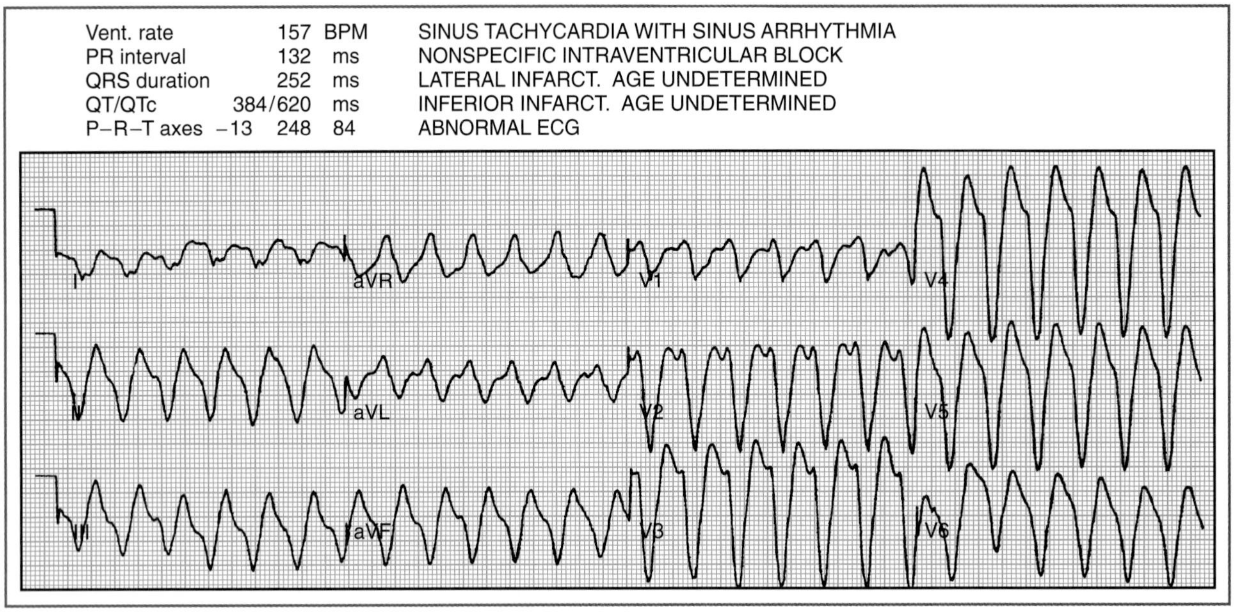
Vent. rate 157 BPM
PR interval 132 ms
QRS duration 252 ms
QT/QTc 384/620 ms
P–R–T axes –13 248 84
SINUS TACHYCARDIA WITH SINUS ARRHYTHMIA
NONSPECIFIC INTRAVENTRICULAR BLOCK
LATERAL INFARCT. AGE UNDETERMINED
INFERIOR INFARCT. AGE UNDETERMINED
ABNORMAL ECG
I
aVR
V1
V4
II
aVL
V2
V5
III
aVF
V3
V6

Figure 6–17.

1. ______________________________

2. ______________________________

3. ______________________________

4. ______________________________

5. ______________________________

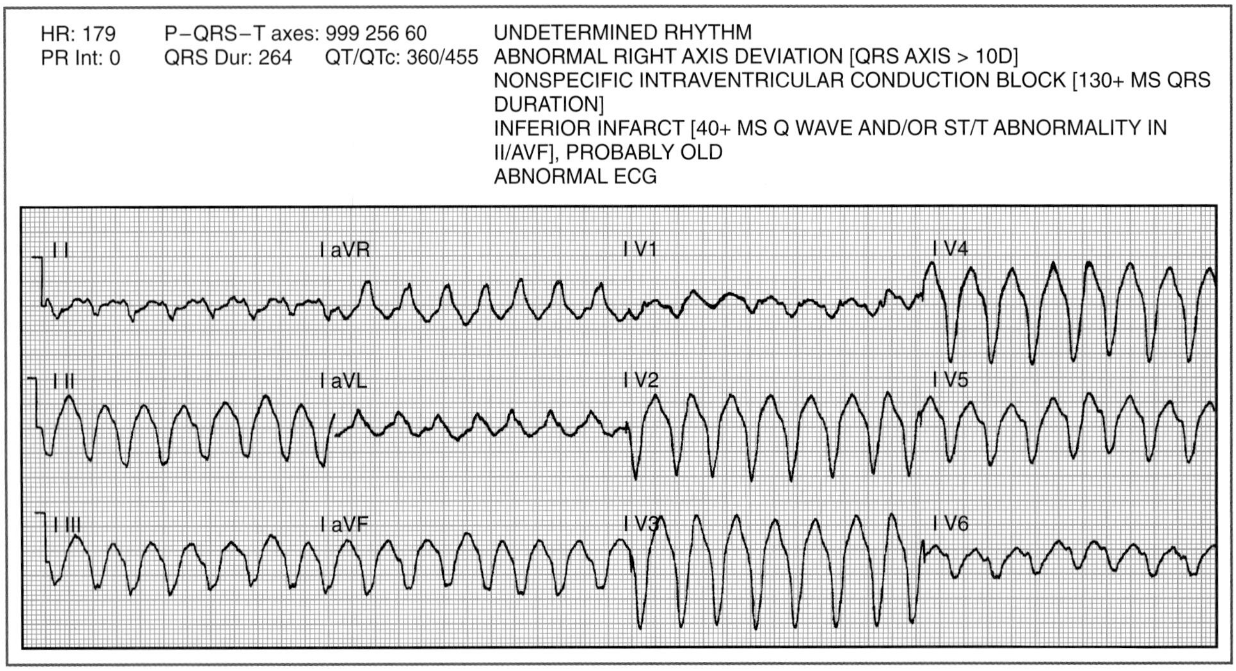
HR: 179
PR Int: 0
P–QRS–T axes: 999 256 60
QRS Dur: 264
QT/QTc: 360/455
UNDETERMINED RHYTHM
ABNORMAL RIGHT AXIS DEVIATION [QRS AXIS > 10D]
NONSPECIFIC INTRAVENTRICULAR CONDUCTION BLOCK [130+ MS QRS DURATION]
INFERIOR INFARCT [40+ MS Q WAVE AND/OR ST/T ABNORMALITY IN II/AVF], PROBABLY OLD
ABNORMAL ECG
I
aVR
V1
V4
II
aVL
V2
V5
III
aVF
V3
V6

Figure 6–18.

1. ______________________________

2. ______________________________

3. ______________________________

4. ______________________________

5. ______________________________

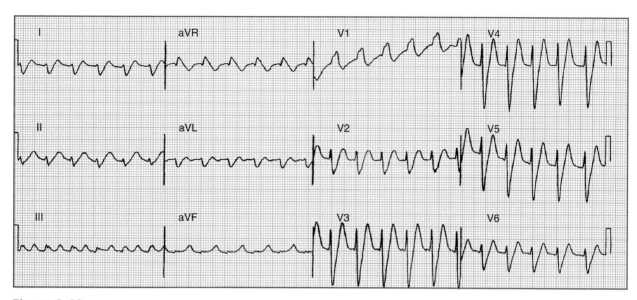

Figure 6–19.

1. _____

2. _____

3. _____

4. _____

5. _____

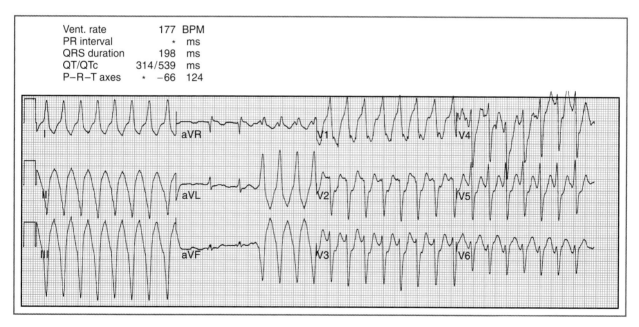

Figure 6–20.

1. _____

2. _____

3. _____

4. _____

5. _____

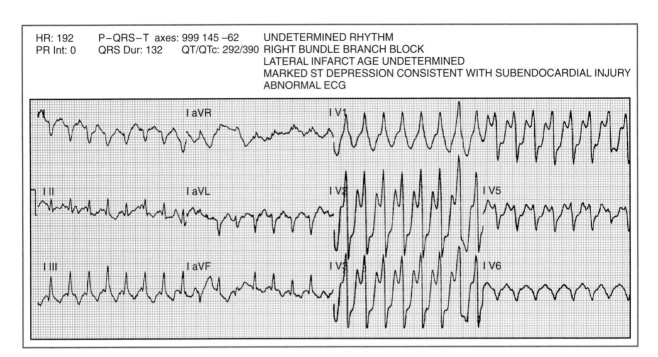

```
HR: 192      P–QRS–T  axes: 999 145 –62     UNDETERMINED RHYTHM
PR Int: 0    QRS Dur: 132   QT/QTc: 292/390  RIGHT BUNDLE BRANCH BLOCK
                                             LATERAL INFARCT AGE UNDETERMINED
                                             MARKED ST DEPRESSION CONSISTENT WITH SUBENDOCARDIAL INJURY
                                             ABNORMAL ECG
```

Figure 6–21.

1. _____
2. _____
3. _____
4. _____
5. _____

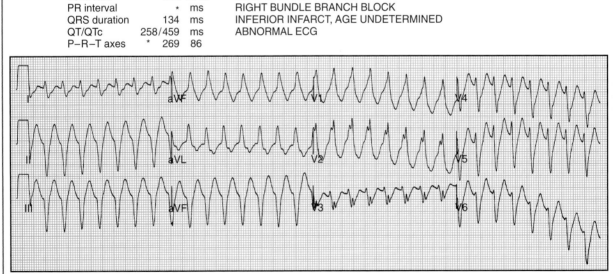

```
Vent. rate         150  BPM     WIDE QRS TACHYCARDIA
PR interval          *  ms      RIGHT BUNDLE BRANCH BLOCK
QRS duration       134  ms      INFERIOR INFARCT, AGE UNDETERMINED
QT/QTc        258/459  ms      ABNORMAL ECG
P–R–T axes      *  269  86
```

Figure 6–22.

1. _____
2. _____
3. _____
4. _____
5. _____

SUMMARY

This chapter has emphasized the importance of a multi-lead approach to ECG interpretation of VT, using explanation and examples. A systematic approach to wide complex tachycardia should include all elements of patient assessment, including history, physical exam, and use of the chart for applying ECG criteria. The result will be sound, rapid identification of this life-threatening arrhythmia, appropriate acute management, and better prognosis for a more permanent solution to the problem.

Following are the key points of this chapter.

- VT occurs more often than SVT.
- VT is usually very regular.
- VT can present with good blood pressure and no symptoms.
- Get a good patient history.
- Do a thorough physical exam.
- Use a systematic approach—Table 6–1—the same way for every patient.
- AV dissociation is worth a look.
- Do not strain yourself by looking too hard for one criterion.
- If the criterion is uncertain, move down the chart to one that is not.

GLOSSARY

AV dissociation a condition in which the atria and ventricles do not activate in a synchronous fashion but beat independent of each other.

cannon A waves pressure waves that shoot up through the jugular veins at irregular intervals.

concordance all the same; that is, precordial leads are up or down, and both conditions suggest VT.

RS interval measures the ventricular activation time; begins at the start of the R wave and continues to the tip, or nadir point, of the S wave.

chapter 7

Acute Myocardial Infarction Pathophysiology

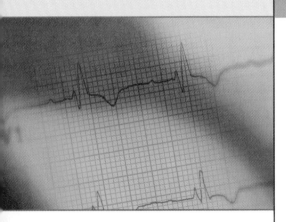

objectives

After reading this chapter, you should be able to:

1. Describe the myocardial coronary blood supply.

2. Name the major coronary arteries and the regions of the heart to which they supply blood.

3. Explain how plaque formation and clot formation relate to the development of myocardial infarction.

4. Describe an intervention plan for managing myocardial infarction.

5. Explain why getting a good medical history is so important in managing the patient with myocardial infarction.

6. List the most common presentations in AMI for women and the elderly.

INTRODUCTION

ECG changes can help you predict which areas of the heart are in trouble, either as an infarct or as a conduction deficit. It always helps to be prepared for the worst. Being able to do that comes from a sound working knowledge of cardiovascular pathophysiology and electrocardiography.

CORONARY ARTERIES

The coronary arteries branch off from the aorta, just above the leaflets of the aortic valve (Figure 7–1). In fact, during systole, or contraction of the ventricles, the pressure opens the valve, shielding the opening to these arteries from the high-pressure surge. After the contraction, the valve closes, and the backflow of blood from the aortic arch flows into the coronary arteries. The coronary arteries, therefore, fill during diastole, or the resting phase of the heart. Myocardial blood is returned to the right atrium of the heart via the coronary sinus and the great cardiac vein.

RIGHT CORONARY ARTERY

Through its marginal branch, the right coronary artery (RCA) (Figure 7–2) supplies the inferior wall of the left ventricle and feeds the right ventricle (Table 7–1). The RCA branches off into the posterior descending coronary artery, which supplies the posterior wall of the left ventricle. Thus, a proximal occlusion could affect all these areas. As a matter of statistics, an inferior wall infarction has posterior and/or right ventricular involvement in 50 percent of the cases.

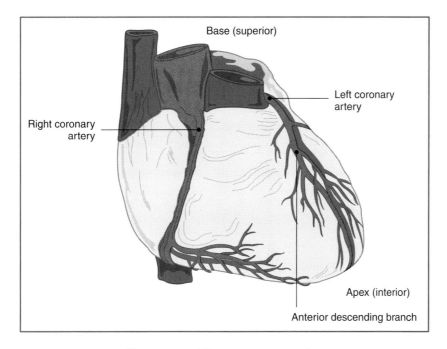

Figure 7–1. The coronary arteries.

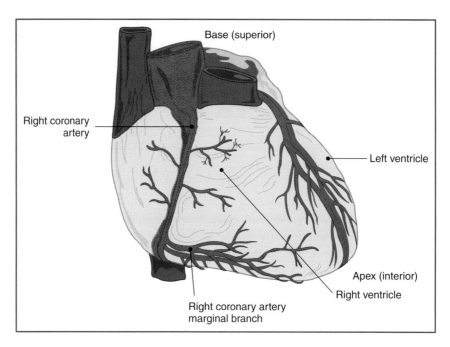

Figure 7–2. The right coronary artery (RCA).

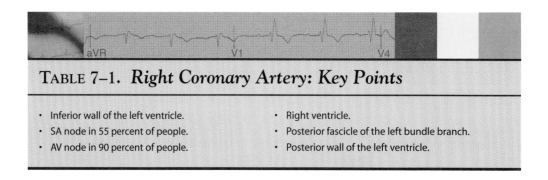

TABLE 7–1. *Right Coronary Artery: Key Points*

- Inferior wall of the left ventricle.
- SA node in 55 percent of people.
- AV node in 90 percent of people.

- Right ventricle.
- Posterior fascicle of the left bundle branch.
- Posterior wall of the left ventricle.

The right coronary artery is also responsible in part for the blood supply to the SA and AV nodes. When blood supply to these areas is compromised, the patient may experience bradycardia (SA node) or AV heart delays (first-degree blocks or second-degree type 1: Wenckebach). The posterior descending branch also feeds part of the left bundle branch.

LEFT CORONARY ARTERY

Left anterior descending branch The left anterior descending (LAD) coronary artery (Table 7–2) is a major branch of the left coronary artery (Figure 7–3) and feeds 40 percent of the left ventricular muscle mass. Because most sudden-death AMIs result from a proximal occlusion of the left anterior descending (LAD) coronary artery, it is known as "the widow maker." Generally, a 40 percent involvement of the left ventricle results in irritation that causes immediate ventricular fibrillation or ventricular tachycardia. The left anterior descending coronary artery feeds the anterior and septal walls of the left ventricle.

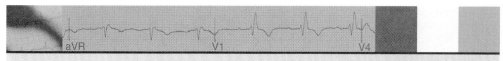

TABLE 7–2. *Left Anterior Descending Coronary Artery: Key Points*

- Anterior wall of the left ventricle.
- Intraventricular septal artery (septum).
- RBB, LBB, and both fascicles of the LBB.

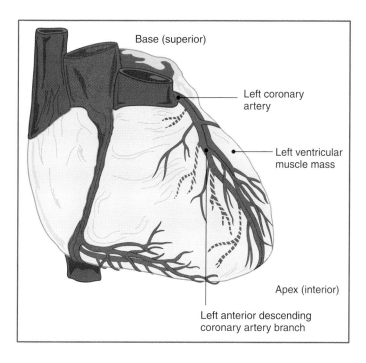

Base (superior)

Left coronary artery

Left ventricular muscle mass

Apex (interior)

Left anterior descending coronary artery branch

Figure 7–3. The left anterior descending branch of the left coronary artery.

The LAD also supplies the bundle of His and both bundle branches through the intraventricular septal perforator artery. That is why some patients may develop complete heart block, bundle branch blocks, or hemiblock as another complication of an LAD proximal occlusion.

Left circumflex artery The left circumflex artery (LCA) is the other major division of the left coronary artery (Figure 7–4). The LCA goes "around" the side and to the back of the heart. The circumflex artery feeds the lateral and posterior walls of the left ventricle.

The circumflex artery feeds the SA node in about 45 percent of the cardiac population and feeds the AV node in about 10 percent of the cardiac patients (Table 7–3). An isolated circumflex artery occlusion is not as common as an occlusion of the RCA or the LAD.

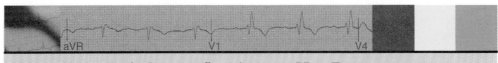

TABLE 7-3. *Left Circumflex Artery: Key Points*

- Lateral wall of the left ventricle.
- SA node in 45 percent of patients.
- AV node in 10 percent of patients.
- Posterior wall of left ventricle.

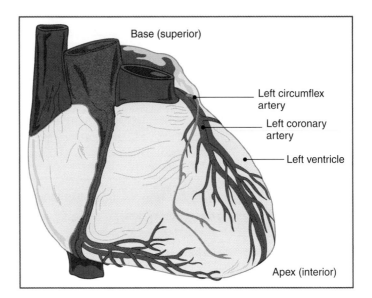

Figure 7–4. The left circumflex artery.

GENESIS OF AN AMI

Various risk factors contribute to the formation of atherosclerotic plaque on the walls of the coronary arteries. Prevention of the plaque formation is a good way to prevent MIs. As a provider, you should be proactive in public education about plaque formation.

Risk factors can be categorized as either nonmodifiable or modifiable. Nonmodifiable risk factors are gender, age, and family history. Other factors, such as hypertension, hyperlipidemia (cholesterol and triglycerides), obesity, stress, drug and alcohol use, and smoking can be altered or controlled.

When taking a patient history, especially for someone with first-time chest pain, risk factors are important, although frequently overlooked. Risk factors can be contributory to the diagnosis.

PLAQUE FORMATION

Plaque forms on vessel walls as a result of low-density lipoprotein (LDL) sticking between layers of the arterial wall. In some cases, such as with smokers, the intimal layer of the artery is permeable and the LDL deposits under it. Over time, this LDL (bad cholesterol) comes into contact with other chemicals and produces the plaque. The plaque continues to build up, narrowing the artery lumen. This condition is known as **atherosclerosis**.

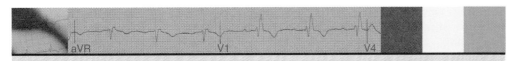

TABLE 7–4. *Occlusion Data*

- In general, the patient with chest pain or symptomatic on exertion had a 70 percent to 85 percent stenosis, or narrowing of the artery.
- The patient who was symptomatic at rest had 90 percent narrowing.
- Symptomatic patients whose symptoms were unrelieved by rest or nitroglycerin were 100 percent occluded.

Atherosclerosis narrows the artery lumen. The narrower the artery, the less blood flow that is available for perfusion of the myocardium. With a decrease in blood supply, any increased demand causes the characteristic angina pectoris, or chest pain. Frequently, patients have temporary chest pain they attribute to indigestion. They say that they sat down, rested, and took some antacid tablets that made the pain go away. In reality, however, the antacids were not as effective as the resting. Resting lowered the demand on the heart; therefore, the blood supply was able to keep up the perfusion. Table 7–4 highlights some interesting data.

CLOT FORMATION

As atherosclerotic plaque hardens, it becomes vulnerable to rupture. When a piece of the plaque ruptures, it breaks off a part of the intimal layer of the blood vessel, causing an injury. The result of this injury is the same as if you cut your arm. At first, you bleed, and then a scab forms, stopping the bleeding and sealing the wound. This same pathophysiology occurs on the inside of a coronary artery.

Clot formation is a natural part of the body's ability to heal itself. When an injury occurs, a chemical, known as thromboplastin, is released. Platelets run into the damaged tissue and are damaged themselves, leading to release of clotting factor #3, which further activates platelets so that they become sticky and can seal the damaged area. With this process comes a complex cascade of chemical reactions that produce fibrin, a kind of mesh framework that aids in clot formation and sealing the wound. The result is a blood clot that traps platelets and red and white blood cells and continues to grow. However, unlike the clot that forms when you cut your arm, a blood vessel completely clots off because it has definitive limits. This total occlusion of the artery is the prelude to an acute myocardial infarction.

A damaged vessel does not immediately totally occlude. Clot formation is a dynamic process, and over time the vessel can occlude. However, knowing about the clot-forming cascade enables one to perhaps intervene in this process. Aspirin and other drugs have been used to deactivate platelets so that they are not sticky and are not contributory to the clot. The standard is two to four tablets of low-strength aspirin (162–325 mg), chewed, to achieve rapid blood levels (about 15 minutes). Heparin, an anticoagulant, slows the chemical cascade that produces fibrin, the other culprit in the clot-forming process. Other medications, including IIb/IIIa glycoprotein inhibitors and low-molecular-weight heparin, are also used as anticoagulants. The end result is interruption of the clot-forming process. The goal is to prevent the artery from becoming totally occluded, allowing perfusion to continue through collateral or main circulation until definitive care—**fibrinolytics** or cardiac cath lab—can eliminate the clot. Using aspirin and heparin buys some time until definitive care can be obtained.

Why not just give heparin and aspirin to everyone who may be having an AMI? Giving aspirin would probably be okay, although aspirin may be harmful to a patient with asthma. The patient history can help determine that factor. But heparin, if given in the wrong setting, can be fatal. In other words, heparin is reserved for a diagnosed evolving AMI. This diagnosis is based on three elements: history of present illness, physical exam, and definitive 12-lead ECG suggesting an acute myocardial infarction.

INTERVENTION PLAN

GET A GOOD HISTORY

Getting a history of the patient's past and present illnesses is an integral part of any patient assessment. With the cardiac patient, the task becomes even more important. Omitted questions, incomplete answers, and failure to explore the details could be devastating to the patient if the wrong treatment modalities are followed. The use of commonly taught memory aids such as OPQRST (Table 7–5) and SAMPLE (Table 7–6) can help you remember what to investigate. However, OPQRST and SAMPLE are not the way or sequence to ask questions. They are only aids meant to help you remember key points.

TABLE 7–5. *OPQRST: How to Investigate the Chief Complaint*

Memory Aid	Meaning	Description
O	Onset time	Pin the patient down on a time.
P	Provoke	Does anything make the "pain" better? Worse?
Q	Quality	Using open-ended questions, ask the patient to describe the pain. "What does the discomfort feel like?" If the patient responds "It just hurts," then ask, "What would I have to do to you to make it feel like that?" Avoid using closed or leading questions. The most common history-taking error is asking, "Is the pain sharp or dull?" This can lead to the wrong impression of the patient's condition. Explore the details. It would be a tragedy to give heparin to a patient who complained of chest pain and then described it as a ripping, tearing sensation.
R	Radiation/region, or the location of discomfort	Ask the patient to draw a circle around the area that hurts. Watch for nonverbal clues. A clenched fist pressing on the chest, for example, is called Levine's sign, indicative of the squeezing sensation that often accompanies an AMI. Ask, "Do you have any other discomfort?" The discomfort in the jaw is an ache, the left arm is numb, and the patient is nauseated.
S	Severity	Ask for the patient's subjective rating of the pain on a scale of 1 to 10, with 10 being the worst ever felt. Asking for severity provides a baseline to compare the effect of pain-reduction therapies.
T	Time, or duration of chest pain	Pain associated with an AMI generally lasts for 30 minutes or more without relief.

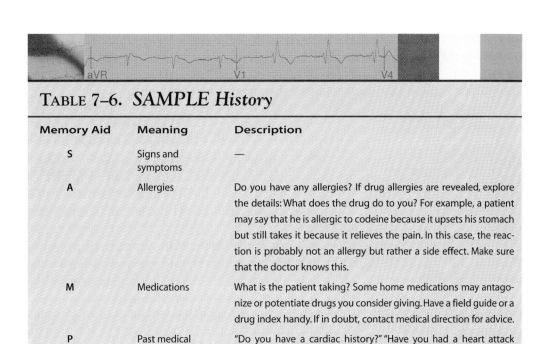

TABLE 7–6. *SAMPLE History*

Memory Aid	Meaning	Description
S	Signs and symptoms	—
A	Allergies	Do you have any allergies? If drug allergies are revealed, explore the details: What does the drug do to you? For example, a patient may say that he is allergic to codeine because it upsets his stomach but still takes it because it relieves the pain. In this case, the reaction is probably not an allergy but rather a side effect. Make sure that the doctor knows this.
M	Medications	What is the patient taking? Some home medications may antagonize or potentiate drugs you consider giving. Have a field guide or a drug index handy. If in doubt, contact medical direction for advice.
P	Past medical history	"Do you have a cardiac history?" "Have you had a heart attack before?" The important thing is to follow up on the details. Ask the patient who has had a heart attack, "Did you go to the hospital, and if so, for how long?" If the patient has no pertinent history, ask about family history or known family diseases, such as cardiac, stroke, or high blood pressure. "Do you smoke? If so, how many packs a day for how long?"
L	Last oral intake	Some studies have shown that a large meal is a precipitating factor for an AMI. Do not dismiss this clue as indigestion.
E	Events leading up to the chief complaint	Having this information will help you see whether the onset was during exertion or at rest.

PHYSICAL EXAM

A general impression of the cardiac patient is essential. Does the patient look sick? What degree of distress is he in? What does the patient's skin look like? Is it cool, pale, sweaty? What nonverbal clues is the patient showing you?

You are the eyes and ears of the physician. A thorough physical exam can help you with a differential diagnosis of the chest discomfort and help the medical direction physician decide on treatment options.

Areas of assessment Assessment of the cardiac patient covers five main areas. First, look for JVD. It can indicate problems with the right ventricle output or perhaps a cardiac tamponade. Listen to lung and heart sounds. Lung sounds may reveal rales, crackles, and wheezing. The crackles can indicate acute pulmonary edema. This complication can occur as a result of a massive AMI, especially if the patient has no history of CHF or fluid retention. Keep in mind that the sensation of being unable to breathe will make the patient with acute pulmonary edema forget that the chest hurts.

Second, auscultate heart sounds, listening for abnormal sounds, such as S3 gallops and murmurs. S3 or S4 heart sounds can indicate poor ejection fraction or ventricular hypertrophy. A murmur can indicate valve problems. A summation gallup can indicate acute failure. (If you are not familiar with heart sounds, use a good CD heart sound self-study module.) Unfortunately, this area of assessment is grossly underused by acute-care providers.

Third, palpate the chest wall to see whether the pain is reproducible. Cardiac chest discomfort is usually not reproducible. Have the patient lean forward and/or change position on the cot. AMI chest pain is not relieved by position changes. In fact, if leaning forward relieves the pain, the condition is likely acute pericarditis.

Fourth, palpate the abdomen for epigastric discomfort, an area of complaint for the cardiac patient. Pressing on that area should not make AMI pain worse. Patients may be nauseated. Also palpate radial pulses in both wrists, feeling for equality and regularity. If pulses differ in intensity, suspect a dissecting aortic aneurysm. When taking a blood pressure in both arms, be suspicious of a difference of more than 15 mmHg. If pulses are irregular, listen to the heart for apical pulses. If different from the radial pulse, a pulse deficit is present. This finding is common in atrial fibrillation and in some other arrhythmias, such as ventricular ectopy.

Fifth, look for peripheral edema. Inspect the ankles of the ambulatory patient or the presacral area of the bedfast patient. Peripheral edema can indicate cardiovascular insufficiency.

Gender and age concerns   Note that the classic signs and symptoms of an MI apply to men, not necessarily to women and the elderly. It is estimated that as many as 50 percent of MIs are missed in women because of this fact. For example, the most common complaints in women with an AMI are weakness and shortness of breath. Seventy-five percent of elderly patients present with shortness of breath as their chief complaint in an AMI. Patients with long-standing diabetes often present with abdominal pain or other nonspecific or atypical complaints. AMIs presenting with such atypical complaints have been referred to as "silent MIs." An estimated 25 percent of all MIs are silent.

12-Lead ECG

Patients with suspected myocardial infarction should have a 12-lead ECG performed as soon as possible. The American Heart Association's guidelines suggest that one should be performed within 10 minutes of patient contact in the emergency department. This standard is also suggested for out-of-hospital providers. Early recognition of an MI can speed the time to diagnosis and can reduce the "door-to-drug time."

Getting a 12-lead ECG is just as important in the out-of-hospital setting, as is prompt notification to the hospital. When the paramedic provides the receiving hospital with all three elements needed for a diagnosis—history, physical exam, and ECG evidence—the physician can order intervention in the form of aspirin and heparin or even fibrinolytic therapy. Whether fibrinolytics are delivered or not, this early notification will allow the hospital to get things ready to intervene and/or, more important, call in the specialist needed for intervention. Whether that intervention is a drug to break up the clot or a cardiologist to take the patient to the cardiac catheterization lab, the door-to-drug or door-to-balloon time can be reduced dramatically.

Out-of-hospital systems should also address the following areas while with the patient. Oxygen, nitroglycerin, and pain control with narcotics are all great ALS support care. The memory aid "MONA greets the MI patient" (MONA stands for morphine, oxygen, nitroglycerin, aspirin) is good to know. Some services also give antiemetics, such as Compazine (prochlorperazine) or Phenergan (promethazine). In addition, where possible, blood samples may be drawn for lab analysis from the IV. This will reduce the number of sticks that are attempted and on the number of sites that are likely to bleed.

Something as simple as completing a fibrinolytic checklist (Figure 7–5) prior to arrival at the hospital has been shown to decrease the time to intervention. Studies have also shown that paramedics and physicians do the checklists with a 98 percent

✝MERCY
ST. JOHN'S
━✦━EMS━✦━

Thrombolytic Checklist

Inclusion / Exclusion Criteria

Pt. Name: _____

Date: _____

MARF: _____

Cardiologist (if known) _____

Indications for Treatment

Yes No

☐ ☐ Ongoing Chest Pain suggestive of an AMI Onset <12 hours

☐ ☐ ECG Evidence of an AMI on 12 or 15 Lead ECG*

☐ ☐ Repeat ECG every 15 minutes if the first is not positive

* ST segment elevation >1mm in limb or posterior leads or
* ST elevation > 2mm in precordial leads in 2 or more related leads
* ST Depression > 2mm leads V1 and V2
* New onset of LBBB

Absolute Contraindications

Yes No

☐ ☐ Active Internal Bleeding

☐ ☐ History of Hemorrhagic CVA or any CVA in the last 2 months

☐ ☐ Recent Brain surgery or trauma (2 months)

☐ ☐ Brain Tumor, Aneurysm, AV malformation

☐ ☐ Known bleeding disorder or Coumadin/warfarin use <3 days

☐ ☐ Severe, uncontrolled hypertension (>180/110)

☐ ☐ Known pericarditis or endocarditis

☐ ☐ High index of suspicion for dissecting aneurysm: tearing pain in back, hypertension, unequal pulses or B/P in arms

☐ ☐ Currently Pregnant

Relative Contraindications

Yes No

☐ ☐ Recent Surgery in the last 10 days

☐ ☐ CPR (traumatic)

☐ ☐ Recent Trauma

☐ ☐ History of hypertension

☐ ☐ GI or GU bleeding in the last 10 days

☐ ☐ History of CVA within the last 6 months

☐ ☐ Intracranial surgery or trauma within the last 6 months

ECG Transmitted	Yes	No
Risk and Benefits Discussed With Patient/Family (see back)	Yes	No
Patient/Family understood risk And benefits	Yes	No
Hospital Destination: _____		
Paramedic: _____		
On-Line Physician: _____		

1st Bolus given by _____ **Time:** _____		
2nd Bolus* given by _____ **Time:** _____		
*Prior to second bolus: If **Yes,** Call Medical Control		
Active Bleeding?	Yes	No
Mental Status Change?	Yes	No
Grips Unequal?	Yes	No
Pupils Unequal?	Yes	No
Neuro Changes?	Yes	No

Figure 7–5. Example of a fibrinolytic checklist.

concurrence. Fibrinolytic checklists can be obtained from numerous sources, including the American College of Cardiologists, drug manufacturers, or area hospitals that use the fibrinolytic agents.

Some ambulances in the United States carry fibrinolytics. Whether a service can do this will be up to the level of commitment of the entire EMS system, from first responders to medical direction to the cardiac care offered by the receiving facilities. Clinical trials are under way to measure the efficacy and benefits of the out-of-hospital administration of fibrinolytic agents.

SUMMARY

Following are the key points of this chapter:

- There are two main coronary arteries.
- Right coronary artery supplies the inferior, posterior wall of the left ventricle and the right ventricle.
- Left anterior descending coronary artery supplies the anterior and septal walls of the left ventricle.
- Circumflex artery feeds the lateral and posterior walls of the left ventricle.
- Clot forming is a dynamic process that, if recognized early, can be interrupted.
- Intervention plan should be a team effort that starts outside of the hospital and continues through the emergency department and through the course of the patient's hospital stay.
- Intervention plan should include steps to intervene as rapidly as possible with drugs or procedures of most likely benefit.
- History taking can be a major factor in the differential diagnosis of chest pain.
- Memory aids, such as OPQRST and SAMPLE, can help the clinician obtain a useful patient history.

GLOSSARY

atherosclerosis the continuous buildup of plaque, resulting in the narrowing of the artery lumen.

fibrinolytics medications such as reteplase and tenecteplase, which stimulate the breakdown of fibrin in blood cells and prevent the polymerization of fibrin into new clots.

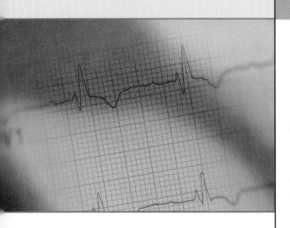

chapter 8

ECG Patterns of Infarction

objectives

After reading this chapter, you should be able to:

1. Discuss the benefits, limitations, and pitfalls of ECG evidence in AMI.

2. Recognize ST segment elevation, ST depression, T wave inversion, and pathological Q wave formation.

3. Describe the ECG changes associated with ischemia, subendocardial injury, myocardial injury, and Q wave infarction.

4. Describe the ECG changes that indicate reciprocal changes on the ECG.

ECG EVIDENCE OF ACUTE MI

BENEFITS OF THE 12-LEAD ECG

The 12-lead ECG is one of the first and best indicators of myocardial injury. At times, however, diagnosing an AMI is elusive because of nonspecific complaints. The 12-lead ECG can be a valuable tool in the early detection of myocardial injury. The benefits of using the 12-lead are summarized in Table 8–1.

A 12-lead ECG is highly specific for confirming an AMI. In fact, if it shows elevation of the standard ST segment or other changes, the ECG is about 90 percent accurate in diagnosing an AMI. With this high a confidence level, patients presenting with a history, a physical exam, and 12-lead ECG evidence are given drugs that could be lethal if given in the wrong diagnosis.

The true benefit of the ECG is speed. ECG evidence is much quicker than evidence from an enzyme analysis. Some cardiac enzymes may take up to four hours or so to show the changes, so valuable time is lost waiting for the results. An ECG can show an evolving AMI in the first minutes following onset, allowing acute-care providers to intervene rapidly and salvage myocardium.

In addition to detecting MI, the 12-lead ECG can be used to determine risk for complete heart block, hemodynamic compromise, and even sudden death. Complications, such as hemiblock and bundle branch blocks, can be identified as well.

LIMITATIONS OF THE 12-LEAD ECG

Although ECG criteria are the first and best indicators of a myocardial infarction, the ECG does have limitations (Table 8–2). The major limitation is its lack of sensitivity, which can be attributed to the machine's inherent capabilities, the "stealth" nature of the injury, and lead misplacement. At best, the ECG's sensitivity rating is a mere 46 to 50 percent. In other words, the ECG may not be able to pick acute changes in about half the cases. The bottom line is that an ECG can never be used to rule out an MI. It can be used only to rule one in. In other words, a patient may have a normal 12-lead with an AMI. Therefore, it is not a good idea to tell a patient, especially one who is in denial, that the ECG is normal. A normal 12-lead does not rule out an AMI.

Many times, the ST segment has subtle changes that represent injury pattern. It is important to ensure that the machine being used has the capability of increased frequency response. This diagnostic quality, as it is often called, will give the clinician a

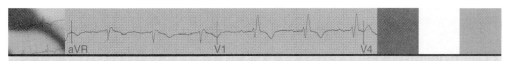

TABLE 8–1. *Benefits of the 12-Lead ECG*

- Is highly specific (90 percent or more confidence).
- Shows the presence of MI.
- Rapid identification possible in early stages.
- Can commit to treat with evidence from ECG, history, and physical exam.
- Identifies complications, such as hemiblocks and bundle branch blocks.

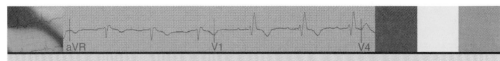

TABLE 8–2. *Limitations of the ECG*

- Sensitive to presence of MI in no more than half the cases.
- Never rules out an MI.
- Diagnostic quality necessary.
- Training required to read the 12-lead ECG.
- Is only one piece of a large puzzle.
- Some non-MI conditions resemble MIs.

more accurate assessment of the ST segment. Without the increased frequency response, the clinician might notice large ST elevation in the V leads in monitor quality; increasing the frequency response will flatten the ST segment. Therefore, it is best to enable diagnostic quality if it is available. Most machines designed to do 12-lead ECGs are diagnostic quality, so no special settings are required.

Clinicians are not born learning how to read ECGs; it is a learned skill. Most basic education programs do not include 12-lead concepts. As a rule, physicians learn the basics of reading 12-lead ECGs in medical school. Depending on what specialty they go into, however, they may not have enough practice in reading ECGs to become proficient. Those who specialize in emergency medicine or cardiology usually have the most experience.

Perhaps the most dangerous combination in 12-lead interpretation is an inexperienced reader and a machine-generated analysis. Although this book will not make you an ECG expert, reading many ECGs will. This book gives you the tools to start reading in a more organized fashion.

The 12-lead ECG is only one part of a large puzzle. Many non-MI conditions look like an AMI. Through a careful and systematic assessment of the 12-lead ECG, getting a good history, and performing a physical exam on the patient, the acute-care provider can accurately determine the patient's cardiac problems.

ECG EVIDENCE OF ACUTE CORONARY SYNDROMES

TRIAGE CRITERIA

Within 10 minutes of patient contact, providers should triage all chest-pain patients by ECG findings. Triage criteria are based on initial ECG presentation, divided into three categories:

- ST segment elevation or new onset of an LBBB.
- T wave inversion or ST segment depression.
- Nondiagnostic ECG.

The criteria are used to screen for patients needing emergent intervention therapy and to initiate that therapy.

ST segment elevation Following are the indicators to look for:

- Injury (damaged but salvageable).
- ST segment elevation >1 mm (>2 mm in septal leads).
- Present in two or more related or anatomically contiguous leads.
- Measure at J point (plus 40 ms) to baseline.

ST segment elevation means acute transmural injury—across the three layers of heart—and is a significant finding. Despite discussion and writings about the shape of the ST segment elevation as a discriminator, clinicians should avoid getting caught up in this debate. In an acute myocardial injury, the shape is not as diagnostic as reciprocal changes, patient history, and presentation. The fact is that patterns, or shapes, of ST segment elevation are as unique as fingerprints. Only the elevation is constant (Figures 8–1 and 8–2). Acute-injury patterns are confirmed by finding reciprocal changes (ST segment depression) in particular leads.

ST depression Any deviation to the ST segment catches the clinician's eye. However, when **ST segment depression** appears, realize that ST segment elevation is more significant and may also be found. If it is, the ST segment depression is considered reciprocal to the elevation, and this clue confirms the diagnosis of a myocardial injury (Figure 8–3).

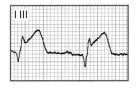

Figure 8–1. ST segment elevation in upright complex.

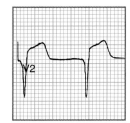

Figure 8–2. ST segment elevation in negative complex.

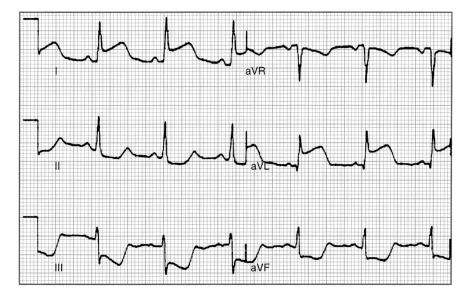

Figure 8–3. ST segment depression in Leads II, III, and aVF. Note the ST elevation in Leads I and aVL.

The causes of ST depression are as follows (Figure 8–4):

- Reciprocal changes to ST elevation.
- Ischemia or subendocardial injury.
- Certain medications, such as digitalis.

If ST segment depression does not appear to be reciprocal—that is, if it occurs without any ST elevation—the patient may be experiencing myocardial ischemia or injury to a subendocardial wall, which involves a single layer of the heart muscle. These types are not triaged for emergent reperfusion strategy as ST segment elevation would be but nonetheless are still treated with anticoagulant therapy and by MONA.

Inverted T waves One early sign of an acute coronary syndrome and myocardial ischemia is the **T wave inversion** (Figure 8–5). Because at times, the ST changes may disappear as the area is reperfused after nitroglycerin, a baseline 12-lead ECG should be acquired before administering nitroglycerin. Thus, nitroglycerin can be diagnostic as well as therapeutic, proving that an acute coronary syndrome exists.

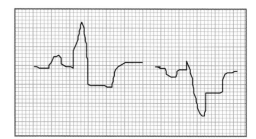

Figure 8–4. ST segment depression.

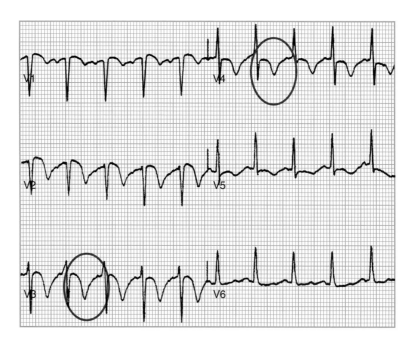

Figure 8–5. 12-Lead ECG showing myocardial ischemia. Note inverted T waves in Leads V2 through V5.

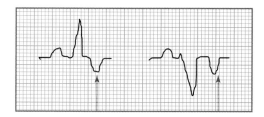

Figure 8–6. Inverted T-waves showing ischemia.

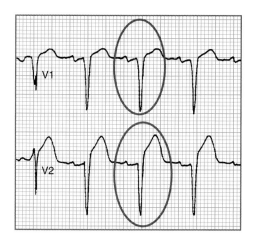

Figure 8–7. Infarction. Note the Q waves in Leads V1 and V2 and the ST segment elevation in the same.

Following are the key points about inverted T waves (Figure 8–6):

- Ischemia (transient reduction in blood flow).
- Symmetrical inverted T waves in two or more related leads.
- Inverted T waves normal in Leads V1 and III.

PATHOLOGICAL Q WAVES

Some injury patterns, if left untreated, may develop infarction patterns, or **pathological Q waves**. A pathological Q wave signifies infarction, or death of the tissue. A Q wave is considered pathological if it is more than 40 ms wide, or one third of the R wave height. The combination of a Q wave and ST segment elevation represents an acute myocardial infarction.

Following are the ECG indicators of infarct (necrosis or death) (Figure 8–7):

- Pathologic Q waves.
- >40 ms, or 0.04 sec wide, or one-third of R wave height.
- When seen with ST elevation, indicates acute ongoing myocardial infarction.

PRACTICE: ECG EVIDENCE OF ACUTE CORONARY SYNDROMES

Work the following examples, looking for ECG evidence of acute coronary syndromes. Identify ST segment elevation, ST segment depression, and T wave inversion (Figures 8–8 through 8–17). Answers are provided in the Answer Key at the back of the book.

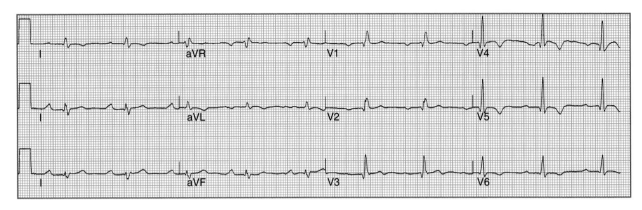

Figure 8–8.

ST elevation: _____

ST depression: _____

T wave inversion: _____

Pathological Q waves: _____

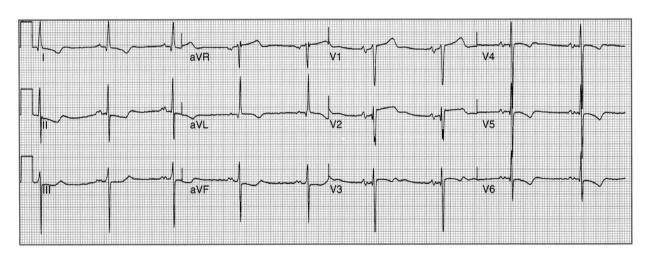

Figure 8–9.

ST elevation: _____

ST depression: _____

T wave inversion: _____

Pathological Q waves: _____

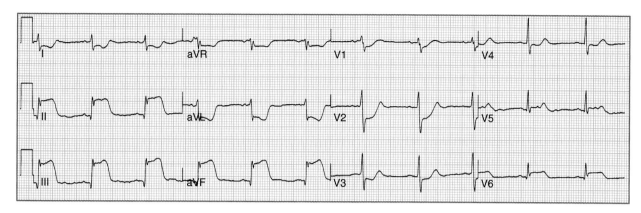

Figure 8–10.

ST elevation: _____

ST depression: _____

T wave inversion: _____

Pathological Q waves: _____

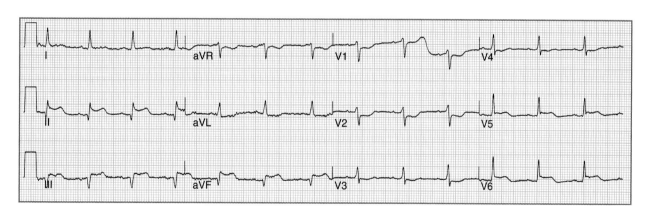

Figure 8–11.

ST elevation: _____

ST depression: _____

T wave inversion: _____

Pathological Q waves: _____

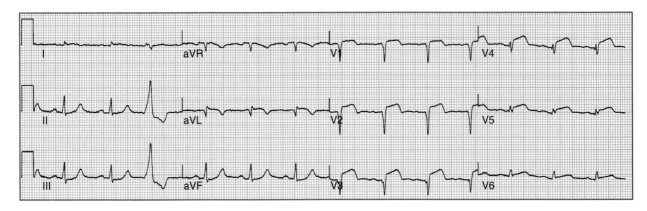

Figure 8–12.

ST elevation: _____

ST depression: _____

T wave inversion: _____

Pathological Q waves: _____

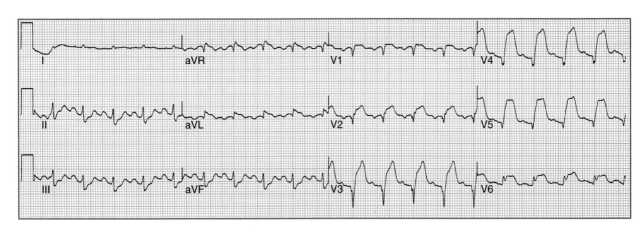

Figure 8–13.

ST elevation: _____

ST depression: _____

T wave inversion: _____

Pathological Q waves: _____

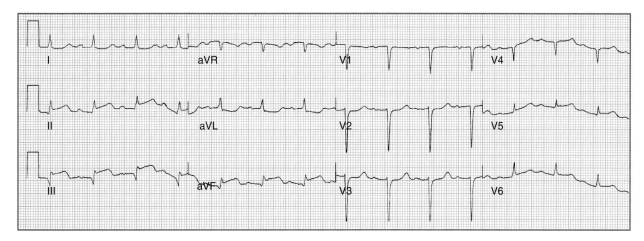

Figure 8–14.

ST elevation: _____

ST depression: _____

T wave inversion: _____

Pathological Q waves: _____

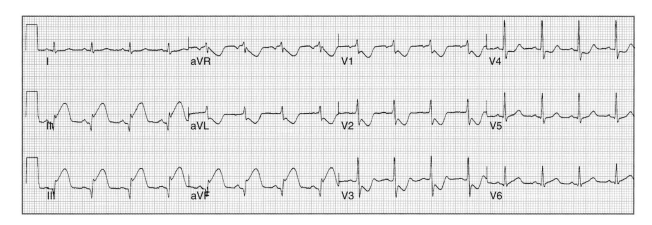

Figure 8–15.

ST elevation: _____

ST depression: _____

T wave inversion: _____

Pathological Q waves: _____

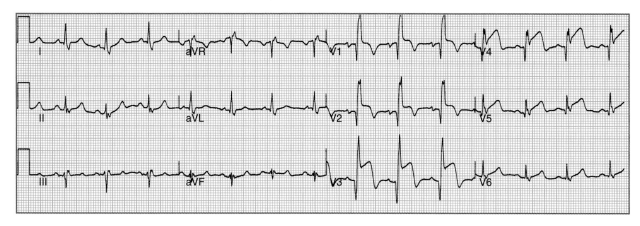

Figure 8–16.

ST elevation: _____

ST depression: _____

T wave inversion: _____

Pathological Q waves: _____

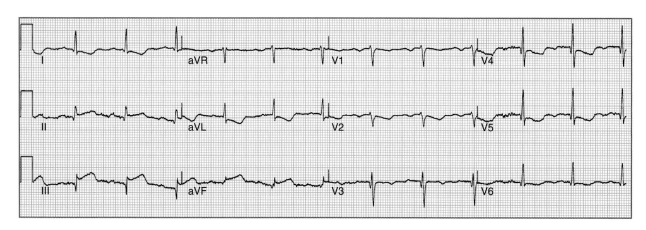

Figure 8–17.

ST elevation: _____

ST depression: _____

T wave inversion: _____

Pathological Q waves: _____

SUMMARY

Following are the key points of this chapter.

- ECG criteria are the first and best indicators of a myocardial infarction.
- Normal ECG does not rule out an AMI.
- Training is needed to read the ECG.
- ECG criteria, a patient history, and physical exam help ensure rapid treatment.
- Chest-pain patients can be triaged by 12-lead ECG findings.
- ST elevation is the most important thing to look for in the acute setting.
- ST depression is usually reciprocal to the ST elevation and confirms the diagnosis of an AMI.

GLOSSARY

pathological Q wave signifies infarction, or death of the tissue; the pathological Q wave is more than 40 ms wide, or one-third of the R wave height.

ST segment depression when reciprocal to ST segment elevation, confirms the diagnosis of a myocardial injury. In cases without ST segment elevation, indicates ischemia or subendocardial (single-layer thick) injury.

ST segment elevation a significant finding that indicates acute transmural injury across the three layers of heart.

T wave inversion an early sign of acute coronary syndrome and myocardial ischemia.

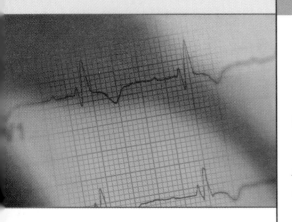

chapter 9

Locating the AMI:
The Secondary Survey

objectives

After reading this chapter, you should be able to:

1. Describe which leads are related to the various areas of the heart.

2. Describe a systematic approach to assessing a 12-lead ECG for acute myocardial infarction.

3. Use the Acute MI Locator Chart to identify the location of the area of injury or ischemia.

4. Use the Acute MI Locator Chart to identify the areas of reciprocal changes associated with acute myocardial infarction.

5. Use the Acute MI Locator Chart to describe what other areas of the heart could be affected by a specific location of infarction.

INTRODUCTION

Chapter 8 explained how to recognize ECG changes related to myocardial infarction. This chapter introduces and describes an organized approach to locating an AMI. Just as a secondary survey of a trauma patient is a detailed exam looking for injuries, a 12-lead ECG can be used to assess for "injuries."

USING ISAL

The secondary survey involves a head-to-toe exam of the patient in order to look for injuries. Using this strategy provides organization and movement in a logical direction so that hidden injuries can be detected.

The secondary survey of a 12-lead ECG is accomplished by using the phrase "I See All Leads." This phrase can be divided into sections by the first letter of each word, representing the order of lead groups to look at for the ST changes related to acute MI: ISAL (Figure 9–1).

This system was developed primarily to establish a head, or starting point, for beginning an assessment of a 12-lead ECG. The paradigm of Lead II would always have clinicians looking there first. Therefore, with Lead II representing the inferior lead group, the other leads were added in a logical progression around the 12-lead ECG to develop ISAL. The phrase also reminds the clinician to look at all leads rather than stop at the first sign of trouble.

After watching how thousands of providers learn how to read a 12-lead ECG, I have discovered, through much trial and error, that this system of reading one for AMI has performed with excellent results. This system is found in the Acute MI Locator Chart, which uses the ISAL guidelines (Table 9–1).

USING THE ACUTE MI LOCATOR CHART

When assessing the 12-lead ECG for evidence of an AMI, start in the inferior leads—II, III, and aVF—looking for evidence of ST segment elevation. If you see the elevation, write it down or circle the lead(s) that show it. Next, move to the septal leads—V1 and

I	Inferior Leads	II, III, aVF
S	Septal Leads	V1, V2
A	Anterior Leads	V3, V4,
L	Lateral Leads	V5, V6, I, aVL

Figure 9–1. Using ISAL for the secondary survey. The color coding identifies the lead group: green, inferior; blue, septal; red, anterior; yellow, lateral.

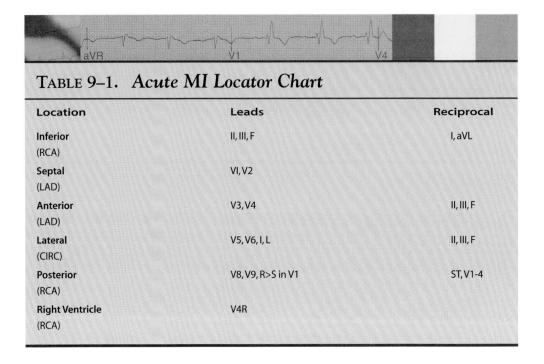

TABLE 9–1. *Acute MI Locator Chart*

Location	Leads	Reciprocal
Inferior (RCA)	II, III, F	I, aVL
Septal (LAD)	VI, V2	
Anterior (LAD)	V3, V4	II, III, F
Lateral (CIRC)	V5, V6, I, L	II, III, F
Posterior (RCA)	V8, V9, R>S in V1	ST, V1-4
Right Ventricle (RCA)	V4R	

V2—again inspecting for ST segment elevation. If you see it, write it down or circle the lead. Continue by inspecting the anterior leads—V3 and V4—looking for ST segment elevation. Continue through the lateral leads—V5, V6, I, and aVL—still looking for ST elevation.

When you have scanned all 12 leads, compare the ones you have written down or circled to the Acute MI Locator Chart. Leads with indicative ST elevation will list the location of the injury.

Then, the Acute MI Locator Chart shows you which leads to look in for reciprocal ST segment depression, thus confirming the diagnosis of an MI. Furthermore, the Acute MI Locator Chart suggests which coronary artery is involved, so you can determine the extent of occlusion.

The Acute MI Locator Chart also includes the elements found in the 15-lead ECG, which is discussed in Chapter 10. The right ventricle lead V4R and the posterior leads V8 and V9 are listed on the chart as well.

The column labeled "Location" lists the area of the heart corresponding to the indicated leads. In parentheses below the name of the location is the coronary artery involved. The "Leads" column identifies the area of the ST segment elevation. The "Reciprocal" column shows which leads to inspect for reciprocal (ST segment depression) changes for AMI (Figures 9–2 and 9–3).

Armed with this new information about what to look for and how to go about, get right to it by trying the practice problems that follow.

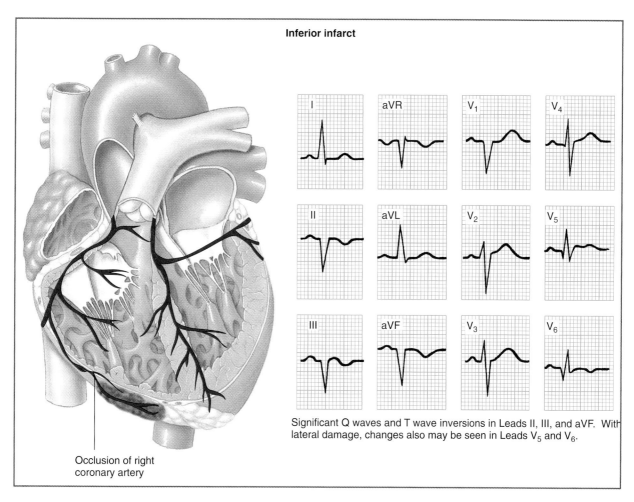

Inferior infarct

Significant Q waves and T wave inversions in Leads II, III, and aVF. With lateral damage, changes also may be seen in Leads V_5 and V_6.

Occlusion of right coronary artery

Figure 9–2. Acute inferior MI.

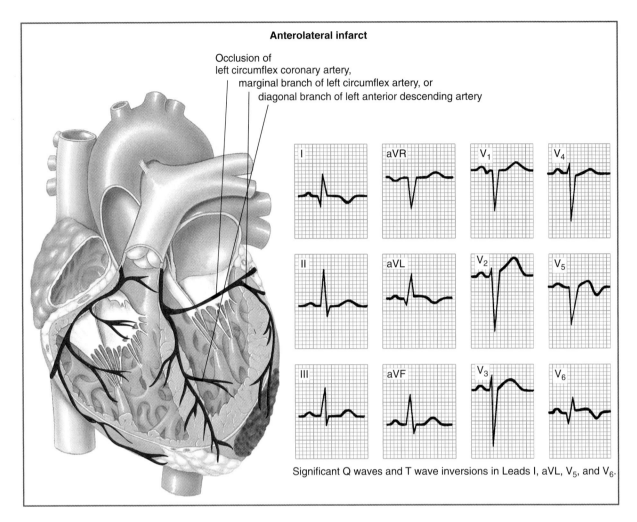

Figure 9–3. Acute anterior MI.

PRACTICE: USING THE ACUTE MI LOCATOR CHART

See Figures 9–4 through 9–12 for practice using the Acute MI Locator Chart to locate an AMI. All answers are provided in the Answer Key at the back of the book.

PR 0. 184s   QRS 0.102s
QT/QTc   0.402s/0.421s
P−QRS−T Axes   79° −69° 41°

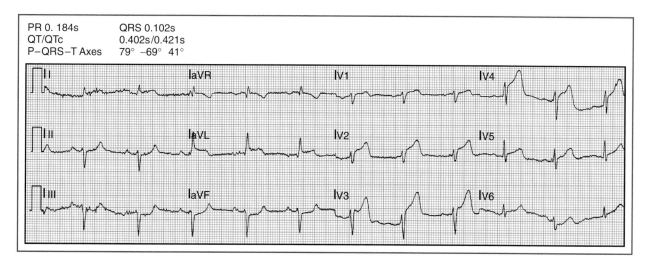

Figure 9–4.

Location: _____

Rationale: _____

HR: 96   P−QRS−T axes: 122 195 181
PR Int: 176 QRS Dur: 84   QT/QTc: 356/409

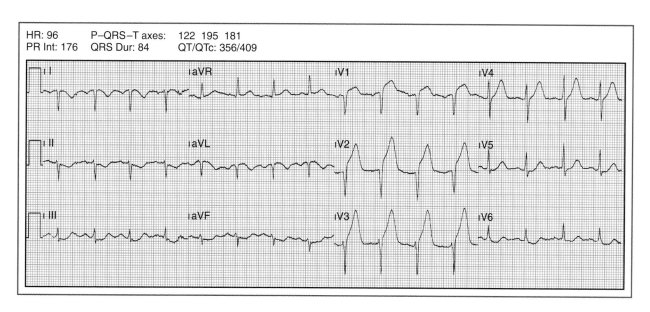

Figure 9–5.

Location: _____

Rationale: _____

PR 0. 124s   QRS 0.092s
QT/QTc   0.390s/0.408s
P−QRS−T Axes 60° 6° 27°

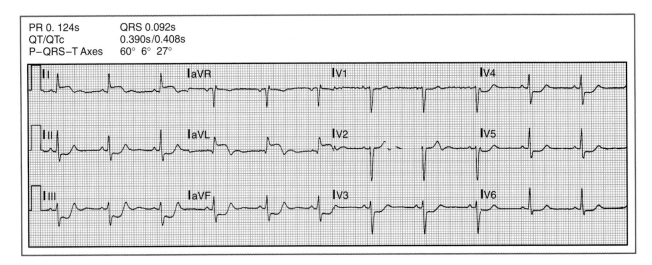

Figure 9–6.

Location: _____

Rationale: _____

PR 0. 140s   QRS 0.088s
QT/QTc   0.358s/0.426s
P−QRS−T Axes 55° 61° 102°

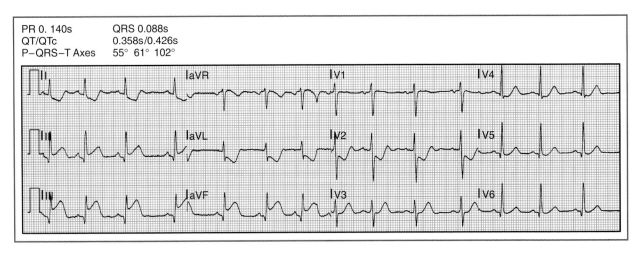

Figure 9–7.

Location: _____

Rationale: _____

HR: 87 P–QRS–T axes: 33 –9 77
PR Int: 164 QRS Dur: 80 QT/QTc: 348/392

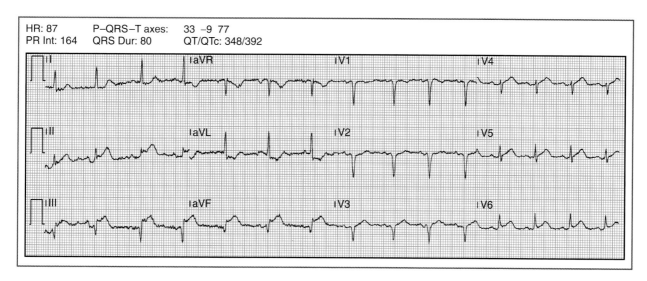

Figure 9–8.

Location: _____

Rationale: _____

HR: 52 P–QRS–T axes: 69 93 94
PR Int: 220 QRS Dur: 104 QT/QTc: 408/387

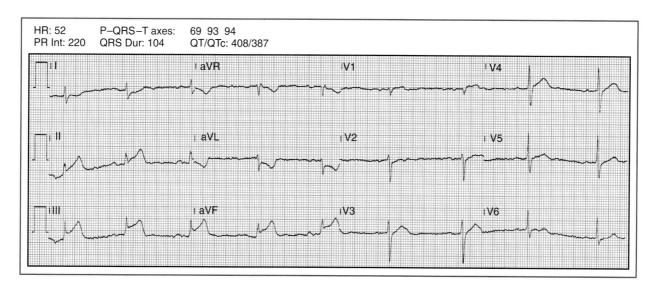

Figure 9–9.

Location: _____

Rationale: _____

PR 0.170s   QRS 0.102s
QT/QTc   0.360s/0.425s
P–QRS–T Axes   71° −19° 38°

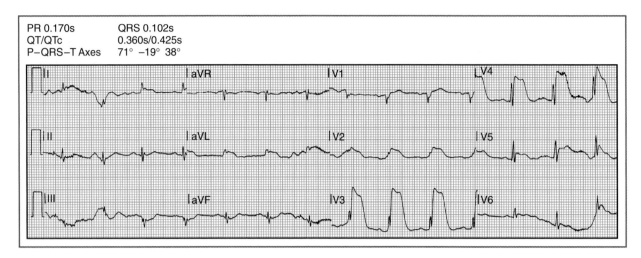

Figure 9–10.

Location:_____

Rationale:_____

HR: 57   P–QRS–T axes: 999 85 180
PR Int: 0   QRS Dur: 100   QT/QTc: 368/362

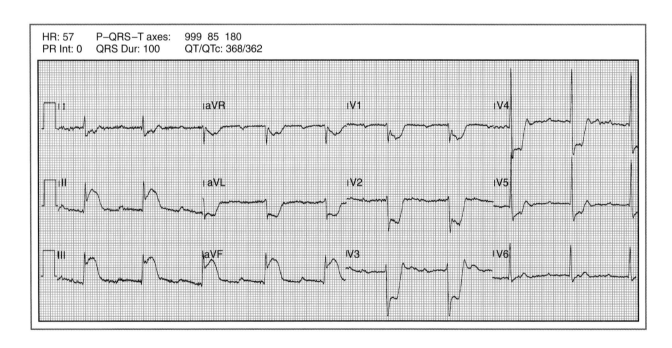

Figure 9–11.

Location:_____

Rationale:_____

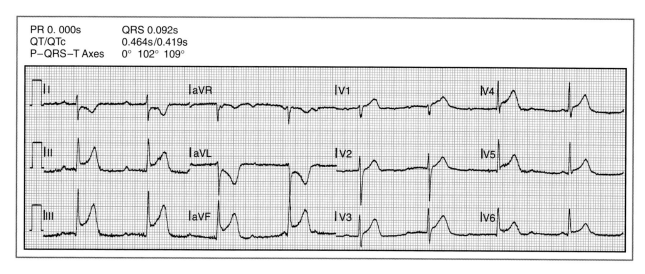

PR 0. 000s   QRS 0.092s
QT/QTc   0.464s/0.419s
P–QRS–T Axes   0° 102° 109°

Figure 9–12.

Location:_____

Rationale:_____

chapter 10

The 15-Lead ECG

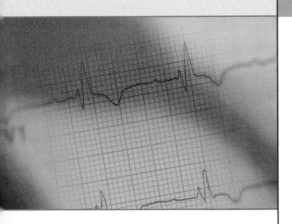

objectives

After reading this chapter, you should be able to:

1. Describe the benefits of acquiring a 15-lead ECG.

2. Describe the proper placement for acquiring Leads V4R, V8, and V9.

3. Describe the hemodynamic problems associated with a right ventricular infarction.

4. List three clinical signs of a right ventricular infarction.

5. On a 15-lead ECG, recognize ECG changes related to RVI and posterior MI.

INTRODUCTION

A 12-lead ECG has a high degree of accuracy when ST changes are present. In about 50 percent of the cases, however, the machine has limited ability to pick up the infarct. In other words, of 100 people having an AMI, 50 of them would show a normal 12-lead. The benefit of a 15-lead ECG is that it increases the sensitivity of the ECG by 23 percent. Thus, 23 more people can be aggressively managed. Table 10–1 specifies the conditions for running a 15-lead ECG.

ACQUIRING THE 15-LEAD ECG

To acquire the 15-lead ECG, follow these steps:

1. Run the initial 12-lead ECG as usual.
2. Place an electrode pad on the midclavicular line at the fifth intercostal space on the right side of the patient—the same as V4 on the left side (Figure 10–1).
3. On the back, place an electrode pad in the fifth intercostal space, midscapular line: the Lead V8 (posterior) position. This lead lines up with V4 on the front of the patient's chest at the same height.
4. Place another electrode between V8 and the spine in the same intercostal space: the Lead V9 (posterior) position (Figure 10–2).
5. Remove the electrode wires for Leads V4, V5, and V6.
6. Attach the V4 wire to the V4R lead placement.
7. Attach the V5 wire to the Lead V8 placement and the V6 wire to the Lead V9 placement.
8. Run a second 12-lead ECG with the new lead placements.
9. Label the second 12-lead ECG to reflect the new leads: V4 as V4R, V5 as V8, and V6 as V9.

Alternatively, a standard 3-lead monitor can be used. Recall that the multi-lead (9-lead) ECG is acquired by moving the red electrode wire to each of the V lead positions while keeping the monitor in Lead III. To get the extra leads, simply place the red electrode wire on the position for V4R first, then on V8, and then on V9. These three leads, added to the nine acquired earlier, make up a 12-lead ECG. Be sure to label the leads to identify which lead is being examined.

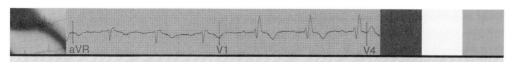

TABLE 10–1. *Indications for Running a 15-Lead ECG*

- Normal 12-lead ECG.
- ECG evidence of an acute inferior infarction.
- ST depression in Leads V1 to V4, suggesting posterior infarction.

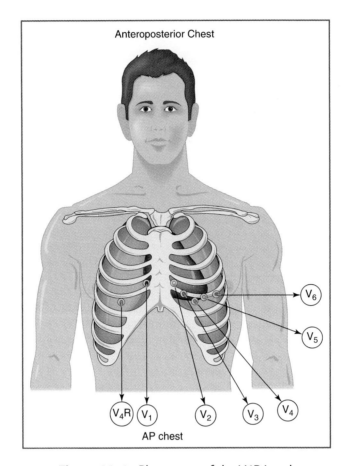

Figure 10–1. Placement of the V4R Lead.

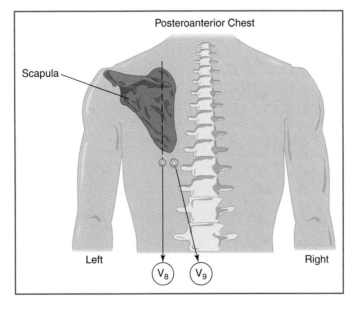

Figure 10–2. Placement of Leads V8 and V9.

RIGHT VENTRICULAR INFARCTION

The right ventricle, responsible for the heart's preload, gets its blood supply from the right coronary artery, which also feeds the inferior and posterior walls. Whenever damaged, the right ventricle can dramatically affect the blood available for the left ventricle to pump.

The cardiovascular system can compensate for the reduction in preload by increasing peripheral vascular resistance through vasoconstriction. The patient with **right ventricular infarction** (RVI) can be normotensive or hypotensive on presentation. Clinicians should be aware that nitrates might cause a precipitous drop in blood pressure in the setting of an AMI. This is secondary to nitroglycerin's effect on the afterload.

The right ventricle is involved in an inferior MI 50 percent of the time. Lead V4R looks at the right ventricle. The 15-lead ECG, Lead V4R in particular, can be helpful in discovering the presence of RVI. In addition to 15-lead ECG evidence, the following clinical triad of signs and symptoms provides further clues for the condition:

- Jugular vein distention (JVD).
- Hypotension, either presenting or following nitroglycerin administration.
- Clear lung sounds.

It is important for the clinician to assess for the conditions before giving nitrates or morphine. Patients with RVI frequently require fluids in larger quantity than you would expect to give a patient. Some cases have required up to a liter or more initially just to get a blood pressure that is perfusing.

A right ventricular infarction presents with ST segment elevation in Lead V4R (Figure 10–3). Reciprocal changes will not be seen, owing to the small size of the ventricle and the fact that it is across the septum from a reciprocal lead.

Before administering any nitrate or vasoactive drug, the acute-care provider should assess for lung sounds. A one-liter IV bag with large tubing should be established with an isotonic solution, such as normal saline.

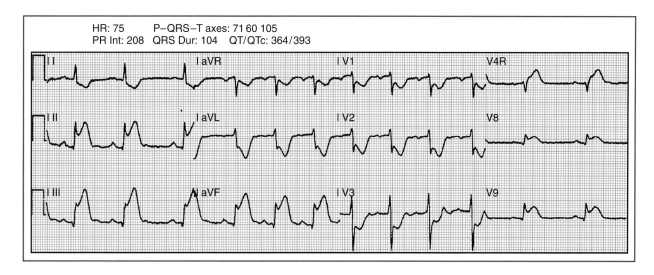

Figure 10–3. V4R with ST segment elevation.

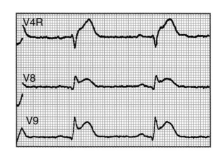

Figure 10–4. Posterior MI with elevation in Leads V8 and V9.

POSTERIOR INFARCTION

Posterior infarcts occur in 50 percent of all inferior MIs. A posterior MI is present in 50 percent of inferior wall MIs. The posterior wall usually does not create the extraordinary hemodynamic effects that an RVI does. However, a posterior MI may present isolated from an inferior MI. In this circumstance, the clinician with only a 12-lead ECG may lack the evidence that the patient is having a posterior infarct. A posterior MI is evidenced on a 15-lead ECG as ST segment elevation in Leads V8 and V9, with reciprocal ST segment depression in Leads V1–V4 (Figure 10–4).

PRACTICE: USING THE 15-LEAD ECG

See Figures 10–5 through 10–10 for practice using the 15-lead ECG. Locate right ventricle and posterior wall ST-T wave changes indicating acute coronary syndrome. All answers are provided in the Answer Key at the back of the book.

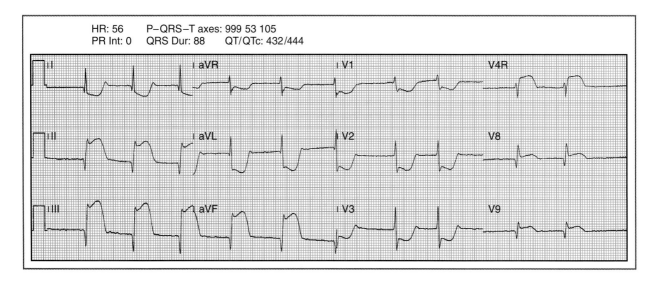

Figure 10–5.

1. ST elevation: _____

2. ST depression: _____

3. T wave inversion: _____

4. Pathological Q waves: _____

5. Location: _____

6. Rationale: _____

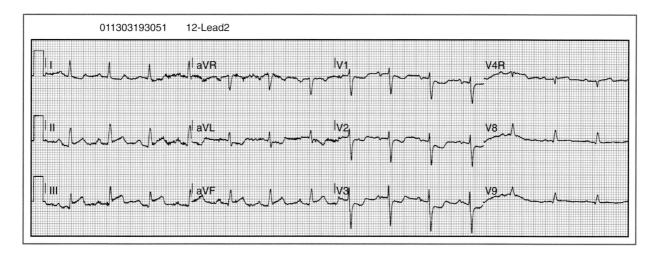

011303193051   12-Lead2

Figure 10–6.

1. ST elevation: _____

2. ST depression: _____

3. T wave inversion: _____

4. Pathological Q waves: _____

5. Location: _____

6. Rationale: _____

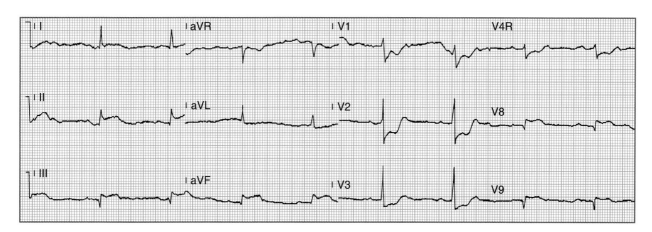

Figure 10–7.

1. ST elevation: _____

2. ST depression: _____

3. T wave inversion: _____

4. Pathological Q waves: _____

5. Location: _____

6. Rationale: _____

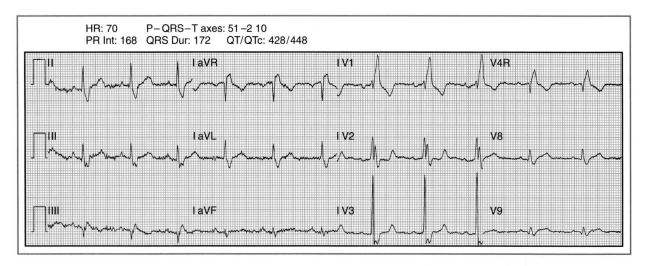

Figure 10–8.

1. ST elevation: _____

2. ST depression: _____

3. T wave inversion: _____

4. Pathological Q waves: _____

5. Location: _____

6. Rationale: _____

Figure 10–9.

1. ST elevation: _____

2. ST depression: _____

3. T wave inversion: _____

4. Pathological Q waves: _____

5. Location: _____

6. Rationale: _____

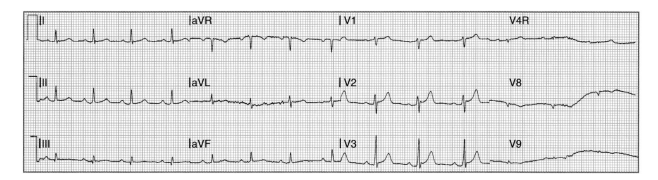

Figure 10–10.

1. ST elevation: _____

2. ST depression: _____

3. T wave inversion: _____

4. Pathological Q waves: _____

5. Location: _____

6. Rationale: _____

SUMMARY

Following are the key points of this chapter:

- 15-lead ECG can increase sensitivity by 23 percent for locating an AMI.
- RVI can have a profound effect on preload and the patient's blood pressure.
- Posterior MI can be isolated and, if recognized early, treated as other MIs.
- Clinical criteria for RVI include JVD, hypotension, and clear lung sounds.

GLOSSARY

right ventricular infarction occurs when there is an occlusion of the right coronary artery proximal to the acute marginal branches.

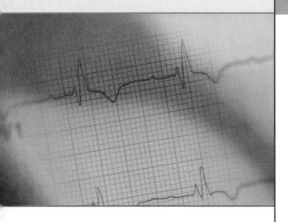

chapter 11

Left Bundle Branch Block and Acute MI

objectives

After reading this chapter, you should be able to:

1. Describe the diagnostic problems associated with LBBB.

2. Describe the criteria for MI in LBBB, using changes in QRS configuration.

3. Use a simple table ECG calculator to determine the probability of AMI in LBBB.

4. Describe the accuracy of the criteria for finding an AMI in LBBB.

INTRODUCTION

An AMI is often difficult to diagnose in the setting of a left bundle branch block. Traditionally, clinicians labeled the LBBB a "nondiagnostic ECG," which sometimes meant that, although the patient was presenting with the signs and symptoms of an AMI, the ECG evidence was inconclusive. In such cases, treatment might be delayed until enzyme tests could be made or an old 12-lead ECG found. Table 11–1 summarizes LBBB facts.

FINDING THE LBBB

Follow these steps:

1. Use Lead V1 (MCL–1).
2. Determine whether QRS is >120 ms.
3. Circle the J point.
4. Draw a line into the complex.
5. Go down with the terminal deflection left turn (LBBB).

In Figure 11–1, the LBBB has ST elevation as a normal finding because of the left ventricle's late repolarization, which does not allow the return to isoelectric. For this reason, the AMI could hide behind the LBBB. Many researchers have been looking into this so-called enigma. Several criteria have been mentioned as an aid in determining the presence of an MI in a left bundle branch block. Remember: *No ECG criterion is foolproof. ECG criteria are not a substitute for clinical assessment and history-taking skills.*

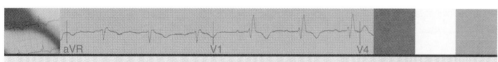

TABLE 11–1. *Facts About a Left Bundle Branch Block*

- Higher mortality than RBBB or no BBB.
- Most often seen in large anterior MIs.
- Lower ejection fractions (<50 percent when QRS is >170 ms).
- Higher left ventricular end diastolic pressures (LVEDP).
- Poorer global left ventricular (LV) function.
- ISIS II showed higher mortality when AMI with LBBB not treated with fibrinolytic agent.
- FTT trial showed mortality within six hours of symptom onset significantly reduced in patients receiving a fibrinolytic agent.

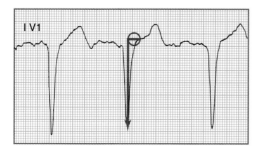

Figure 11–1. Finding the LBBB.

CRITERIA FOR AMI IN LBBB

NEW ONSET OF LBBB

Perhaps the easiest criterion for this condition is a new onset of left bundle branch block, along with signs and symptoms of an AMI. This criterion will generally point to the conclusion that an AMI is present. Of course, one would have to have an old 12-lead ECG demonstrating no LBBB before this episode. In the hospital, medical records may have the relevant chart available. However, in the out-of-hospital setting, that is not usually the case. The prehospital provider should supply the receiving hospital with the information necessary for a rapid search of the records to find the file. In some cases, ambulance paramedics have received a return call by an emergency department physician who found the records and diagnosed the MI based on new onset. This heads-up action will speed the time to intervention with aspirin and heparin and reduce door-to-drug or door-to-balloon time.

CHANGES IN QRS CONFIGURATION

Changes in QRS configuration include (see also Table 11–2):

* Q waves seen in at least two lateral leads (I, aVL, V5, V6) (Figure 11–2).
* R wave regression seen from Leads V1 to V4 (Figure 11–3). Note how the size of the R wave gets progressively smaller from Lead V1 to Lead V4.
* Notching of the S wave in at least two of Leads V3 to V5 (Figure 11–4).

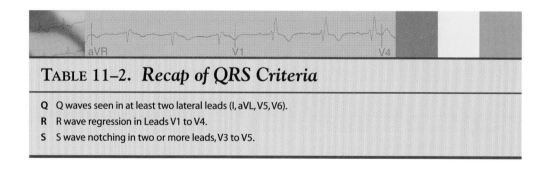

TABLE 11–2. *Recap of QRS Criteria*

Q Q waves seen in at least two lateral leads (I, aVL, V5, V6).
R R wave regression in Leads V1 to V4.
S S wave notching in two or more leads, V3 to V5.

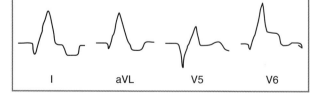

Figure 11–2. Q wave changes in lateral leads.

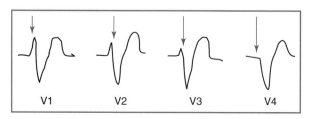

Figure 11–3. R wave regression in V1–V4.

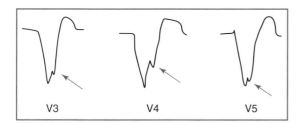

Figure 11–4. S wave notching occurring late on the S wave.

Each of the QRS criteria has a specificity range of 90 percent to 100 percent and a predictive value of 85 percent to 100 percent when combined with criteria from below.

CALCULATING AN AMI IN LBBB

Another way to determine the likelihood of AMI in LBBB and chest pain is to use the chart shown here as Table 11–3. Sgarbossa, Pinski, Barbagetata, et al[1] developed this simple chart. It helps the clinician determine three things on looking at an ECG with an LBBB:

1. *Is ST segment elevation ≥1 mm and concordant with the QRS axis?* This means that the elevation is in the same direction as the QRS deflection (Figure 11–5). This criterion, if met, is worth five points. It is the most heavily weighted of the three.
2. *Is ST segment depression ≥1 mm in V1, V2, or V3?* This simple criterion can be seen in any of these leads. Remember to find the J point when looking for the point of ST depression (Figure 11–6). This criterion, if met, is worth three points.

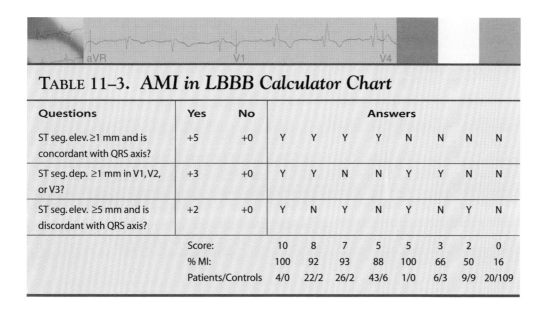

TABLE 11–3. *AMI in LBBB Calculator Chart*

Questions	Yes	No	Answers							
ST seg. elev. ≥1 mm and is concordant with QRS axis?	+5	+0	Y	Y	Y	Y	N	N	N	N
ST seg. dep. ≥1 mm in V1, V2, or V3?	+3	+0	Y	Y	N	N	Y	Y	N	N
ST seg. elev. ≥5 mm and is discordant with QRS axis?	+2	+0	Y	N	Y	N	Y	N	Y	N
		Score:	10	8	7	5	5	3	2	0
		% MI:	100	92	93	88	100	66	50	16
		Patients/Controls	4/0	22/2	26/2	43/6	1/0	6/3	9/9	20/109

[1]Sgarbossa, Pinski, Barbagetata, et al. "Electrocardiographic Diagnosis of Evolving Acute Myocardial Infarction in the Presence of Left Bundle Branch Block," *New England Journal of Medicine*, 334(8), 481-7.

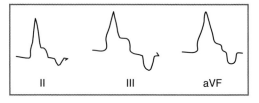

Figure 11–5. Determining the presence of ST segment elevation in upright complexes.

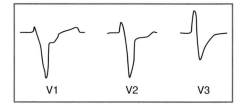

Figure 11–6. Determining the presence of ST segment depression in Leads V1, V2, or V3.

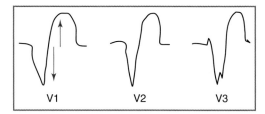

Figure 11–7. Determining ST segment elevation ≥5 mm in a negative complex.

3. *Is ST segment elevation ≥5 mm discordant from the QRS axis?* This means that the ST elevation goes up and the QRS deflection is down (Figure 11–7). This criterion, if present, is worth two points.

Various combinations of these criteria can be present. Using the chart (Table 11–3) will help you determine the likelihood of an AMI. Another benefit of using the chart is its relatively high reliability. If the score total is at least 3, the sensitivity is 78 percent. Thus, 22 percent of MI patients would be missed or would not meet the criteria but nonetheless would be having an AMI. The specificity is 90 percent. In other words, if the score is at least 3, 90 of 100 patients would have the accuracy that the table suggests.

This promising method is easy to use. In light of current practice that renders an ECG with a LBBB nondiagnostic, this new development brings an opportunity to intervene more quickly. It is important to note that the physician will have the ultimate call. In many cases, an LBBB is still an enigma inside a dilemma.

PRACTICE: LBBB AND AMI CASES

See Figures 11–8 through 11–12 for practice using the criteria described in this chapter to determine the possibility of LBBB and AMI. All answers are provided in the Answer Key at the back of the book.

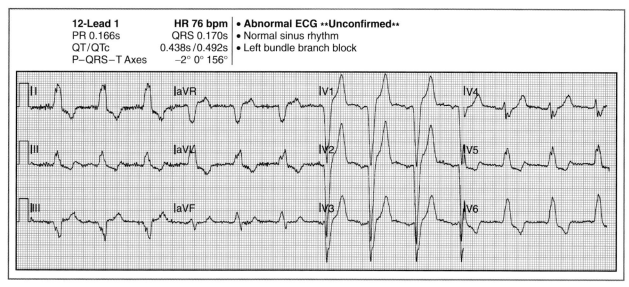

Figure 11-8.

Q waves in lateral leads?_____

R wave regression?_____

S wave notching? _____

ST segment elevation in upright complexes? _____

ST depression in V1, V2, or V3? _____

ST elevation ≥5 mm in negative complexes? _____

Score on calculator: _____

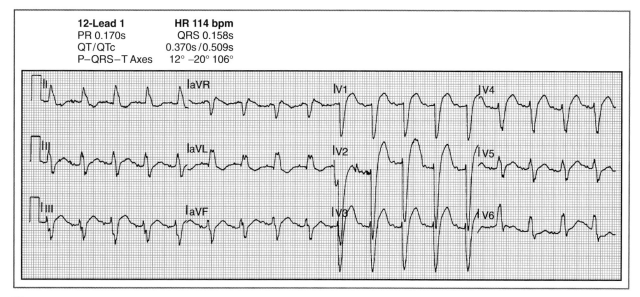

Figure 11-9.

Q waves in lateral leads?_____

R wave regression?_____

S wave notching? _____

ST segment elevation in upright complexes? _____

ST depression in V1, V2, or V3? _____

ST elevation ≥5 mm in negative complexes? _____

Score on calculator: _____

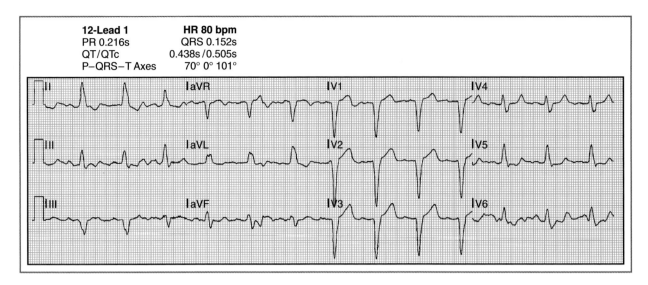

Figure 11–10.

Q waves in lateral leads? _____

R wave regression? _____

S wave notching? _____

ST segment elevation in upright complexes? _____

ST depression in V1, V2, or V3? _____

ST elevation ≥5 mm in negative complexes? _____

Score on calculator: _____

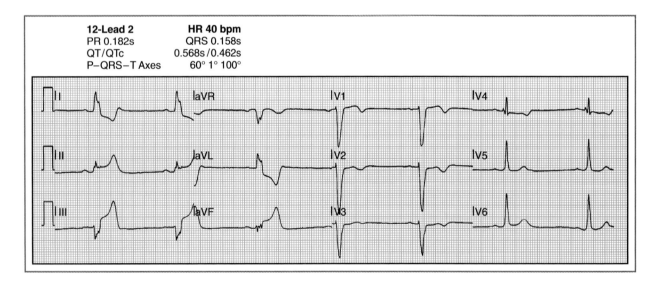

Figure 11–11.

Q waves in lateral leads? _____

R wave regression? _____

S wave notching? _____

ST segment elevation in upright complexes? _____

ST depression in V1, V2, or V3? _____

ST elevation ≥5 mm in negative complexes? _____

Score on calculator: _____

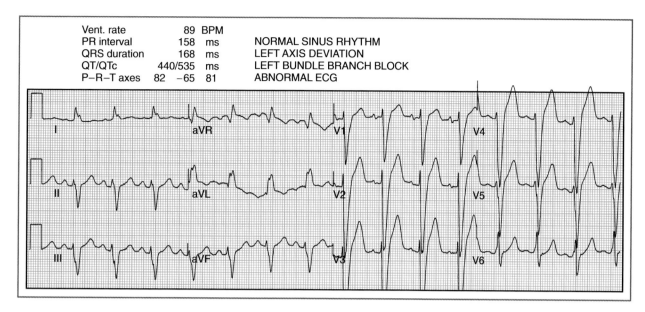

Vent. rate   89 BPM
PR interval   158 ms   NORMAL SINUS RHYTHM
QRS duration   168 ms   LEFT AXIS DEVIATION
QT/QTc   440/535 ms   LEFT BUNDLE BRANCH BLOCK
P–R–T axes   82 –65 81   ABNORMAL ECG

Figure 11–12.

Q waves in lateral leads?_____

R wave regression?_____

S wave notching? _____

ST segment elevation in upright complexes? _____

ST depression in V1, V2, or V3? _____

ST elevation ≥5 mm in negative complexes? _____

Score on calculator: _____

SUMMARY

Following are the key points of this chapter:

- It is now possible to discover an AMI in the setting of an LBBB.
- When faced with an LBBB and a symptomatic patient, think QRS chart (Table 11–3).
- Look at the QRS configurations, and then use the chart for ST segment criteria.
- The more criteria that are met, the greater the probability of a myocardial infarction.

chapter 12

Chamber Enlargement

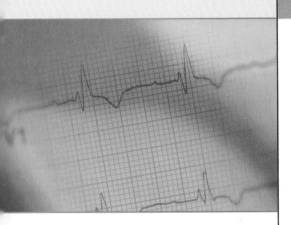

objectives

After reading this chapter, you should be able to:

1. Identify, by criteria, evidence of right and left atrial enlargement.

2. Identify, by criteria, evidence of right and left ventricular hypertrophy and the presence of a strain pattern.

3. Describe the clinical implications of atrial and ventricular enlargement.

ATRIAL ABNORMALITIES

The governing criterion for sinus rhythm, sinus tachycardia, and so on, is that sinus P waves are upright, round, and uniform in shape in Lead II. However, not all P waves look nice and rounded or even normal, for that matter. What determines the shape of a P wave? This chapter presents some simple criteria for determining right and left atrial enlargement.

On an ECG, a normal P wave is rounded, less than 3 mm tall, and less than 120 ms wide. The P wave is upright in Leads II, III, and aVF and upright, negative, or biphasic in Lead V1 (MCL-1) (Figure 12–1).

RIGHT ATRIAL ABNORMALITY

With **right atrial enlargement (RAE)**, the ECG will show tall, pointed P waves in the inferior Leads, II, III, or aVF, and the P wave will be more than 2.5 mm (0.25 mv) (Figure 12–2). Because the right side of the heart is the pulmonary side, the memory aid "3-P" has been used to describe RAE: Pointed, Prominent, Pulmonary or Pulmonale.

RAE may be caused by congenital heart disease, tricuspid or pulmonary valve disease, or pulmonary hypertension (any cause). The clinical implications of RAE are as follows:

- Generally not an acute problem.
- Frequently seen with right ventricular hypertrophy.
- Can been seen with other criteria pointing to other, more severe problems, such as pulmonary embolism.

LEFT ATRIAL ABNORMALITY

With **left atrial enlargement (LAE)**, the ECG will show:

- Lead II: Widened (>120 ms, or 3 mm) P wave with a notched or m-shaped appearance (Figure 12–3).
- Lead V1 (or MCL-1): A broad, terminal negative P deflection of more than 1 mm, or one small square on the ECG (Figure 12–4).

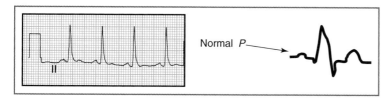

Figure 12–1. A normal P wave.

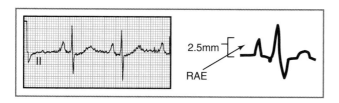

Figure 12–2. Right atrial enlargement.

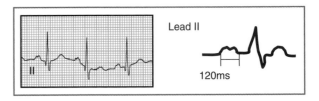

Figure 12–3. LAE: Widened P wave with notched appearance on Lead II.

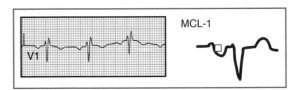

Figure 12–4. Broad, negative P deflection on Lead V1 (MCL-1).

It has been suggested that the criteria demonstrate a conduction abnormality, not necessarily atrial enlargement. The criteria could also mean left atrial dilation, owing to increased pressure, or volume overload.

LAE may be caused by hypertension, pulmonary edema, mitral or aortic valve stenosis, left ventricular hypertrophy (LVH), or acute myocardial infarction. The clinical implications of LAE are as follows:

- Same as the causes.
- No treatment of the specific problem.
- Can give clues as to overall patient hemodynamics.

VENTRICULAR HYPERTROPHY

RIGHT VENTRICULAR HYPERTROPHY

Right ventricular hypertrophy (RVH) is caused by increased pressure, or volume, in the right ventricle. RVH generally occurs in circumstances similar to those mentioned for RAE. RVH is characterized by large forces that go away from the lateral leads and toward Lead V1 (MCL-1) (Figure 12–5).

The ECG criteria for right ventricular hypertrophy are:

- RAE.
- Narrow QRS.
- Right axis deviation.
- R wave height in V1 (MCL-1) is $\supseteq$ 7 mm.
- Asymmetrical downsloping ST segment (strain) in inferior leads.

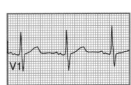

Figure 12–5. Right ventricular hypertrophy.

The clinical implications of RVH are as follows:

* Not an acute problem, with no specific treatment.
* Can be confused with a posterior hemiblock. In the setting of a right bundle branch block and a right-axis deviation, a posterior hemiblock should be assumed in the symptomatic patient until proved otherwise.
* Remember the hemodynamics that caused it.

LEFT VENTRICULAR HYPERTROPHY

Left ventricular hypertrophy (LVH) is usually caused by increased pressure, or volume, in the left ventricle. LVH is often found in mitral or aortic stenosis, hypertension, AMI, cardiomyopathy, or ischemic heart disease.

The ECG criteria are as follows:

* LAE, along with any other QRS voltage criteria, is diagnostic.
* Generally narrow QRS or slightly widened with strain.
* Usually normal axis, although can be physiologic left as it progresses.
* May be the cause of an axis that is –15 degrees or more.

Experts disagree about the accuracy of ECG criteria for diagnosing LVH. Some say that ECG criteria cannot be used with accuracy; others point out that if the criteria show that LVH is present, it is. This issue appears to be the classic case of specificity versus sensitivity. Definitive diagnosis involves other criteria such as echocardiography.

The clinical implications of LVH are as follows:

* Higher incidence of sudden death and ischemic arrhythmias.
* Can mimic the ST depression or elevation seen with myocardial ischemia.
* May be caused by an AMI.
* In the presence of an LBBB, LVH criteria not determined.
* May be a useful clue as to hemodynamic condition.

To determine the "Rule of 35," one of the primary voltage criteria, measure the deepest S wave (in mm from the isoelectric line) from either Lead V1 or V2. Add this number to the tallest R wave of Lead V5 or V6. If the resulting number is greater than 35 and if the patient is at least 35 years old, this voltage criterion has been met.

The other voltage criteria are as follows:

* R wave in Lead aVL is >11 mm (Figure 12–6).
* R wave >20 mm in any inferior lead (II, III, or aVF).
* R wave >20 mm in Lead V6.
* R wave >25 mm in V5.
* S waves >25 mm in Lead V1 or V2.

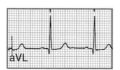

Figure 12–6. R wave in Lead aVL.

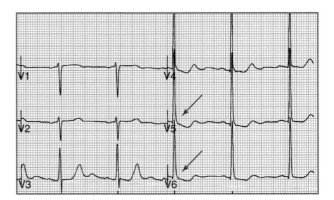

Figure 12–7. Strain. Note the downsloping ST segment and asymmetric T waves.

With so many voltage criteria, you may ask if it is necessary to measure them all. The answer is no. If the complexes look large, assume hypertrophy. Apply whichever criteria you need to make the call.

To confirm LVH, the clinician should look for evidence of strain, the hallmark of hypertrophy (Figure 12–7). A strain pattern to hypertrophy confirms the diagnosis. Many machine-generated analyses print the message "voltage criteria for LVH met." This message means that at least one of the criteria for LVH has been met.

A message stating "repolarization abnormality means "strain." Strain is best seen on the ECG in the lateral or inferior leads (II, III, aVF, V5, or V6). Strain is evidenced by asymmetrical ST depression and T wave inversion that looks almost biphasic.

PRACTICE: CHAMBER ENLARGEMENT

Go to Figures 12–8 through 12–17 to practice identifying chamber enlargement. For example, after studying Figure 12–8, you should write "LVH with strain" and which criterion is positive for hypertrophy in the space provided for you. All answers are provided in the Answer Key at the back of the book.

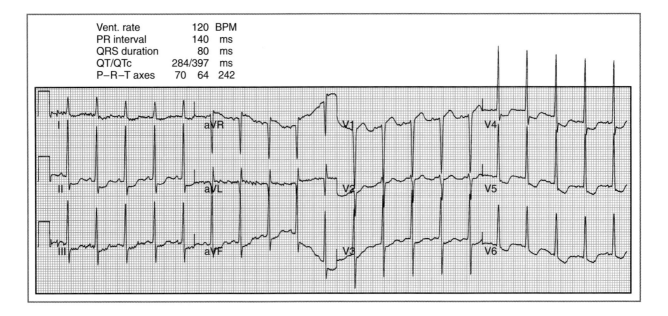

Vent. rate	120	BPM
PR interval	140	ms
QRS duration	80	ms
QT/QTc	284/397	ms
P–R–T axes	70 64	242

Figure 12–8. _____

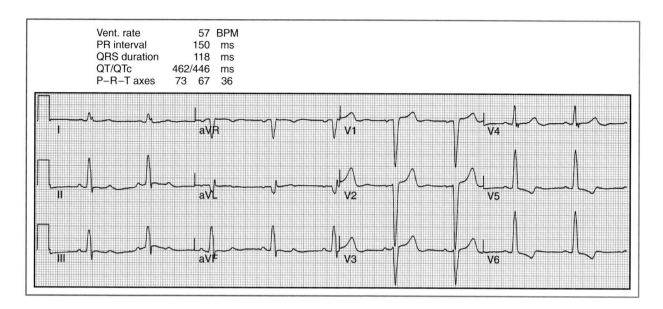

Vent. rate	57	BPM
PR interval	150	ms
QRS duration	118	ms
QT/QTc	462/446	ms
P–R–T axes	73 67 36	

Figure 12–9.

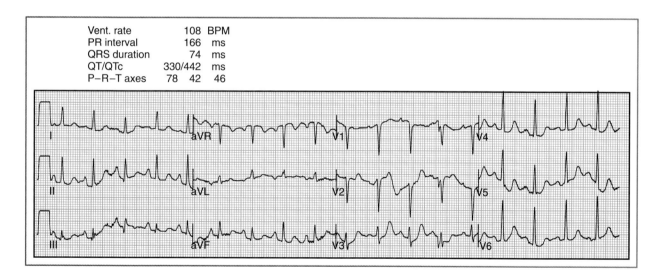

Vent. rate	108	BPM
PR interval	166	ms
QRS duration	74	ms
QT/QTc	330/442	ms
P–R–T axes	78 42 46	

Figure 12–10.

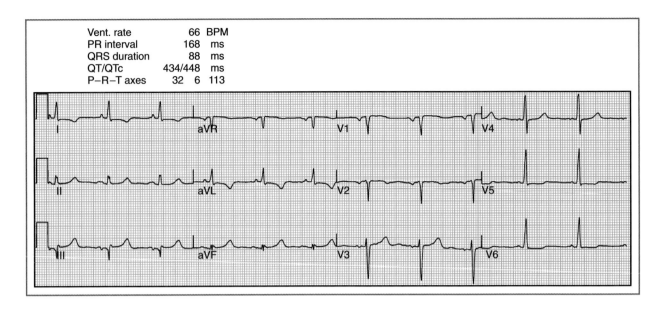

Figure 12–11. _____

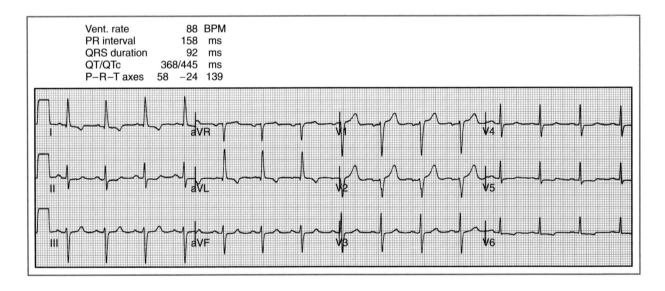

Figure 12–12. _____

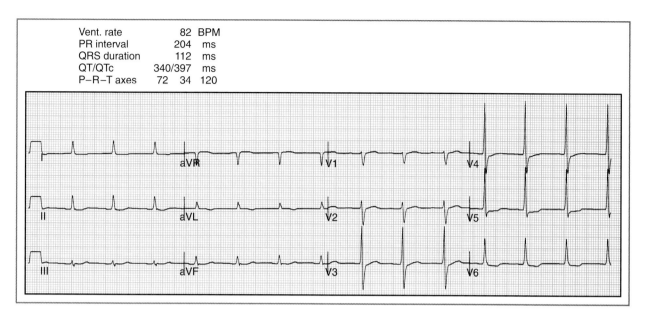

Vent. rate   82 BPM
PR interval   204 ms
QRS duration   112 ms
QT/QTc   340/397 ms
P–R–T axes   72 34 120

Figure 12–13.

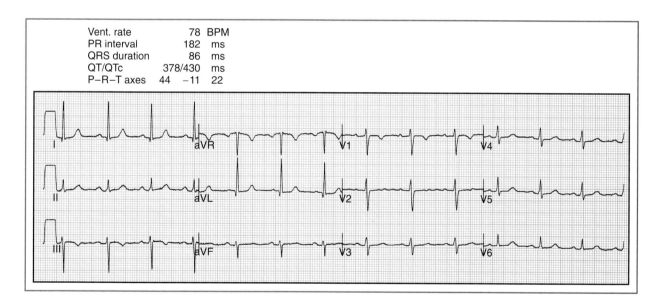

Vent. rate   78 BPM
PR interval   182 ms
QRS duration   86 ms
QT/QTc   378/430 ms
P–R–T axes   44 −11 22

Figure 12–14.

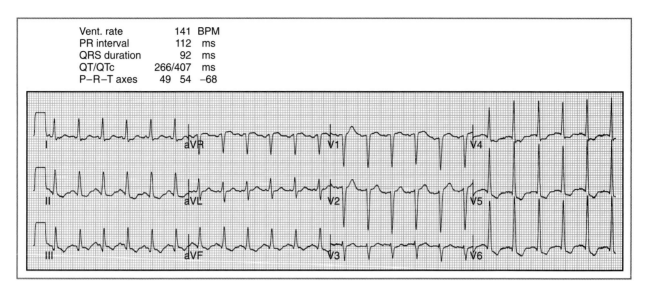

Vent. rate   141   BPM
PR interval   112   ms
QRS duration   92   ms
QT/QTc   266/407   ms
P–R–T axes   49 54 –68

Figure 12–15.

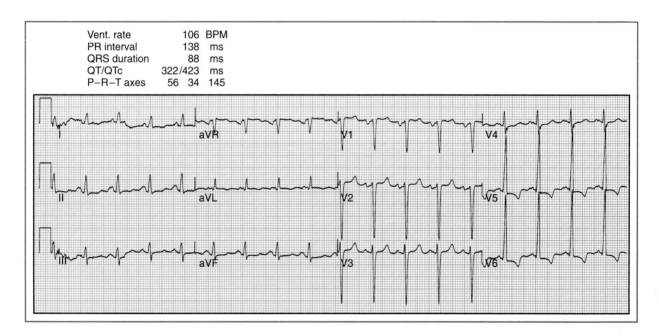

Vent. rate   106   BPM
PR interval   138   ms
QRS duration   88   ms
QT/QTc   322/423   ms
P–R–T axes   56 34 145

Figure 12–16.

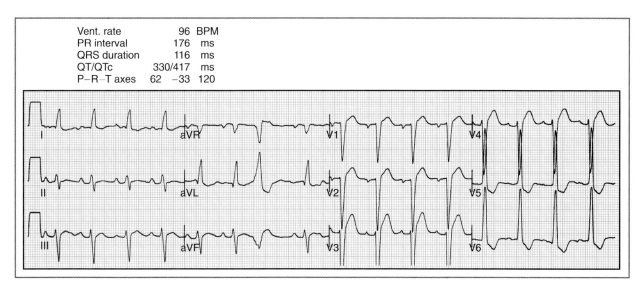

Vent. rate	96	BPM
PR interval	176	ms
QRS duration	116	ms
QT/QTc	330/417	ms
P–R–T axes	62 –33	120

Figure 12–17.

SUMMARY

Following are the key points of this chapter:

- Although not usually clinically significant alone, atrial abnormalities can help the clinician discover more serious conditions.
- Pointed P waves: P-pulmonale = RAE.
- M-shaped P waves: M-mitrale = LAE.
- If the complexes are large, think hypertrophy and measure.
- Table 12–1 can be helpful in organizing your search for LVH.
- When voltage criteria have been met, look for strain pattern and atrial enlargement.

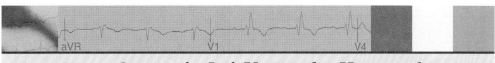

TABLE 12–1. *Criteria for Left Ventricular Hypertrophy*

- Rule of 35: Deepest S wave of Lead V1 or V2 plus the tallest R wave of Lead V5 or V6.
- Lead aVL R wave is >11 mm tall.
- R wave >20 mm in any inferior lead, II, III, or aVF.
- R wave >20 mm in lead V6.
- R wave >25 mm in V5.
- S wave >25 mm in V1 or V2.

- If >35 mm and if the patient is older than 35, LVH voltage criterion met.
- Voltage criteria for LVH present.

GLOSSARY

left atrial enlargement (LAE) a condition caused by hypertension, pulmonary edema, mitral or aortic valve stenosis, left ventricular hypertrophy (LVH), or acute myocardial infarction.

right atrial enlargement (RAE) a condition caused by congenital heart disease, tricuspid or pulmonary valve disease, or pulmonary hypertension (any cause).

left ventricular hypertrophy (LVH) a condition in which the cardiac muscle responds to increased resistance in the circulation by becoming enlarged.

right ventricular hypertrophy (RVH) caused by increased pressure, or volume, in the right ventricle.

chapter 13

Electrolyte, Drug, and Other ECG Changes

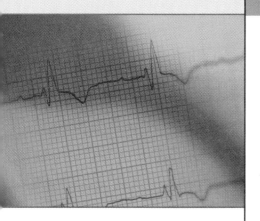

objectives

After reading this chapter, you should be able to:

1. List the causes and clinical implications of various electrolyte abnormalities.

2. Describe the ECG changes that suggest hypokalemia, hyperkalemia, hypocalcemia, and hypercalcemia.

3. Explain how and why to measure the QT/QTc interval.

4. Describe the clinical implications of a prolonged QT interval.

5. Describe the effects of digitalis on the ECG.

6. Describe the ECG evidence of pericarditis and the early repolarization variant.

7. Describe the ECG findings that suggest pulmonary embolism.

INTRODUCTION

Electrolytes are extremely important to the body's electrical system. They are responsible for the heart's polarity changes that are picked up by the ECG machine. Most criteria for interpreting electrolyte changes are based on the assumption of homeostasis, the normal electrolyte ranges for an individual.

The electrolytes potassium and calcium have strong influences over the cardiac cycle. Abnormalities sometimes may be seen on the ECG. It is important to note that an ECG is not a substitute for blood studies to determine the serum level. These criteria are designed as guidelines to aid in discovering possibly covert conditions.

POTASSIUM (K+)

Potassium has the following major benefits:

- Prevents action potential from being too short (QT interval).
- Allows for organized fast heart rates.
- Protects from excitability.
- Slows the heart rate in vagal conditions.

HYPOKALEMIA

Hypokalemia has the following characteristics:

- Serum levels below 3.5 to 5 mEq/L.
- Most commonly caused by vomiting, diarrhea, diuretics, and gastric suctioning.
- Hypomagnesemia, or low magnesium, which has the same ECG characteristics.
- Muscle weakness and polyuria as common signs and symptoms.
- Digitalis resulting from hypokalemia, causing serious dysrhythmias (Torsades de pointes).
- Atrial flutter, heart blocks, and bradycardia.

ECG changes Figure 13–1 shows hypokalemia-induced ECG changes:

- ST segment depression.
- T waves flattened or joined with U waves.
- U waves getting larger than the T waves as the potassium level falls.
- QT interval appearing to lengthen as T combines with U.
- PR interval increases.

Needed actions
- Monitor ECG.
- Increase dietary intake of potassium.

HYPERKALEMIA

Figure 13–2 shows typical hyperkalemia ECG patterns:

- Serum levels above the normal range.
- Most commonly caused by renal failure.
- Possible sinus node quit at 7.5 mEq/L.
- VF, or asystole, at 10 to 12 mEq/L.

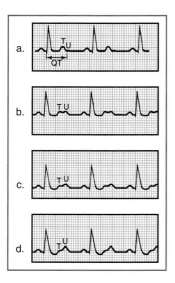

Figure 13–1. Hypokalemia-induced ECGs. (a) shows normal serum potassium levels (3.5 to 5.0 mEq/L); (b) shows about 3.0 mEq/L; (c) shows 2.0 mEq/L; and (d) shows 1.0 mEq/L.

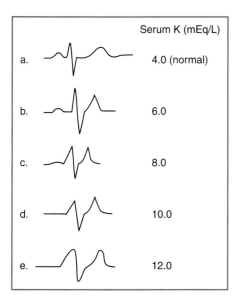

Figure 13–2. Hyperkalemia ECG patterns.

ECG changes Figure 13–3 shows hyperkalemia-induced ECG changes:

Mild cases (less than 6.5 mEq/L).
- Tall, tented, peaked T waves with a narrow base (QTc is still normal).
- Best seen in Leads II, III, V2, and V4.
- Normal P waves.

Moderate cases (less than 8 mEq/L).
- QRS widens.
- Broad S wave in V leads.
- Left-axis deviation.
- ST segment is gone, contiguous with the peaked T wave.
- P wave starts to flatten and diminish.

Severe cases (more than 8 mEq/L).
- P waves disappear.
- Sine waves.

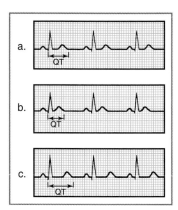

Figure 13–3. Hyperkalemia-induced ECG changes. (a) shows normal serum potassium levels (3.5 to 5.0 mEq/L); (b) shows about 7.0 mEq/L; (c) shows 8.0 to 9.0 mEq/L; and (d) shows more than 10.0 mEq/L.

Figure 13–4. Calcium-related ECG patterns. (a) shows normal QT interval within a range of 0.32 to 0.39 sec for a heart rate of 80; (b) shows hypercalcemia, a QT interval below normal range; and (c) shows hypocalcemia, a QT interval above normal range.

CALCIUM

Figure 13–4 shows characteristic calcium-related ECG patterns. On an ECG, **hypercalcemia** is suggested by a shortened QT interval (QTc for heart rate). **Hypocalcemia** is suggested by a prolonged QT interval (**QTc** for heart rate).

EFFECTS OF DRUGS

QT INTERVAL

The QT interval represents the time from the start of depolarization of the ventricles to the end of repolarization. This is, in effect, the refractory period. The QT interval is measured from the start of the QRS complex to the end of the T wave. This distance is done on the vital signs part of the 12-lead ECG. Note on the 12-lead the QT/QTc interval: the QT is the measurement; the QTc represents the corrected QT interval for the current heart rate. It is determined from the following formula: QTc = QT interval/$\sqrt{\text{R-R interval}}$. In other words, QTc equals the QT interval divided by the square root of the R-R interval. To determine whether a QT is prolonged, refer to Table 13–1 and Figure 13–5.

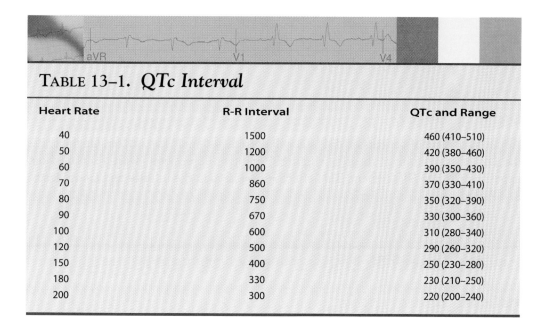

TABLE 13–1. *QTc Interval*

Heart Rate	R-R Interval	QTc and Range
40	1500	460 (410–510)
50	1200	420 (380–460)
60	1000	390 (350–430)
70	860	370 (330–410)
80	750	350 (320–390)
90	670	330 (300–360)
100	600	310 (280–340)
120	500	290 (260–320)
150	400	250 (230–280)
180	330	230 (210–250)
200	300	220 (200–240)

Vent. rate	81	BPM
PR interval	194	ms
QRS duration	100	ms
QT/QTc	446/512	ms
P–R–T axes	71 –48	71

Figure 13–5. Example of QT measurement.

Another way to determine whether the QT is prolonged is to check if more than half the R-R interval is prolonged. This concept works only when the heart rate is between 60 and 100.

Another easy method of detecting a prolonged QT is to look at the QTc number. A QTc over 0.47, or 470 ms, is prolonged in heart rates between 60 and 100.

The QT interval does not include the U wave, if present. If a U wave is present, the measurement ends before the U wave starts. Also, if the QRS complex is more than 80 ms, this excess must be subtracted from the QT measurement. QTc takes this into consideration.

Prolonged QT interval has the following causes:

- Hypokalemia, hypocalcemia.
- Drugs: quinidine, amiodarone, procainamide, tricyclics, disopyramide, phenothiazines, and digitalis.
- Liquid protein diets, myocarditis, AMI, LVH, and hypothermia.

Prolonged QT interval can also be a normal variant in an asymptomatic patient. It might also lead to Torsades de pointes, an ominous polymorphic, potentially lethal form of ventricular tachycardia.

The QT interval may also be shortened. In such cases, the cause may be hypercalcemia or digitalis therapy.

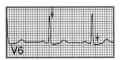

Figure 13–6. The digitalis effect.

DIGITALIS EFFECT

About 60 percent of patients on digitalis will present with the "Dig" effect. On the ECG, the Dig effect manifests itself as slight ST segment depression, with a scooped-out appearance to the ST segment. This effect is best seen in the inferior and lateral leads. See Figure 13–6.

OTHER CONDITIONS WITH ECG CRITERIA

PERICARDITIS

Pericarditis, or inflammation of the pericardium, usually occurs in younger patients without cardiac risk factors. Pericarditis has the following signs and symptoms:

- Chest pain, dyspnea, tachycardia, fever, weakness, and chills.
- Sharp, severe chest pain radiating to the back, neck, and jaw.
- Symptoms made worse by lying flat; better, by sitting up.
- Often pleuritic pain, made worse by breathing.
- Pain that lasts for hours and days.
- Pericardial friction rub, heard along the lower left sternal border.

ECG clues Ninety percent of pericarditis cases have ECG evidence (Figure 13–7):

- ST segment elevation.
- Concave (curved up) in almost all leads, except aVR and V1.
- T wave elevation starting above the isoelectric line.
- ST segment depression, or T wave inversion.
- Almost all leads down (later stage).

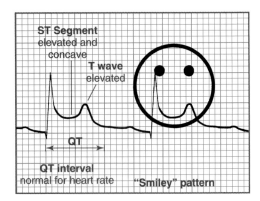

Figure 13–7. ECG evidence of pericarditis.

Diagnosis Pericarditis can be diagnosed as follows:

- Physical criteria: chest pain, pleuritic, relieving factors.
- No response to nitroglycerin.
- Pericardial rub.
- ECG changes that do not localize an artery (everything up!).

Early repolarization variant This condition can occur in young healthy individuals. It is characterized by a notched J point and concave upward ST elevation. This condition is best seen in the inferior and lateral leads (II, III, aVF, V4, V5, and V6) (Figure 13–8).

ACUTE PULMONARY EMBOLISM

An acute pulmonary embolism is a diagnosis of exception. The condition has no unique signs and symptoms. The best clues for finding an acute pulmonary embolism are a history of recent surgery or anticoagulant drugs in a patient with chronic atrial fibrillation.

ECG changes can occur with a large embolism. ECG evidence must be considered only with a complete history and a physical exam of the patient. Alone, these criteria are inconclusive (Figure 13–9):

- Sinus tachycardia.
- Right atrial enlargement.
- Right-axis deviation.
- Right bundle branch block (possible).

NONSPECIFIC ST-T WAVE CHANGES

This book includes many 12-lead ECGs and many forms and shapes of ECG complexes. It comes close to explaining nearly every abnormality. However, some abnormalities defy explanation or identification. Known as nonspecific ST-T wave changes, flattened T waves, biphasic T waves, and unrelated ST depression are just a few of those abnormalities. Fortunately, not many of them have cardiac causes.

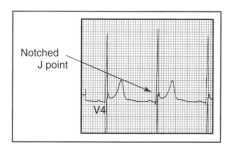

Figure 13–8. Early repolarization variant.

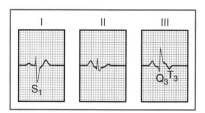

Figure 13–9. S1, Q3, T3 pattern. Notice the deep S wave in Lead I and the abnormal Q waves and inverted T waves in Lead III suggestive of pulmonary embolism.

SUMMARY

Following are the key points of this chapter:

- ECG criteria are not a laboratory diagnosis of electrolyte imbalances.
- ECG criteria are designed to alert the clinician to the possibility of drug or electrolyte problems.
- QTc is the rate-corrected QT interval.
- QTc can be prolonged in asymptomatic patients for various unknown reasons.
- Prolonged QT interval in a patient who has a history of MI or is on antiarrhythmic medication can be significant.
- Pericarditis can mimic an MI but can be distinguished by relieving factors of pain, concave ST segment elevation, and the lack of reciprocal changes.
- ECG changes in pulmonary embolism may not be apparent in smaller embolisms.

GLOSSARY

hypercalcemia a condition in which there is an excessive amount of calcium in the blood.

hyperkalemia a condition in which there is an excessive amount of potassium in the blood.

hypocalcemia a condition in which there is abnormally low blood calcium.

hypokalemia a condition in which there is abnormally low concentration of potassium in the blood.

QTc the rate-corrected QT interval.

chapter 14

Putting It All Together

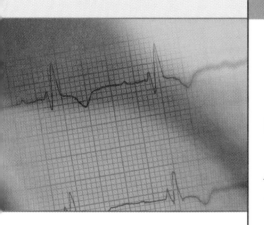

objectives

After reading this chapter, you should be able to:

1. Describe the importance of a systematic approach to the 12-lead ECG.

2. Use a simple algorithm for a time-saving approach to reading 12-lead ECGs.

GETTING A RAPID, ACCURATE 12-LEAD ECG READING

The book has presented a great deal of information about reading 12-lead ECGs. It is now time to bring everything together into an organized system. Table 14–1 lists the steps to rapidly and properly perform a comprehensive assessment of a 12-lead ECG. The table is like a road map through the ECG, ordered to prevent backtracking or having conditions farther down the line rule out the higher-priority ones.

It is important to note that this table puts together all that you have learned for a comprehensive assessment of the 12-lead ECG. The acute-care provider should realize that some acute and serious conditions might preclude a comprehensive assessment of the 12-lead ECG. In this case, steps 1 through 5 are the most appropriate before starting intervention.

The bottom line is: You should take no longer than 90 to 120 seconds to get the information you need from the 12-lead ECG before intervention.

Step 1: Analyze rhythm (15 seconds).

- If the rhythm is a wide complex tachycardia, go to VT algorithm. If the rhythm is determined to be ventricular tachycardia, terminate it and return only after you have a supraventricular rhythm. Return to step 2 after the VT is resolved.

Step 2: Determine axis and hemiblock (5–10 seconds).

- Use the Rapid Axis and Hemiblock Chart to determine the axis and the presence of hemiblock. This can help you find those patients who are at high risk for complete heart block.

TABLE 14–1. *Steps to a Rapid, Accurate 12-Lead ECG Reading*

Step	Rationale
1. Analyze rhythm.	Decide on VT or life threats.
	Use the VT algorithm.
2. Determine axis and hemiblocks.	Risk for CHB, drug contraindications.
3. Determine bundle branch block.	Risk for CHB, drug contraindications.
4. ISAL: Look for ST elevation.	Locate the AMI.
	Use the Acute MI Locator Chart.
5. 15-lead ECG: V4R, V8, V9.	If 12-lead normal/inferior MI or ST depression in V1–V4.
Comprehensive Assessment	
6. LBBB and AMI.	Early recognition is good. Early intervention is better.
7. Subendocardial injury?	ST depression only with ST elevation in lead aVR.
8. Chamber enlargement.	If large complexes seen, use "35."
	If not, measure aVL or other criteria.
9. QTc interval.	If you are going to give antiarrhythmics, diuretics, stimulants.
10. PRN: Pericarditis, early repolarization.	If needed, you may apply these criteria.

Step 3: Bundle branch blocks (5–10 seconds).

- If the QRS complex is less than 120 ms, skip this step and go to the AMI Locator Chart.
- Use the turn-signal theory to determine the presence of left or right bundle branch block. This information can be useful in determining who is at risk for complete heart block and also, in the case of a very wide complex, it can help determine those with a high risk for hemodynamic compromise.
- If an LBBB is present, proceed to the LBBB and AMI criteria.
- If an RBBB is present, proceed to the Acute MI Locator Chart and look for ST segment elevation.

Step 4: The Acute MI Locator Chart (30 seconds).

- I See All Leads.
- Look for ST elevation and then reciprocal changes.
- If ECG is normal or an inferior MI is found, proceed to step 5.

Step 5: The 15-lead ECG (10 seconds).

- If the 12-lead ECG is normal or if there is evidence of an inferior MI or possibility of a posterior MI, run the 15-lead ECG.
- Look in Leads V4R, V8, and V9 for ST elevation.
- Compare it on the AMI Locator Chart.
- If an AMI is found, you have concluded your acute-care assessment. At this point, your attention should be focused on managing the AMI.

Step 6: LBBB and AMI (60 seconds).

- If the patient is presenting symptomatic for an AMI, use the QRS Chart criteria to determine the probability.
- Once done with this step, your acute assessment is complete. Do not delay intervention for other comprehensive assessment unless absolutely needed.

Step 7: Subendocardial injury or ischemic changes.

- If ST segment elevation is not found, yet the patient is still symptomatic, look for ST depression in some leads and elevation only in Lead aVR. Otherwise, are there symmetrically inverted T waves?

Step 8: Chamber enlargement.

- Atrial abnormalities are not of high importance in the acute patient.
- Ventricular hypertrophy can be a clue as to underlying conditions that may affect cardiac output.
- Use the table of hypertrophy to help you locate it quickly.

Step 9: QTc interval.

- This is nice-to-know information rather than need-to-know information.
- Prolonged QTc interval is important to know if the patient is taking a digitalis-type preparation, such as digoxin, lanoxin, or digitalis.
- If you are going to give an antiarrhythmic, such as lidocaine or procainamide, you will want to know this information.
- Look at the QTc interval on the 12-lead ECG. Compare it to the QTc chart supplied.

Step 10: PRN conditions: pericarditis, early repolarization, pulmonary embolism.

• If needed, this would be the time to apply this criterion.
• Clinical criteria for these conditions usually outweigh the ECG evidence.

Figure 14–1 reflects the entire process in algorithm format.

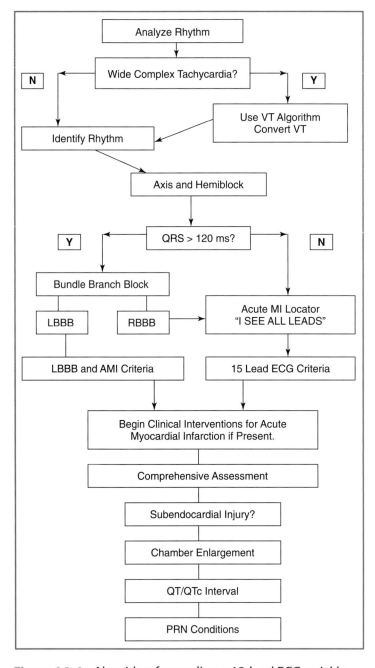

Figure 14–1. Algorithm for reading a 12-lead ECG quickly.

PRACTICE: PUTTING IT ALL TOGETHER

See Figures 14–2 through 14–301 for practice reading an ECG. Study each ECG and write your response in the space provided. For example, for Figure 14–2, you might write, "Atrial fibrillation, right-axis deviation, posterior hemiblock, right bundle branch block." All answers are printed in the Answer Key at the back of the book.

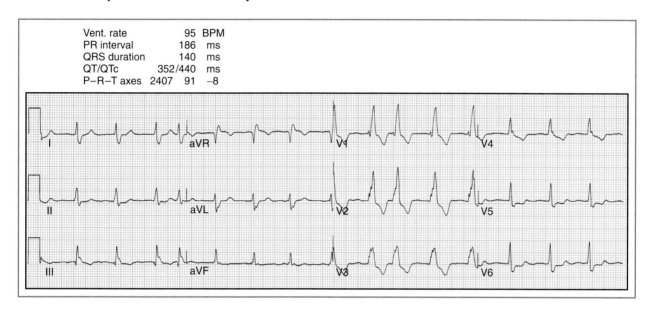

Vent. rate   95   BPM
PR interval   186   ms
QRS duration   140   ms
QT/QTc   352/440   ms
P–R–T axes 2407 91 –8

Figure 14–2.

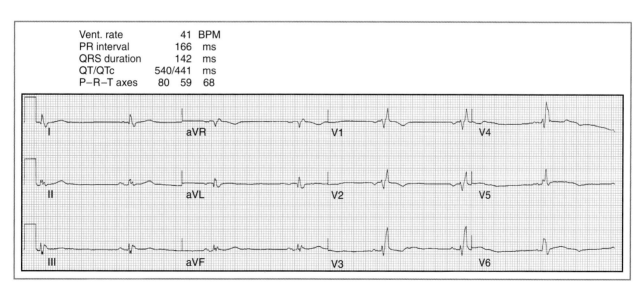

Vent. rate   41   BPM
PR interval   166   ms
QRS duration   142   ms
QT/QTc   540/441   ms
P–R–T axes   80   59   68

Figure 14–3.

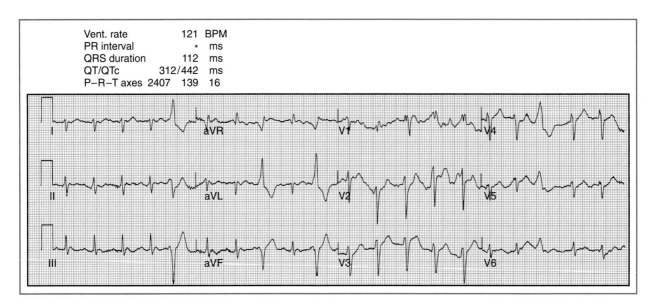

Vent. rate	121	BPM	
PR interval	*	ms	
QRS duration	112	ms	
QT/QTc	312/442	ms	
P–R–T axes 2407	139	16	

Figure 14–4.

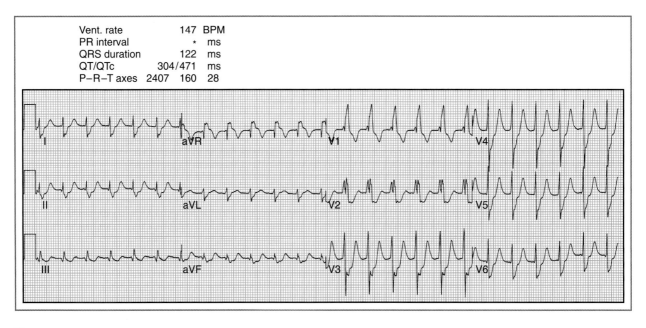

Vent. rate	147	BPM	
PR interval	*	ms	
QRS duration	122	ms	
QT/QTc	304/471	ms	
P–R–T axes 2407	160	28	

Figure 14–5.

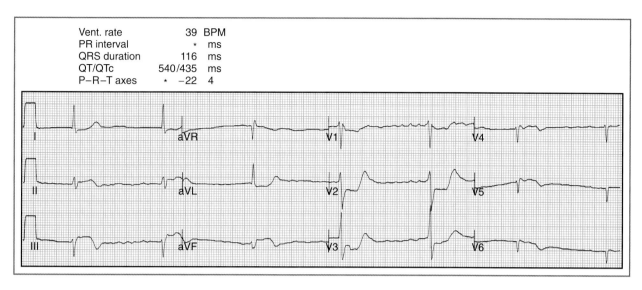

Vent. rate	39	BPM
PR interval	*	ms
QRS duration	116	ms
QT/QTc	540/435	ms
P–R–T axes	* –22	4

Figure 14–6.

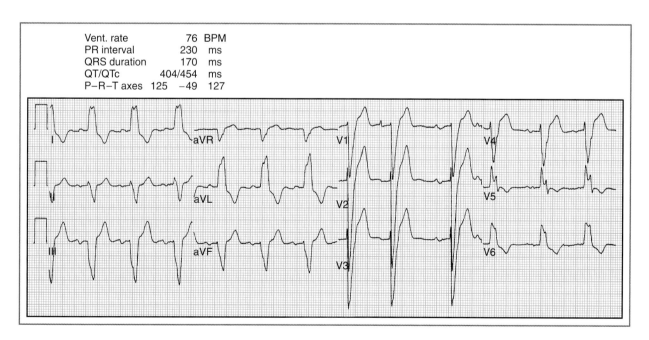

Vent. rate	76	BPM
PR interval	230	ms
QRS duration	170	ms
QT/QTc	404/454	ms
P–R–T axes	125 –49	127

Figure 14–7.

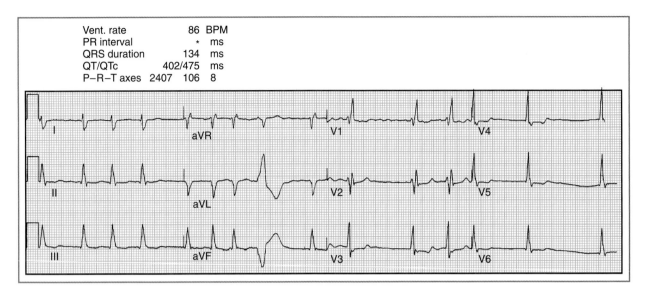

Vent. rate   86 BPM
PR interval   * ms
QRS duration   134 ms
QT/QTc   402/475 ms
P–R–T axes 2407 106 8

Figure 14–8.

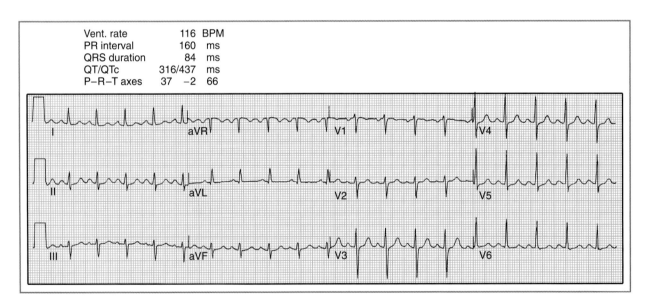

Vent. rate   116 BPM
PR interval   160 ms
QRS duration   84 ms
QT/QTc   316/437 ms
P–R–T axes   37 –2 66

Figure 14–9.

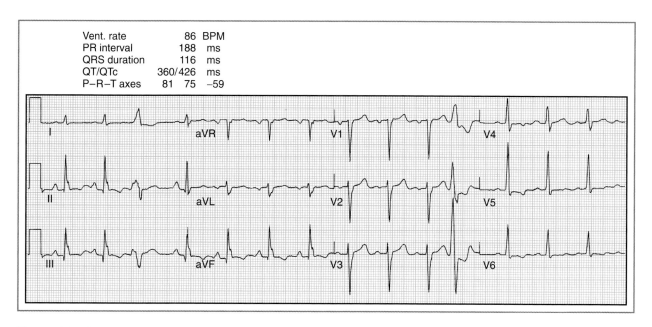

Vent. rate 86 BPM
PR interval 188 ms
QRS duration 116 ms
QT/QTc 360/426 ms
P–R–T axes 81 75 –59

Figure 14–10.

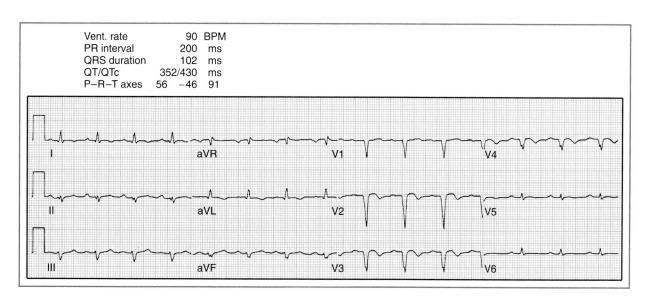

Vent. rate 90 BPM
PR interval 200 ms
QRS duration 102 ms
QT/QTc 352/430 ms
P–R–T axes 56 –46 91

Figure 14–11.

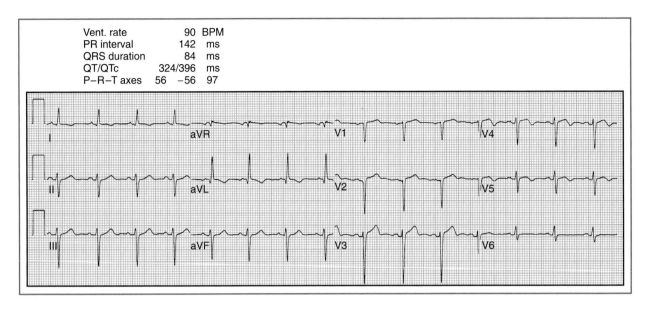

Vent. rate	90	BPM
PR interval	142	ms
QRS duration	84	ms
QT/QTc	324/396	ms
P–R–T axes	56 –56 97	

Figure 14–12.

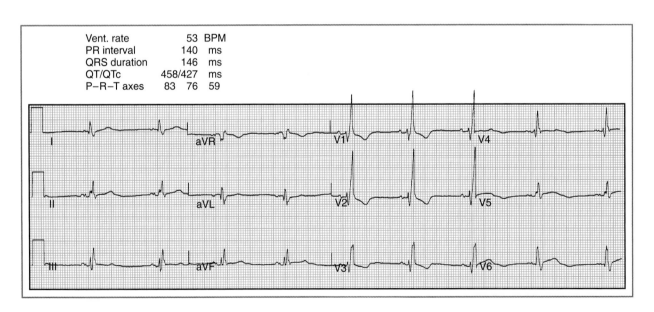

Vent. rate	53	BPM
PR interval	140	ms
QRS duration	146	ms
QT/QTc	458/427	ms
P–R–T axes	83 76 59	

Figure 14–13.

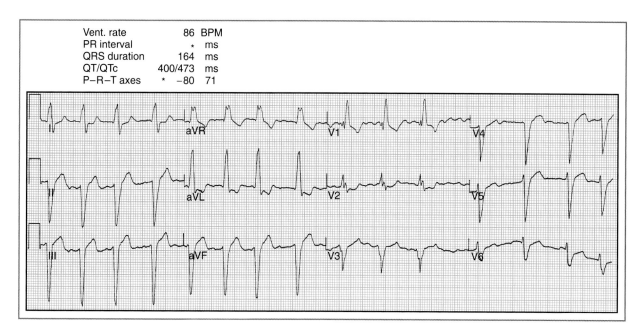

```
Vent. rate        86  BPM
PR interval        *  ms
QRS duration     164  ms
QT/QTc       400/473  ms
P–R–T axes    *  –80  71
```

Figure 14–14.

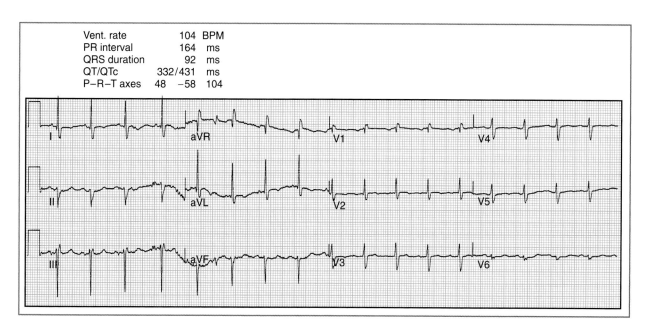

```
Vent. rate       104  BPM
PR interval      164  ms
QRS duration      92  ms
QT/QTc       332/431  ms
P–R–T axes  48  –58  104
```

Figure 14–15.

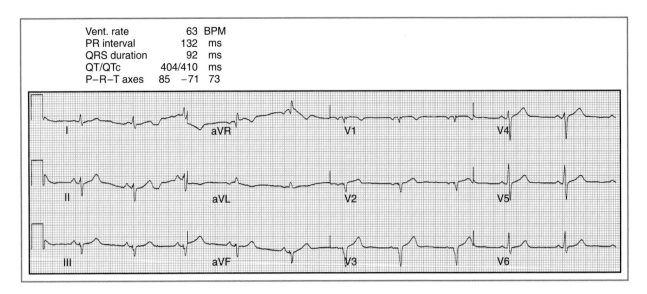

Vent. rate	63	BPM
PR interval	132	ms
QRS duration	92	ms
QT/QTc	404/410	ms
P–R–T axes	85 –71	73

Figure 14–16.

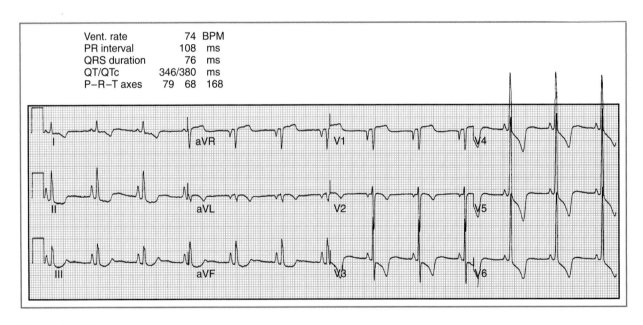

Vent. rate	74	BPM
PR interval	108	ms
QRS duration	76	ms
QT/QTc	346/380	ms
P–R–T axes	79 68	168

Figure 14–17.

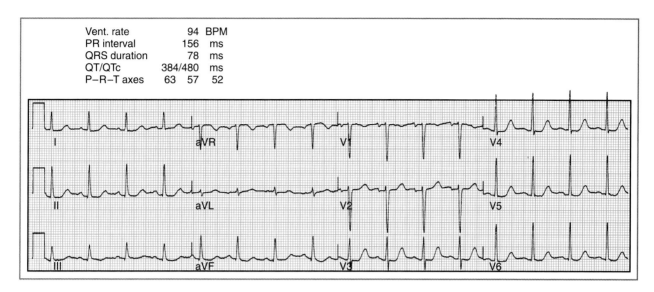

Vent. rate	94	BPM
PR interval	156	ms
QRS duration	78	ms
QT/QTc	384/480	ms
P–R–T axes	63 57 52	

Figure 14–18.

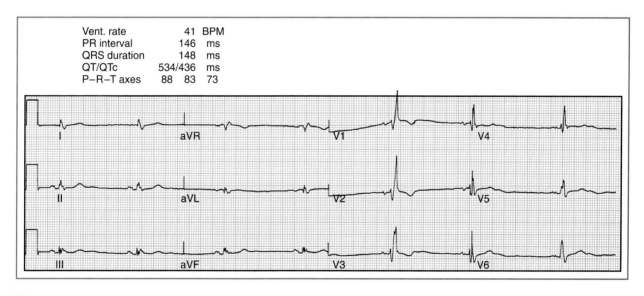

Vent. rate	41	BPM
PR interval	146	ms
QRS duration	148	ms
QT/QTc	534/436	ms
P–R–T axes	88 83 73	

Figure 14–19.

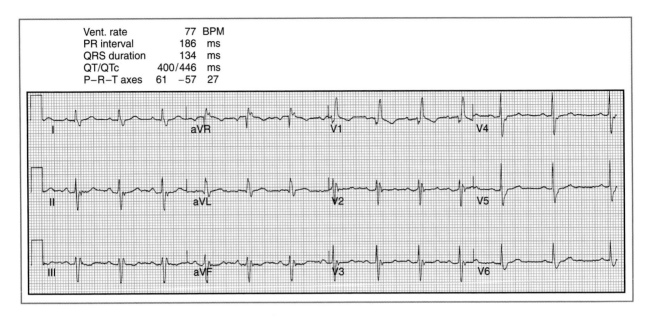

Vent. rate	77	BPM
PR interval	186	ms
QRS duration	134	ms
QT/QTc	400/446	ms
P–R–T axes	61 –57 27	

Figure 14–20.

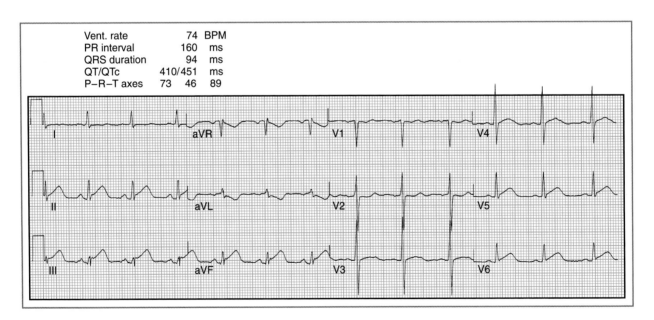

Vent. rate	74	BPM
PR interval	160	ms
QRS duration	94	ms
QT/QTc	410/451	ms
P–R–T axes	73 46 89	

Figure 14–21.

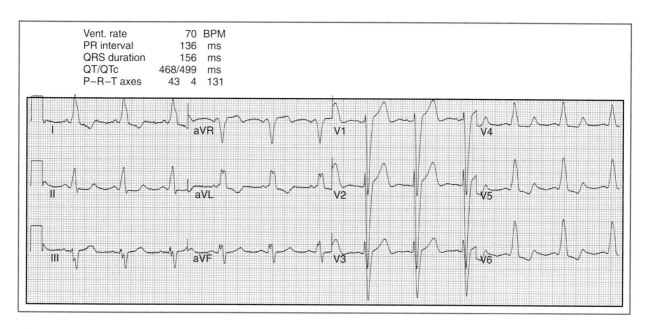

Vent. rate	70	BPM
PR interval	136	ms
QRS duration	156	ms
QT/QTc	468/499	ms
P–R–T axes	43 4	131

Figure 14–22.

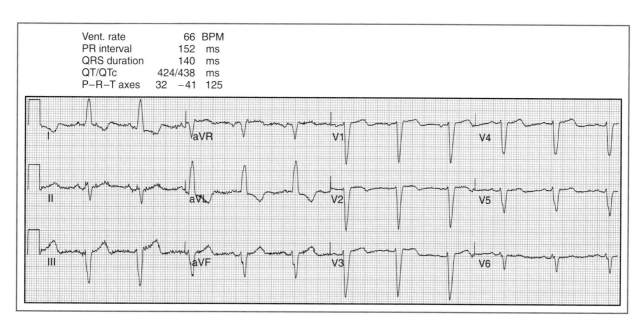

Vent. rate	66	BPM
PR interval	152	ms
QRS duration	140	ms
QT/QTc	424/438	ms
P–R–T axes	32 −41	125

Figure 14–23.

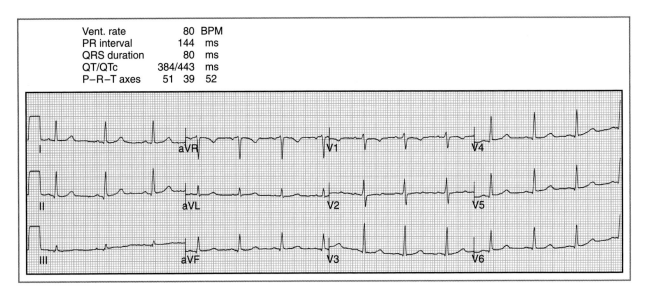

Vent. rate	80	BPM
PR interval	144	ms
QRS duration	80	ms
QT/QTc	384/443	ms
P–R–T axes	51 39 52	

Figure 14–24.

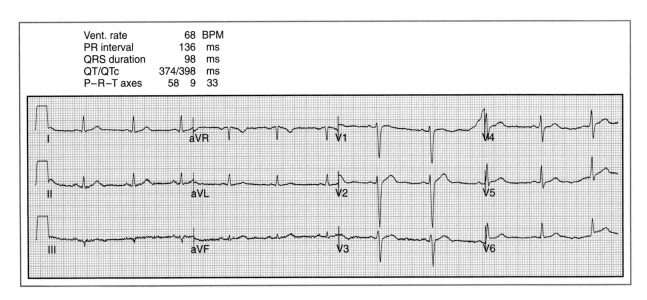

Vent. rate	68	BPM
PR interval	136	ms
QRS duration	98	ms
QT/QTc	374/398	ms
P–R–T axes	58 9 33	

Figure 14–25.

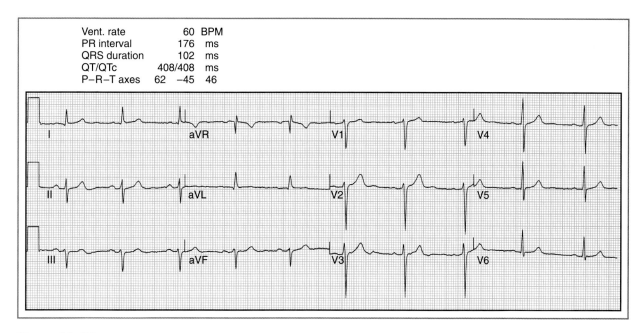

Vent. rate	60	BPM
PR interval	176	ms
QRS duration	102	ms
QT/QTc	408/408	ms
P–R–T axes	62 −45 46	

Figure 14–26.

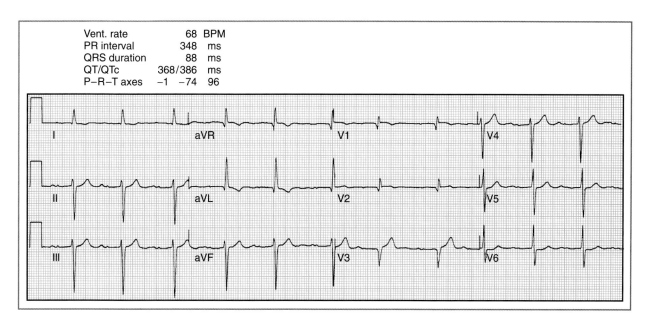

Vent. rate	68	BPM
PR interval	348	ms
QRS duration	88	ms
QT/QTc	368/386	ms
P–R–T axes	−1 −74 96	

Figure 14–27.

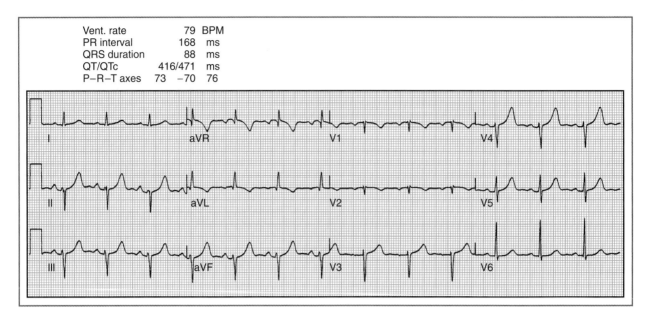

Vent. rate	79	BPM
PR interval	168	ms
QRS duration	88	ms
QT/QTc	416/471	ms
P–R–T axes	73 –70 76	

Figure 14–28.

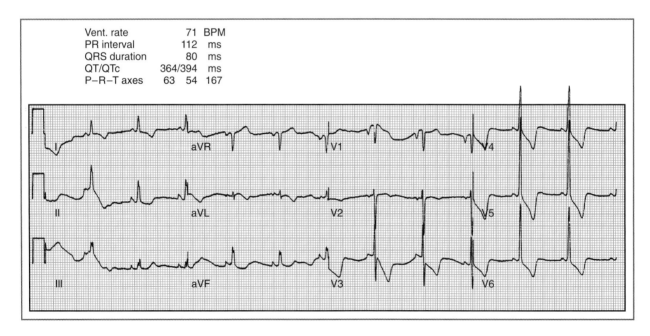

Vent. rate	71	BPM
PR interval	112	ms
QRS duration	80	ms
QT/QTc	364/394	ms
P–R–T axes	63 54 167	

Figure 14–29.

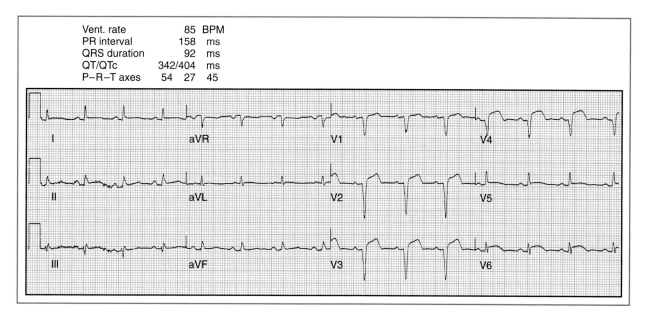

```
Vent. rate        85  BPM
PR interval      158  ms
QRS duration      92  ms
QT/QTc       342/404  ms
P–R–T axes    54  27  45
```

Figure 14–30.

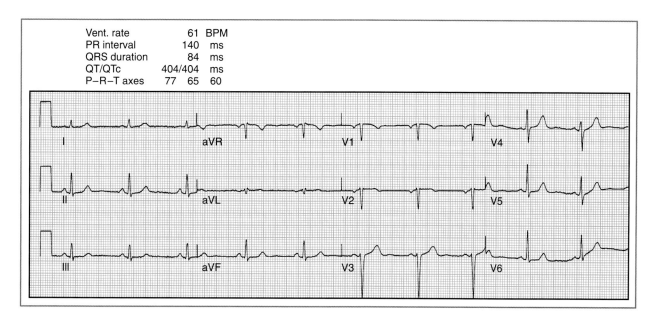

```
Vent. rate        61  BPM
PR interval      140  ms
QRS duration      84  ms
QT/QTc       404/404  ms
P–R–T axes    77  65  60
```

Figure 14–31.

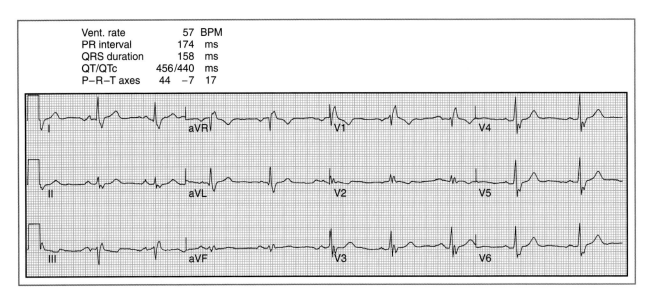

Figure 14–32.

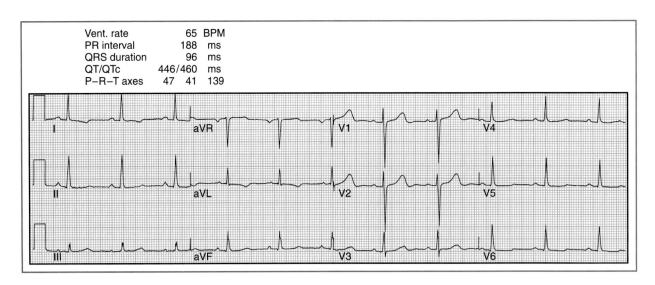

Figure 14–33.

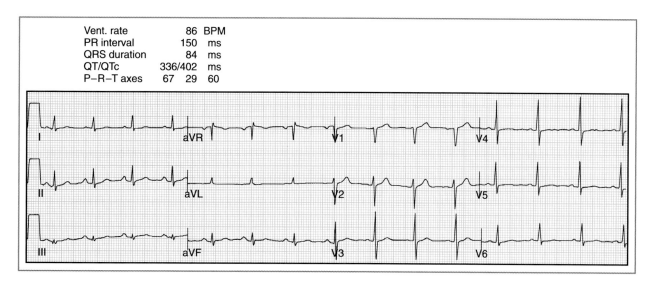

Figure 14–34.

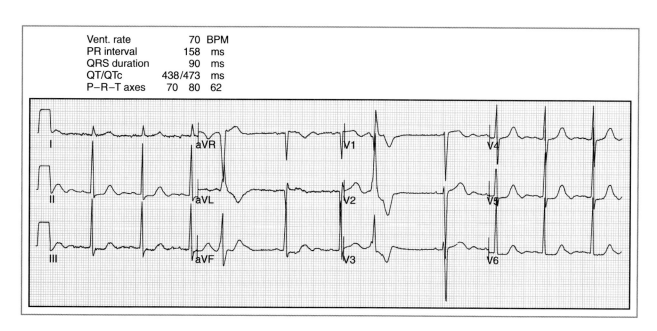

Figure 14–35.

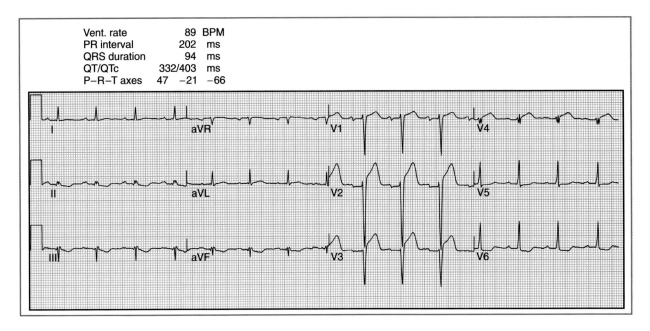

Vent. rate	89	BPM
PR interval	202	ms
QRS duration	94	ms
QT/QTc	332/403	ms
P–R–T axes	47 –21 –66	

Figure 14–36.

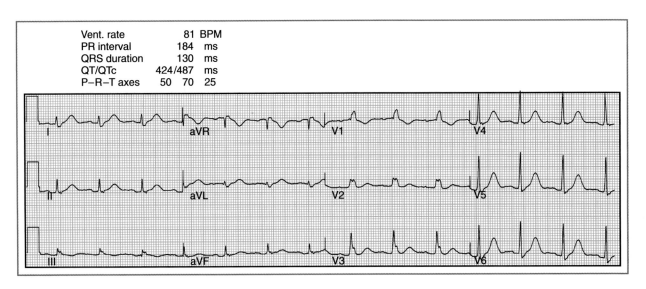

Vent. rate	81	BPM
PR interval	184	ms
QRS duration	130	ms
QT/QTc	424/487	ms
P–R–T axes	50 70 25	

Figure 14–37.

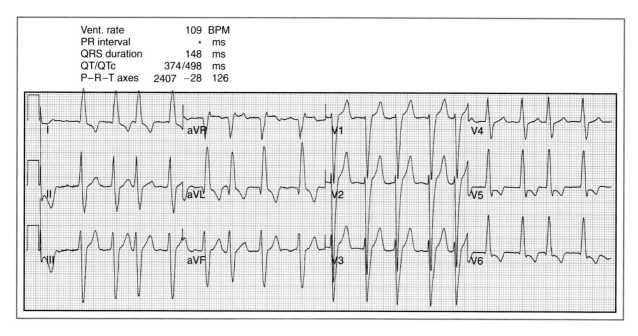

Figure 14–38.

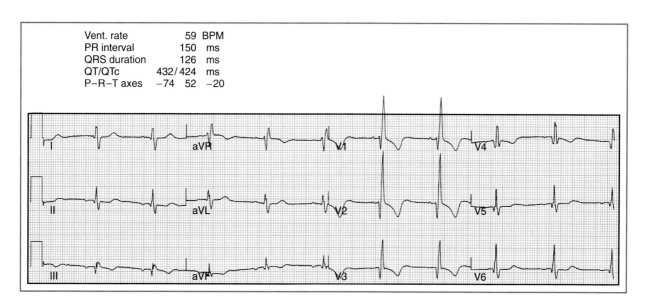

Figure 14–39.

Vent. rate	104	BPM
PR interval	162	ms
QRS duration	156	ms
QT/QTc	382/496	ms
P–R–T axes	64 –27 93	

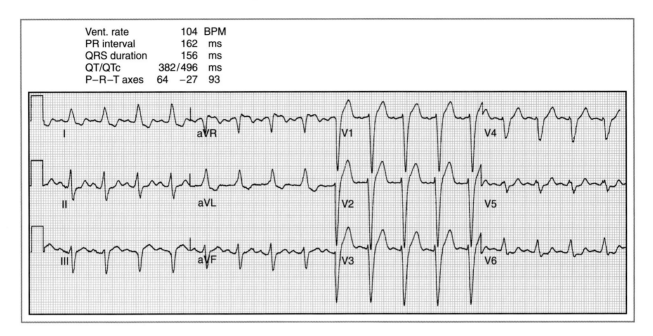

Figure 14–40.

Vent. rate	80	BPM
PR interval	*	ms
QRS duration	108	ms
QT/QTc	438/503	ms
P–R–T axes	81 –20 0	

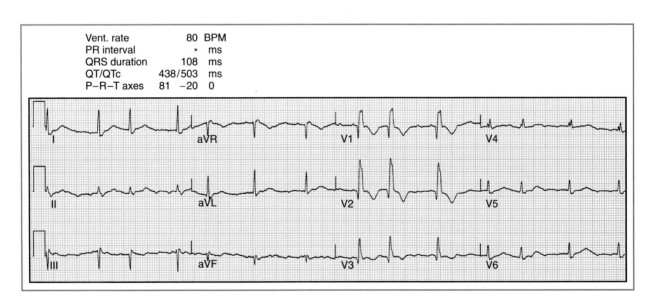

Figure 14–41.

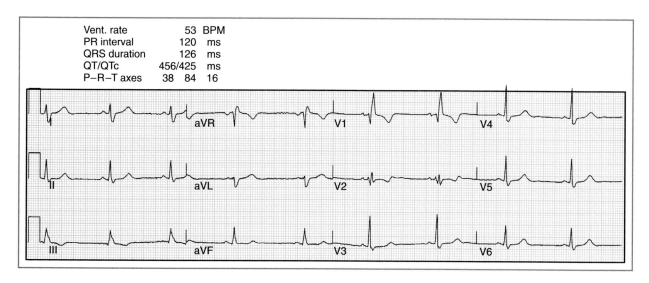

Figure 14–42.

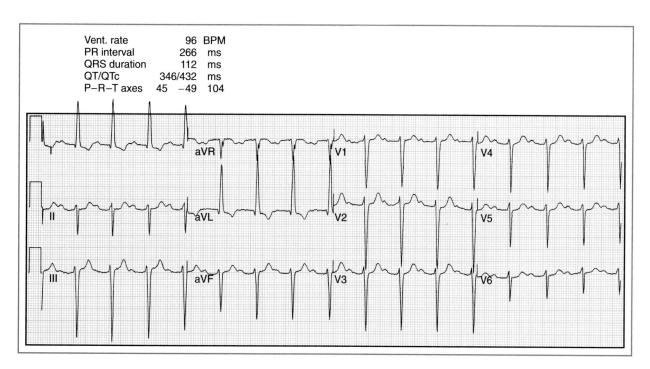

Figure 14–43.

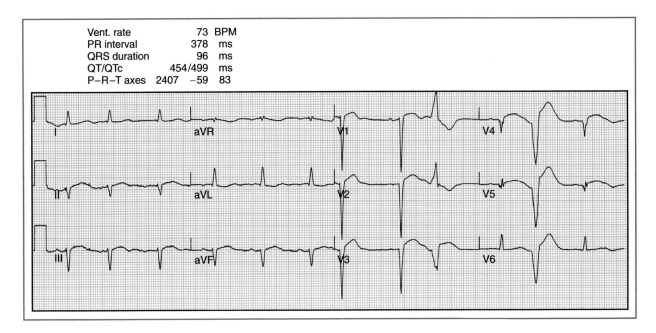

Vent. rate	73	BPM
PR interval	378	ms
QRS duration	96	ms
QT/QTc	454/499	ms
P–R–T axes	2407 –59	83

Figure 14–44.

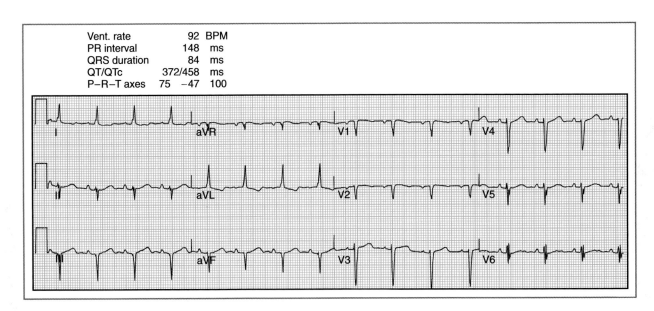

Vent. rate	92	BPM
PR interval	148	ms
QRS duration	84	ms
QT/QTc	372/458	ms
P–R–T axes	75 –47	100

Figure 14–45.

Vent. rate	79	BPM
PR interval	180	ms
QRS duration	96	ms
QT/QTc	366/419	ms
P–R–T axes	−3 38	91

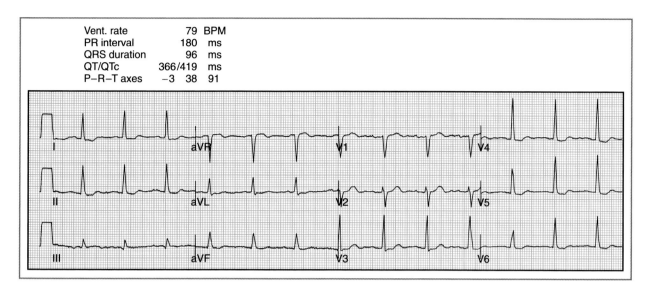

Figure 14–46.

Vent. rate	69	BPM
PR interval	116	ms
QRS duration	82	ms
QT/QTc	378/403	ms
P–R–T axes	85 65	66

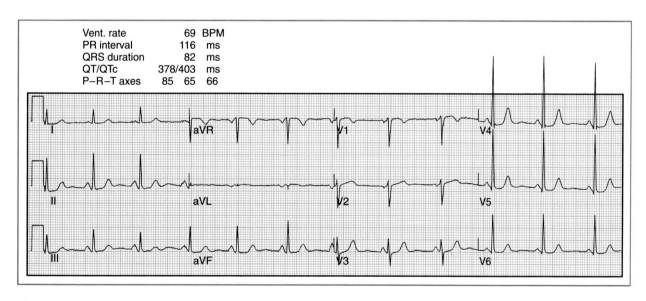

Figure 14–47.

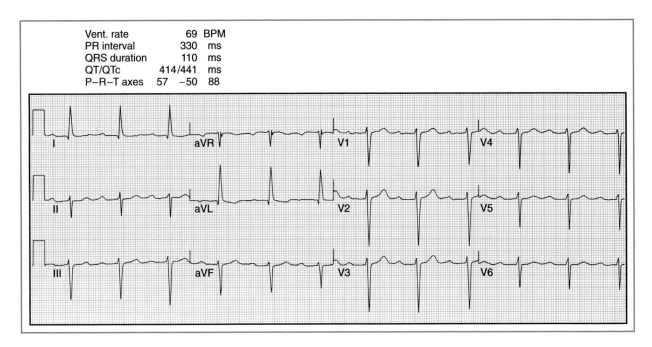

Vent. rate   69 BPM
PR interval   330 ms
QRS duration   110 ms
QT/QTc   414/441 ms
P–R–T axes   57 –50 88

Figure 14–48.

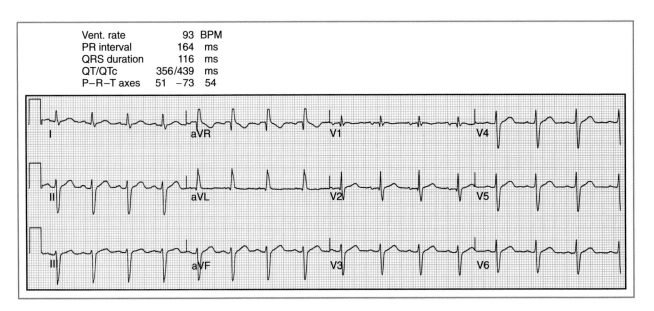

Vent. rate   93 BPM
PR interval   164 ms
QRS duration   116 ms
QT/QTc   356/439 ms
P–R–T axes   51 –73 54

Figure 14–49.

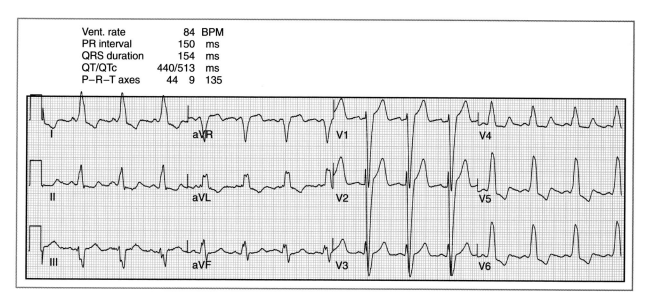

Vent. rate	84	BPM
PR interval	150	ms
QRS duration	154	ms
QT/QTc	440/513	ms
P–R–T axes	44 9 135	

Figure 14–50.

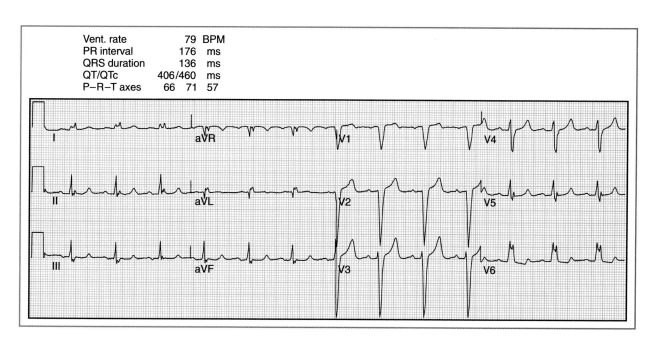

Vent. rate	79	BPM
PR interval	176	ms
QRS duration	136	ms
QT/QTc	406/460	ms
P–R–T axes	66 71 57	

Figure 14–51.

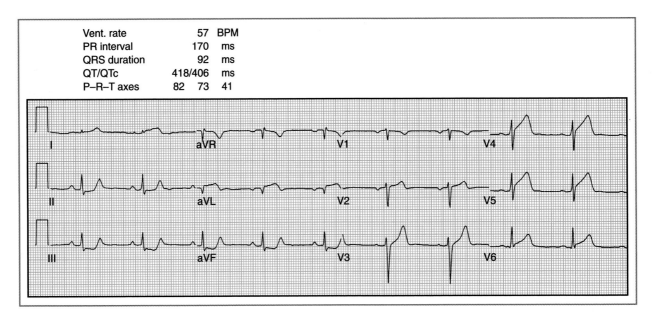

Vent. rate	57	BPM
PR interval	170	ms
QRS duration	92	ms
QT/QTc	418/406	ms
P–R–T axes	82 73 41	

Figure 14–52.

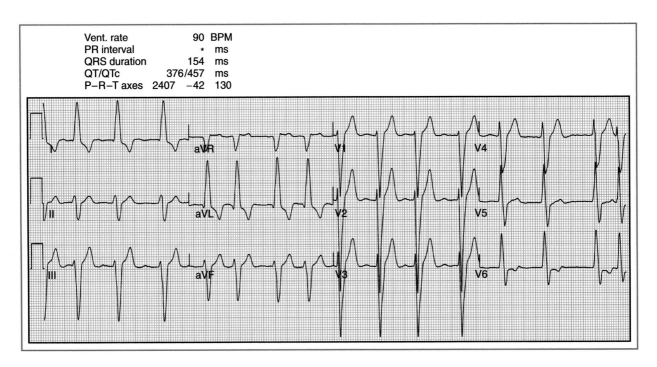

Vent. rate	90	BPM
PR interval	*	ms
QRS duration	154	ms
QT/QTc	376/457	ms
P–R–T axes	2407 −42 130	

Figure 14–53.

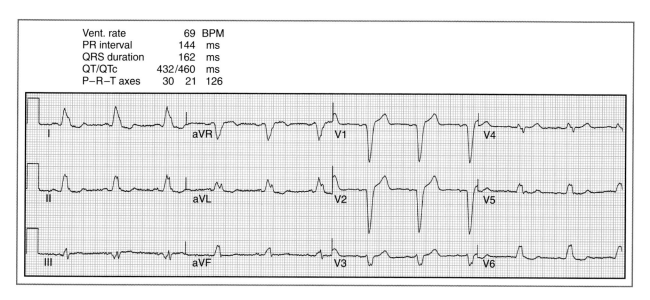

Vent. rate	69	BPM
PR interval	144	ms
QRS duration	162	ms
QT/QTc	432/460	ms
P–R–T axes	30 21 126	

Figure 14–54.

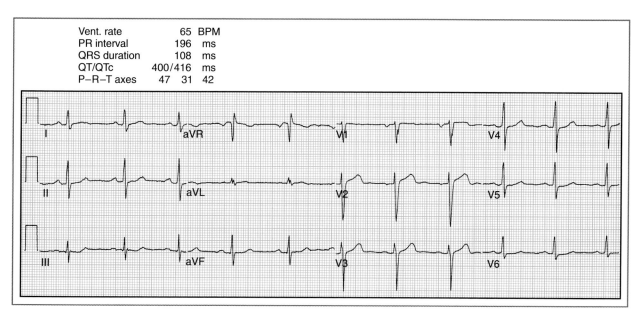

Vent. rate	65	BPM
PR interval	196	ms
QRS duration	108	ms
QT/QTc	400/416	ms
P–R–T axes	47 31 42	

Figure 14–55.

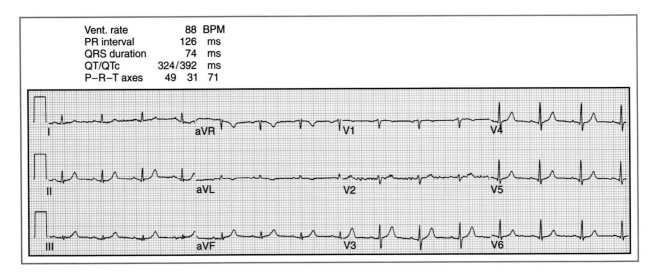

Vent. rate	88	BPM
PR interval	126	ms
QRS duration	74	ms
QT/QTc	324/392	ms
P–R–T axes	49 31 71	

Figure 14–56.

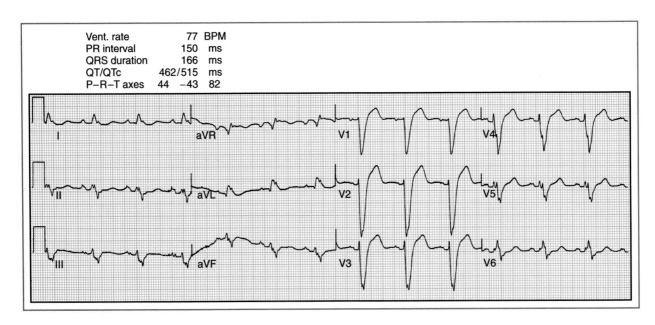

Vent. rate	77	BPM
PR interval	150	ms
QRS duration	166	ms
QT/QTc	462/515	ms
P–R–T axes	44 –43 82	

Figure 14–57.

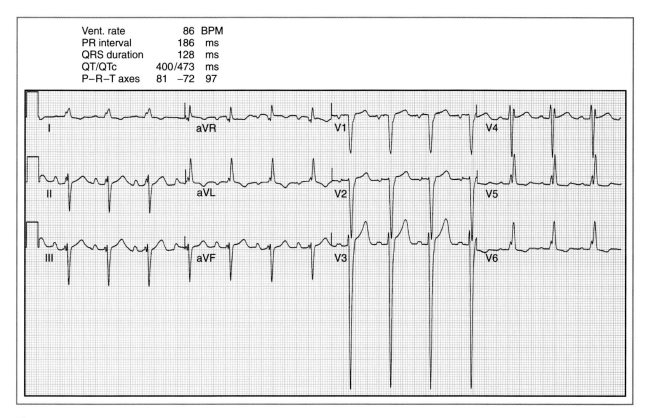

Vent. rate	86	BPM
PR interval	186	ms
QRS duration	128	ms
QT/QTc	400/473	ms
P–R–T axes	81 –72	97

Figure 14–58.

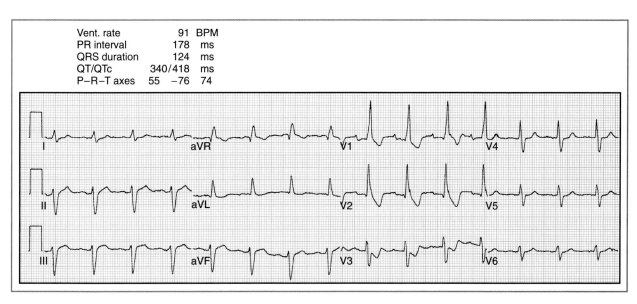

Vent. rate	91	BPM
PR interval	178	ms
QRS duration	124	ms
QT/QTc	340/418	ms
P–R–T axes	55 –76	74

Figure 14–59.

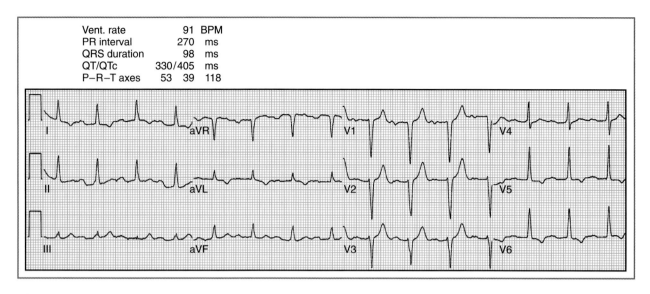

Vent. rate	91	BPM
PR interval	270	ms
QRS duration	98	ms
QT/QTc	330/405	ms
P–R–T axes	53 39 118	

Figure 14–60.

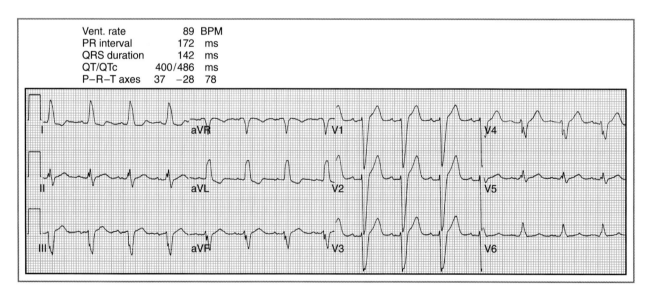

Vent. rate	89	BPM
PR interval	172	ms
QRS duration	142	ms
QT/QTc	400/486	ms
P–R–T axes	37 −28 78	

Figure 14–61.

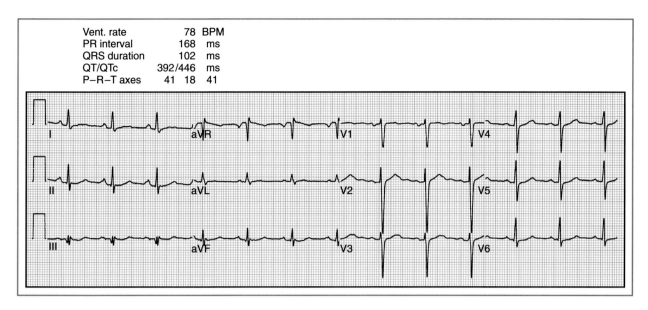

Vent. rate   78 BPM
PR interval   168 ms
QRS duration   102 ms
QT/QTc   392/446 ms
P–R–T axes   41 18 41

Figure 14–62.

Vent. rate   87 BPM
PR interval   196 ms
QRS duration   96 ms
QT/QTc   384/460 ms
P–R–T axes   72 –43 25

Figure 14–63.

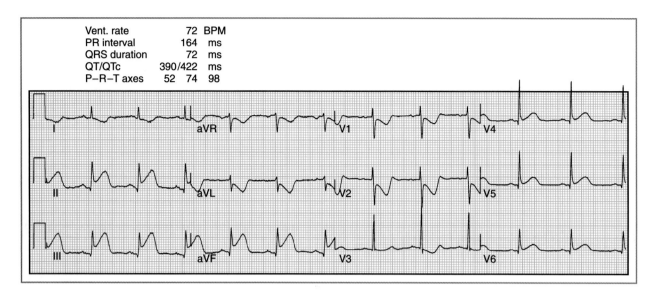

Vent. rate	72	BPM
PR interval	164	ms
QRS duration	72	ms
QT/QTc	390/422	ms
P–R–T axes	52 74 98	

Figure 14–64.

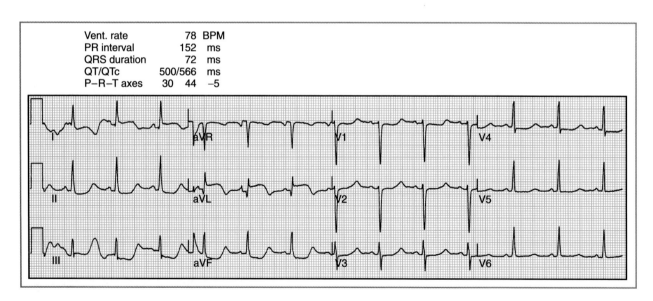

Vent. rate	78	BPM
PR interval	152	ms
QRS duration	72	ms
QT/QTc	500/566	ms
P–R–T axes	30 44 −5	

Figure 14–65.

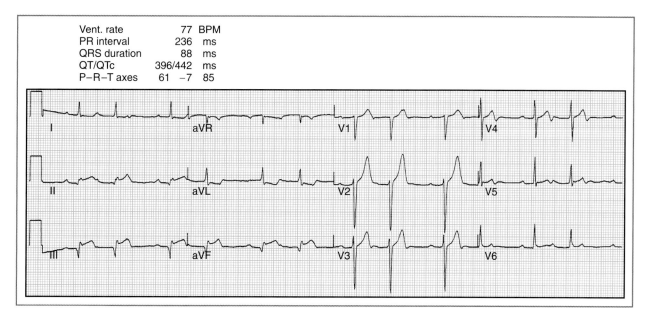

Figure 14–66.

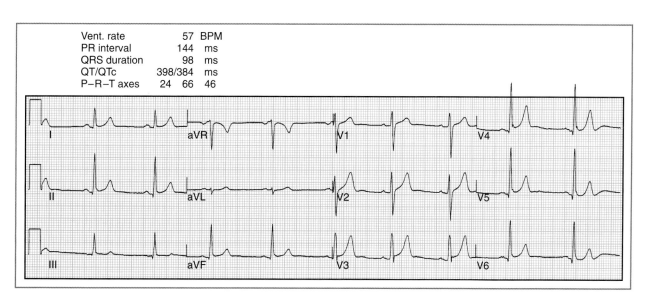

Figure 14–67.

Vent. rate	58	BPM
PR interval	154	ms
QRS duration	84	ms
QT/QTc	414/407	ms
P–R–T axes	47 93 92	

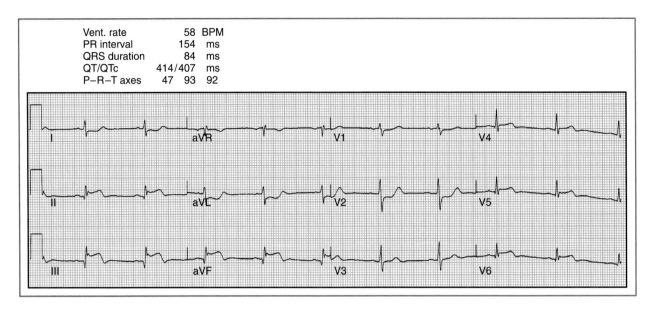

Figure 14–68.

Vent. rate	65	BPM
PR interval	156	ms
QRS duration	90	ms
QT/QTc	394/409	ms
P–R–T axes	75 77 72	

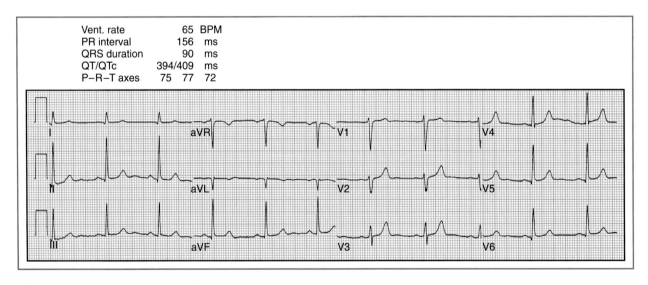

Figure 14–69.

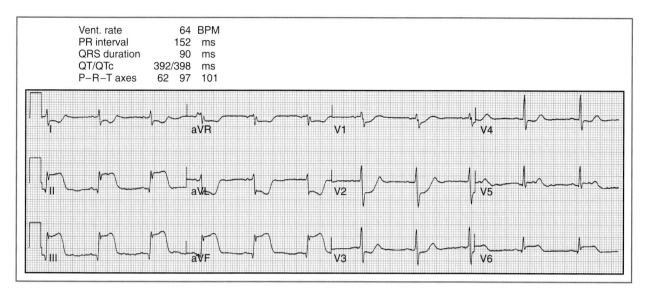

```
Vent. rate        64  BPM
PR interval      152  ms
QRS duration      90  ms
QT/QTc       392/398  ms
P–R–T axes    62  97  101
```

Figure 14–70.

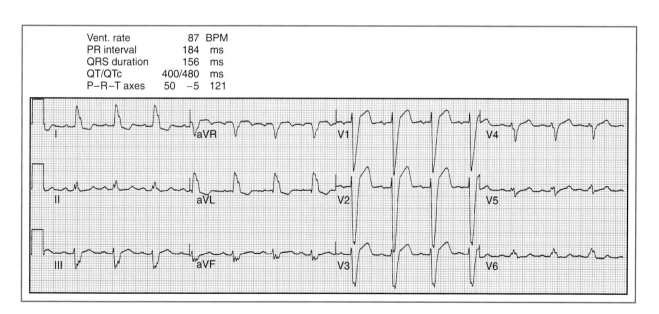

```
Vent. rate        87  BPM
PR interval      184  ms
QRS duration     156  ms
QT/QTc       400/480  ms
P–R–T axes    50  –5  121
```

Figure 14–71.

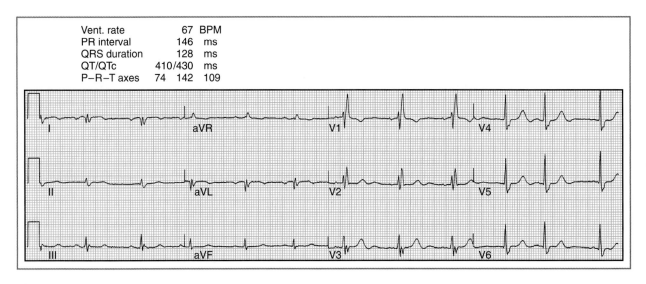

Vent. rate	67	BPM
PR interval	146	ms
QRS duration	128	ms
QT/QTc	410/430	ms
P–R–T axes	74 142 109	

Figure 14–72.

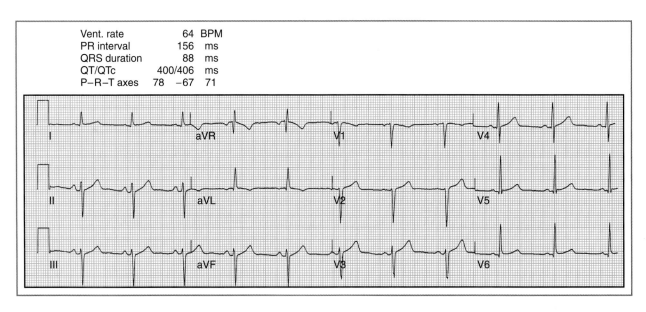

Vent. rate	64	BPM
PR interval	156	ms
QRS duration	88	ms
QT/QTc	400/406	ms
P–R–T axes	78 –67 71	

Figure 14–73.

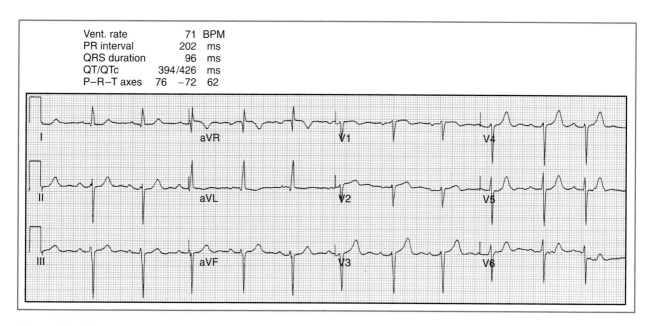

Vent. rate	71	BPM
PR interval	202	ms
QRS duration	96	ms
QT/QTc	394/426	ms
P–R–T axes	76	−72	62

Figure 14–74.

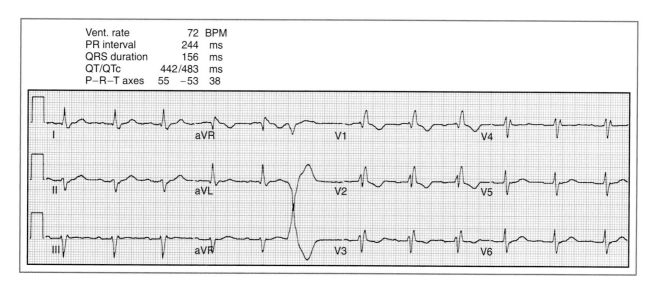

Vent. rate	72	BPM
PR interval	244	ms
QRS duration	156	ms
QT/QTc	442/483	ms
P–R–T axes	55	−53	38

Figure 14–75.

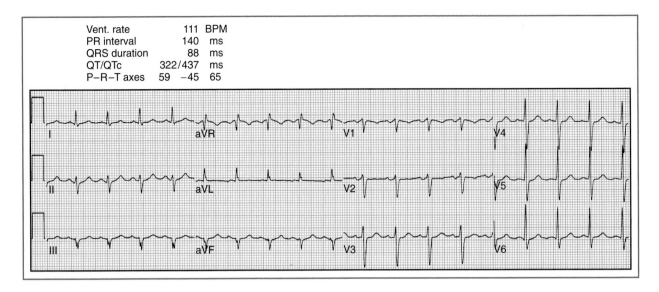

Vent. rate   111 BPM
PR interval   140 ms
QRS duration   88 ms
QT/QTc   322/437 ms
P–R–T axes 59 –45 65

Figure 14–76.

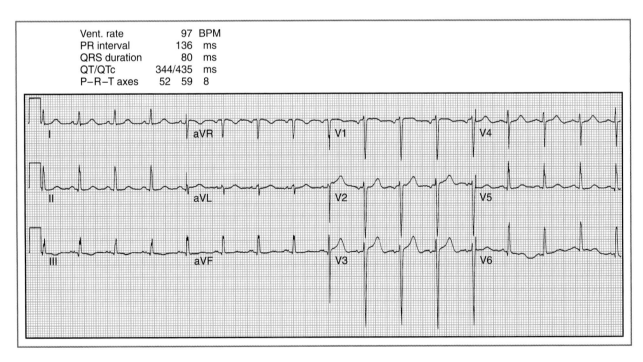

Vent. rate   97 BPM
PR interval   136 ms
QRS duration   80 ms
QT/QTc   344/435 ms
P–R–T axes 52 59 8

Figure 14–77.

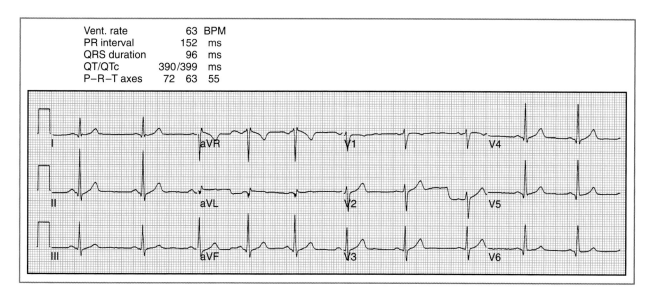

Vent. rate	63	BPM
PR interval	152	ms
QRS duration	96	ms
QT/QTc	390/399	ms
P–R–T axes	72 63 55	

Figure 14–78.

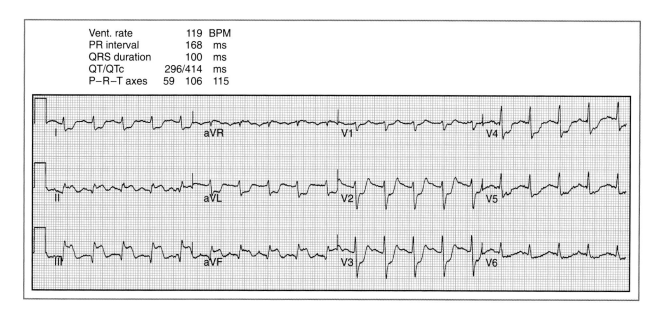

Vent. rate	119	BPM
PR interval	168	ms
QRS duration	100	ms
QT/QTc	296/414	ms
P–R–T axes	59 106 115	

Figure 14–79.

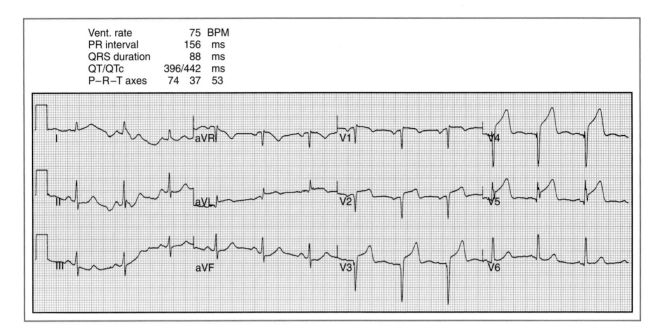

Vent. rate	75	BPM
PR interval	156	ms
QRS duration	88	ms
QT/QTc	396/442	ms
P–R–T axes	74 37 53	

Figure 14–80.

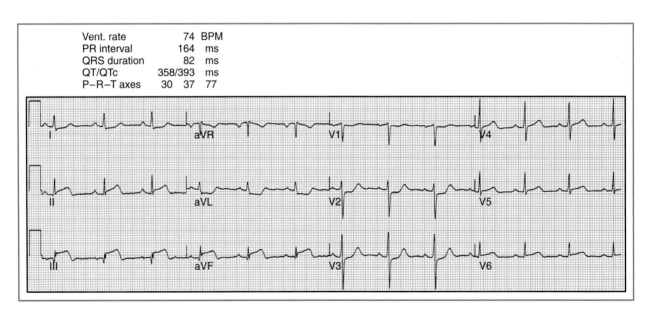

Vent. rate	74	BPM
PR interval	164	ms
QRS duration	82	ms
QT/QTc	358/393	ms
P–R–T axes	30 37 77	

Figure 14–81.

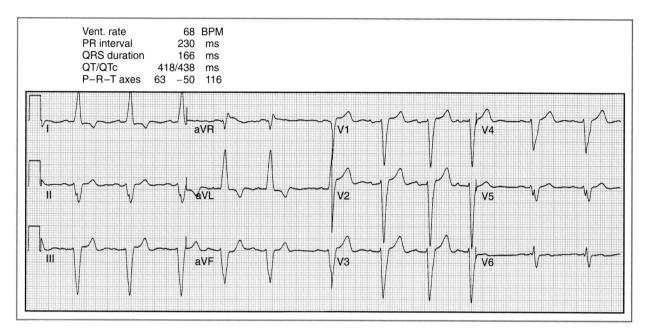

Figure 14–82.

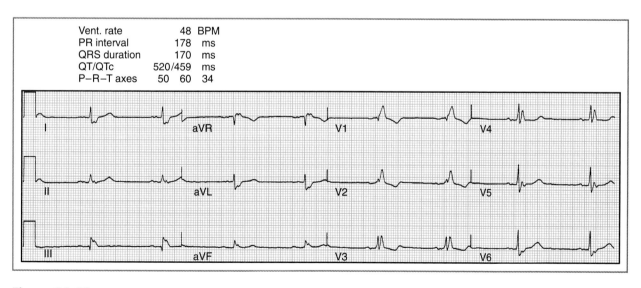

Figure 14–83.

Vent. rate	55	BPM
PR interval	142	ms
QRS duration	126	ms
QT/QTc	464/440	ms
P–R–T axes	67 48 10	

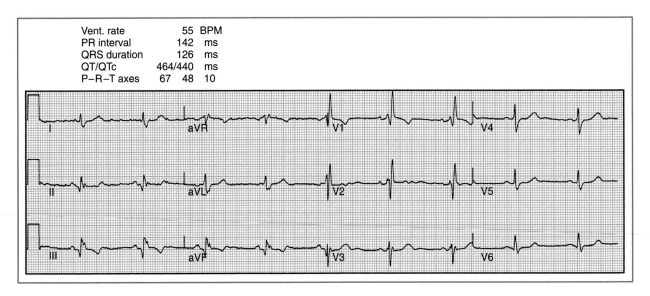

Figure 14–84.

Vent. rate	83	BPM
PR interval	168	ms
QRS duration	132	ms
QT/QTc	378/441	ms
P–R–T axes	57 51 38	

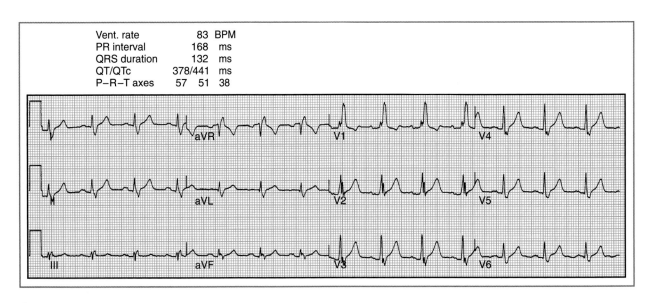

Figure 14–85.

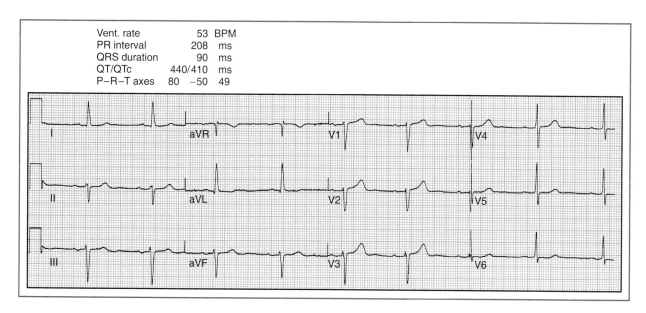

Vent. rate	53	BPM
PR interval	208	ms
QRS duration	90	ms
QT/QTc	440/410	ms
P–R–T axes	80 −50	49

Figure 14–86.

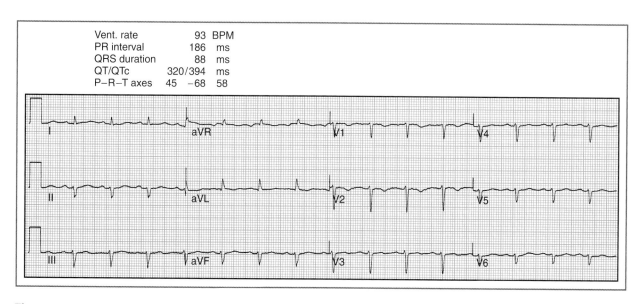

Vent. rate	93	BPM
PR interval	186	ms
QRS duration	88	ms
QT/QTc	320/394	ms
P–R–T axes	45 −68	58

Figure 14–87.

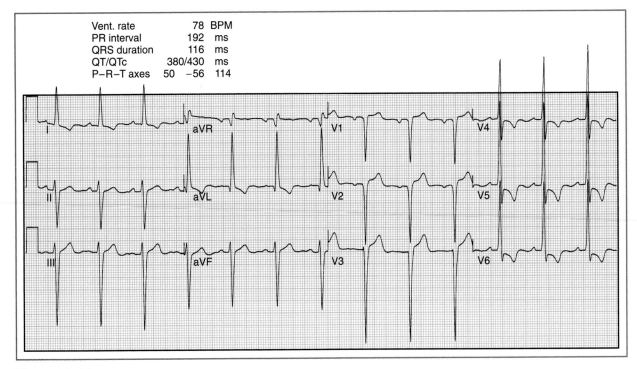

Vent. rate	78	BPM
PR interval	192	ms
QRS duration	116	ms
QT/QTc	380/430	ms
P–R–T axes	50 –56	114

Figure 14–88.

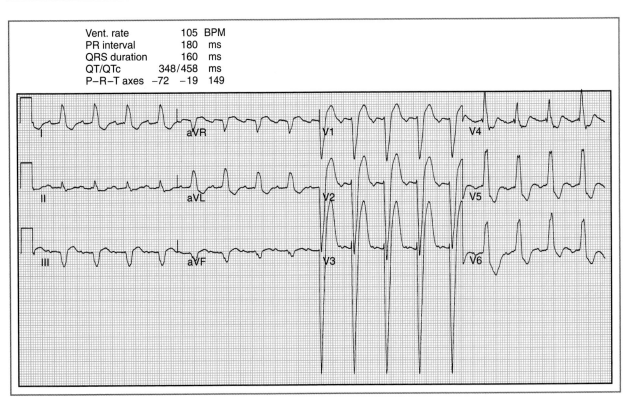

Vent. rate	105	BPM
PR interval	180	ms
QRS duration	160	ms
QT/QTc	348/458	ms
P–R–T axes	–72 –19	149

Figure 14–89.

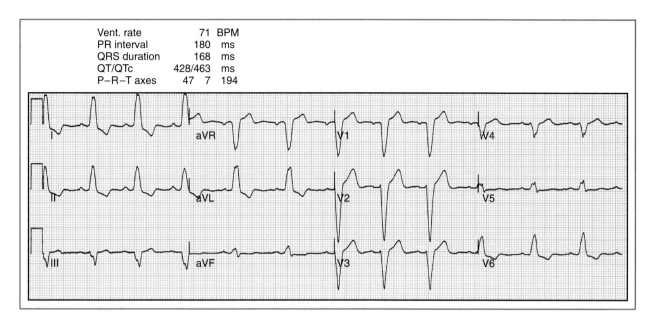

Vent. rate	71	BPM
PR interval	180	ms
QRS duration	168	ms
QT/QTc	428/463	ms
P–R–T axes	47 7	194

Figure 14–90.

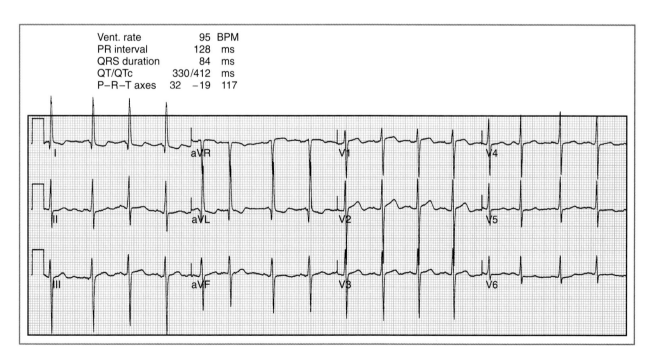

Vent. rate	95	BPM
PR interval	128	ms
QRS duration	84	ms
QT/QTc	330/412	ms
P–R–T axes	32 –19	117

Figure 14–91.

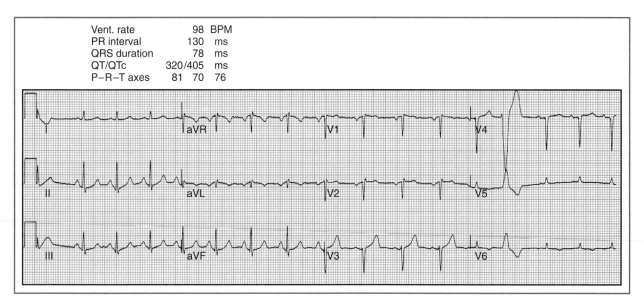

Vent. rate	98	BPM
PR interval	130	ms
QRS duration	78	ms
QT/QTc	320/405	ms
P–R–T axes	81 70 76	

Figure 14–92.

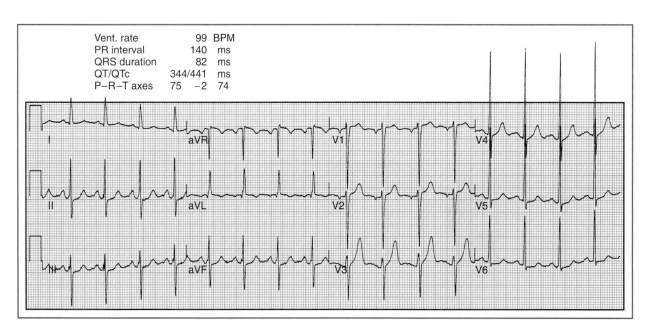

Vent. rate	99	BPM
PR interval	140	ms
QRS duration	82	ms
QT/QTc	344/441	ms
P–R–T axes	75 –2 74	

Figure 14–93.

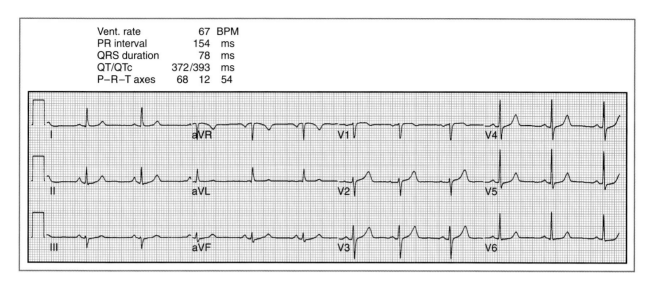

Vent. rate	67	BPM
PR interval	154	ms
QRS duration	78	ms
QT/QTc	372/393	ms
P–R–T axes	68	12	54

Figure 14–94.

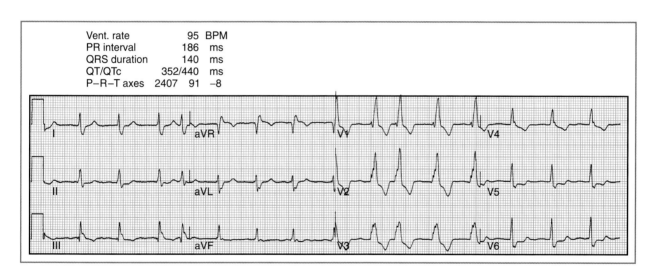

Vent. rate	95	BPM
PR interval	186	ms
QRS duration	140	ms
QT/QTc	352/440	ms
P–R–T axes	2407	91	–8

Figure 14–95.

Vent. rate	110	BPM
PR interval	*	ms
QRS duration	92	ms
QT/QTc	320/432	ms
P–R–T axes	* 118	–62

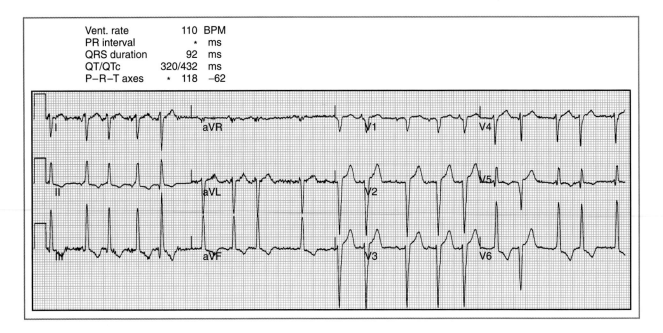

Figure 14–96.

Vent. rate	107	BPM
PR interval	156	ms
QRS duration	156	ms
QT/QTc	358/477	ms
P–R–T axes	55 15	159

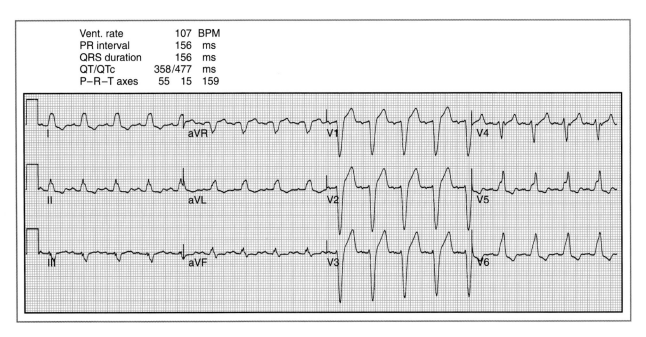

Figure 14–97.

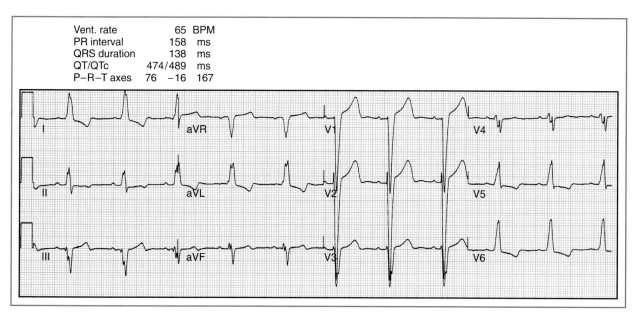

Vent. rate 65 BPM
PR interval 158 ms
QRS duration 138 ms
QT/QTc 474/489 ms
P–R–T axes 76 –16 167

Figure 14–98.

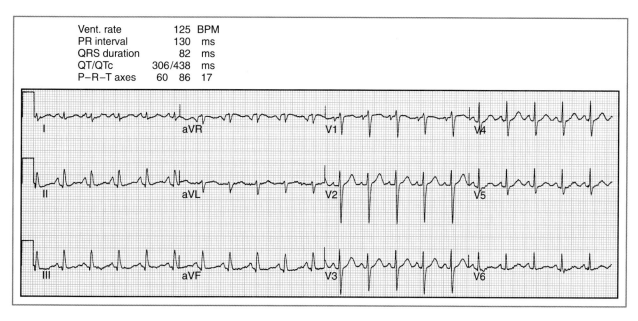

Vent. rate 125 BPM
PR interval 130 ms
QRS duration 82 ms
QT/QTc 306/438 ms
P–R–T axes 60 86 17

Figure 14–99.

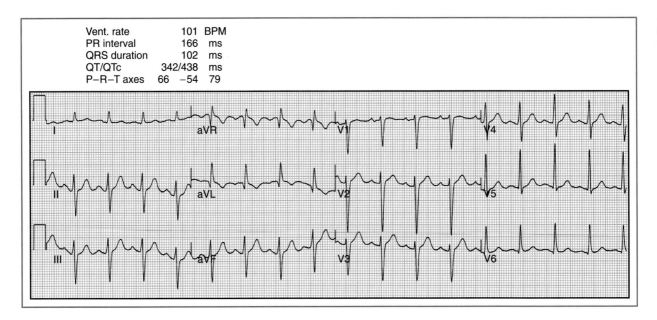

Figure 14–100.

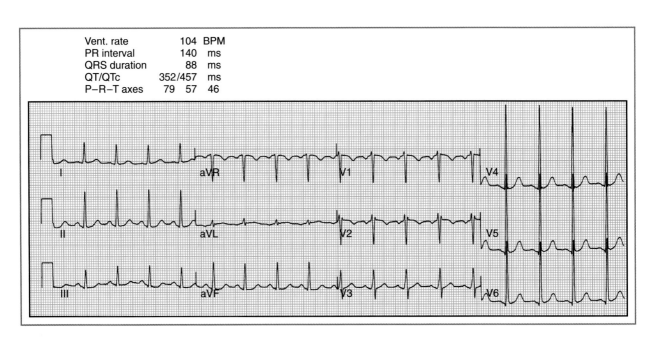

Figure 14–101.

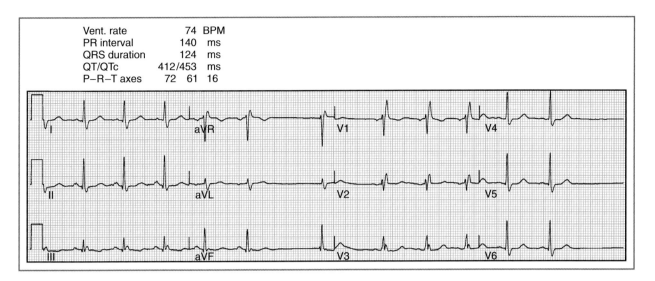

Vent. rate	74	BPM
PR interval	140	ms
QRS duration	124	ms
QT/QTc	412/453	ms
P–R–T axes	72 61 16	

Figure 14–102.

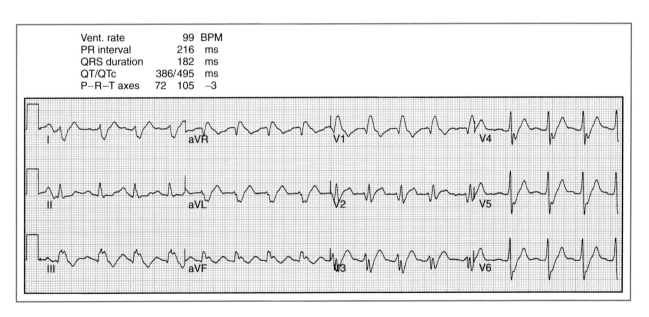

Vent. rate	99	BPM
PR interval	216	ms
QRS duration	182	ms
QT/QTc	386/495	ms
P–R–T axes	72 105 –3	

Figure 14–103.

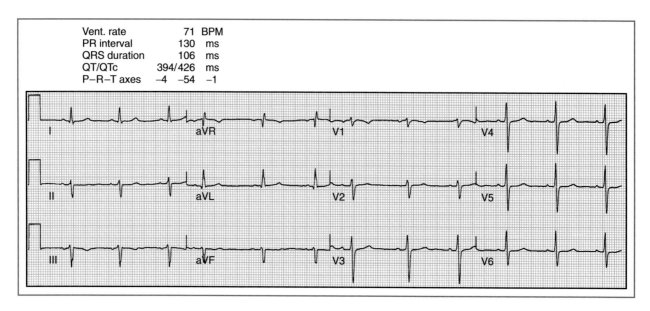

Vent. rate	71	BPM
PR interval	130	ms
QRS duration	106	ms
QT/QTc	394/426	ms
P–R–T axes	–4 –54 –1	

Figure 14–104.

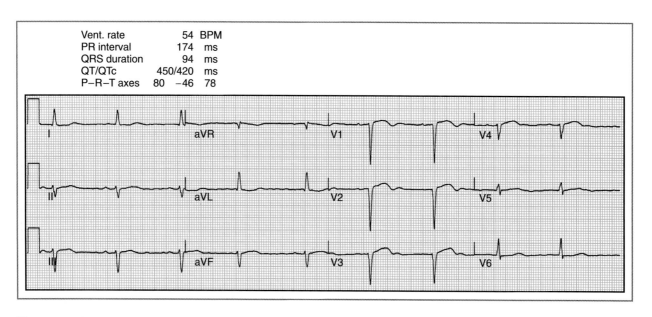

Vent. rate	54	BPM
PR interval	174	ms
QRS duration	94	ms
QT/QTc	450/420	ms
P–R–T axes	80 –46 78	

Figure 14–105.

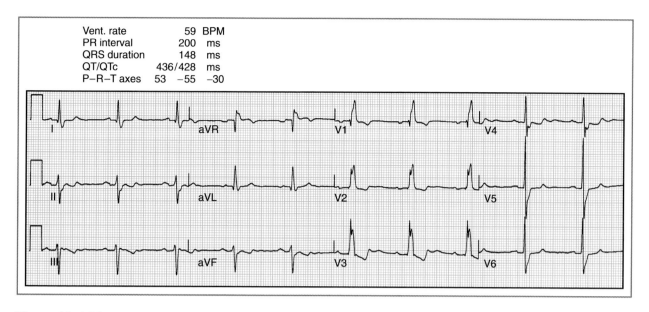

Vent. rate	59	BPM
PR interval	200	ms
QRS duration	148	ms
QT/QTc	436/428	ms
P–R–T axes	53 –55 –30	

Figure 14–106.

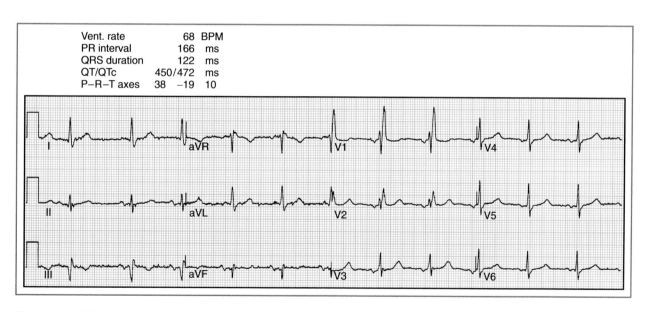

Vent. rate	68	BPM
PR interval	166	ms
QRS duration	122	ms
QT/QTc	450/472	ms
P–R–T axes	38 –19 10	

Figure 14–107.

Vent. rate	94	BPM
PR interval	174	ms
QRS duration	88	ms
QT/QTc	344/430	ms
P–R–T axes	35 50	152

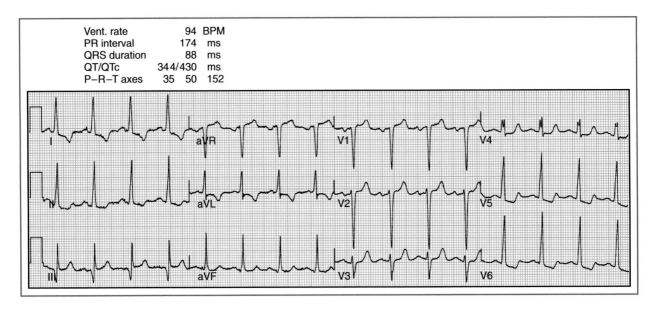

Figure 14–108.

Vent. rate	68	BPM
PR interval	*	ms
QRS duration	90	ms
QT/QTc	410/430	ms
P–R–T axes	2407 30	107

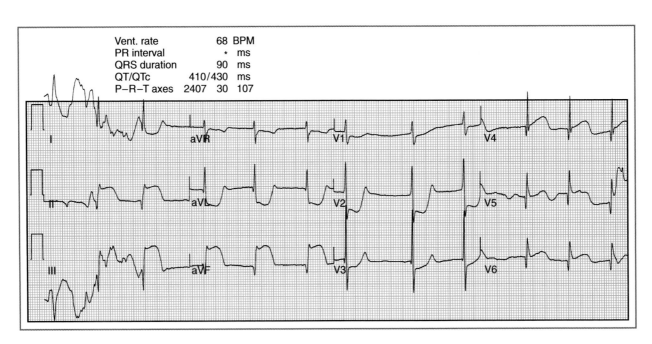

Figure 14–109.

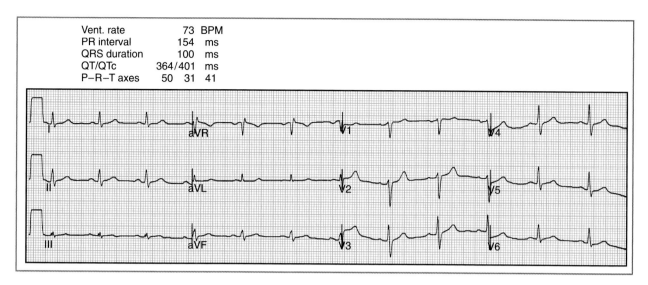

Vent. rate	73	BPM
PR interval	154	ms
QRS duration	100	ms
QT/QTc	364/401	ms
P–R–T axes	50 31 41	

Figure 14–110.

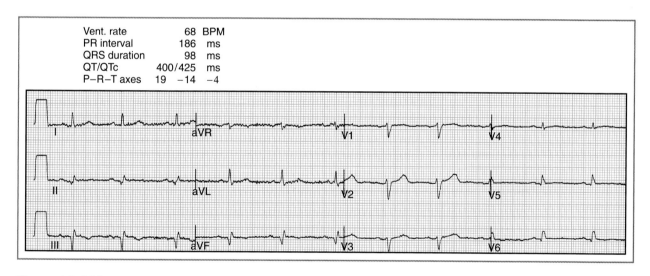

Vent. rate	68	BPM
PR interval	186	ms
QRS duration	98	ms
QT/QTc	400/425	ms
P–R–T axes	19 −14 −4	

Figure 14–111.

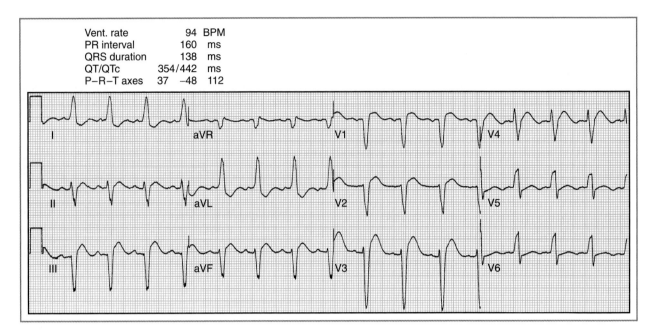

Vent. rate	94	BPM	
PR interval	160	ms	
QRS duration	138	ms	
QT/QTc	354/442	ms	
P–R–T axes	37	–48	112

Figure 14–112.

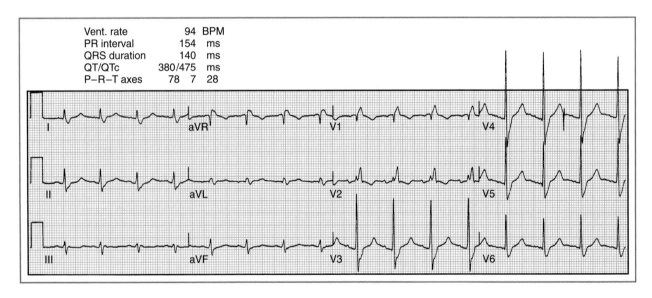

Vent. rate	94	BPM	
PR interval	154	ms	
QRS duration	140	ms	
QT/QTc	380/475	ms	
P–R–T axes	78	7	28

Figure 14–113.

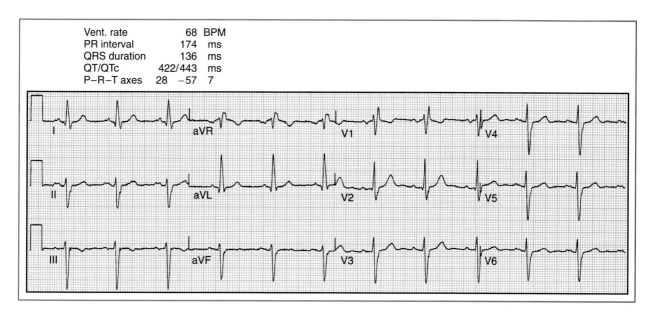

Vent. rate   68   BPM
PR interval   174   ms
QRS duration   136   ms
QT/QTc   422/443   ms
P–R–T axes   28   −57   7

Figure 14–114.

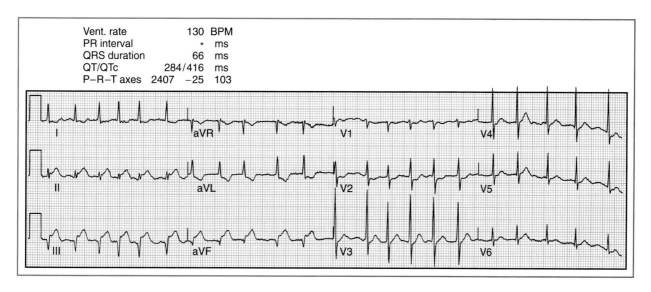

Vent. rate   130   BPM
PR interval   *   ms
QRS duration   66   ms
QT/QTc   284/416   ms
P–R–T axes   2407   −25   103

Figure 14–115.

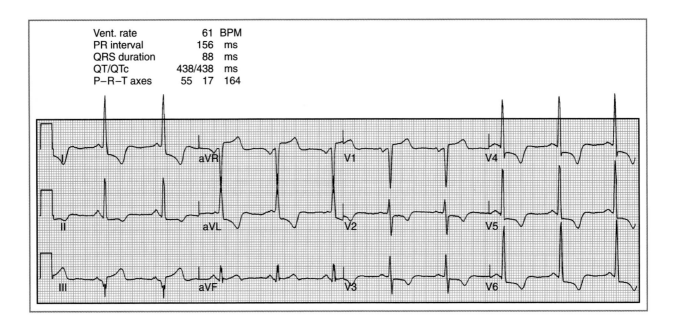

Vent. rate	61	BPM
PR interval	156	ms
QRS duration	88	ms
QT/QTc	438/438	ms
P–R–T axes	55	17	164

Figure 14–116.

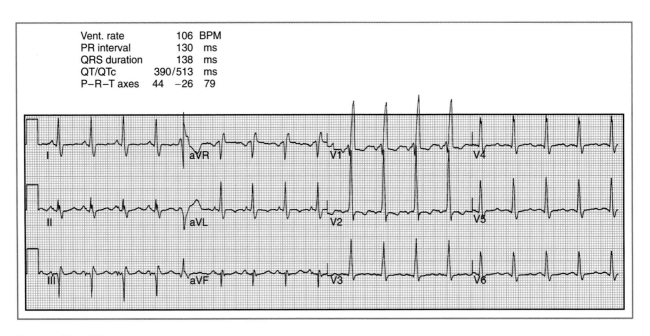

Vent. rate	106	BPM
PR interval	130	ms
QRS duration	138	ms
QT/QTc	390/513	ms
P–R–T axes	44	−26	79

Figure 14–117.

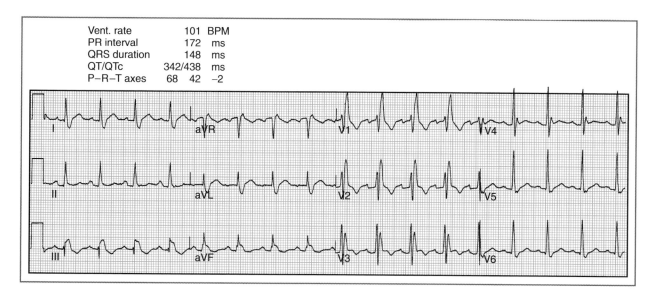

Vent. rate	101	BPM
PR interval	172	ms
QRS duration	148	ms
QT/QTc	342/438	ms
P–R–T axes	68 42 –2	

Figure 14–118.

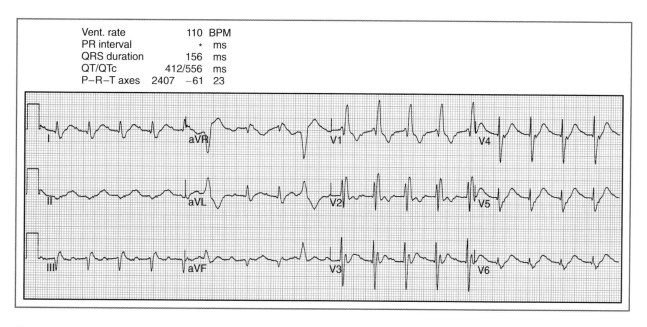

Vent. rate	110	BPM
PR interval	*	ms
QRS duration	156	ms
QT/QTc	412/556	ms
P–R–T axes	2407 –61 23	

Figure 14–119.

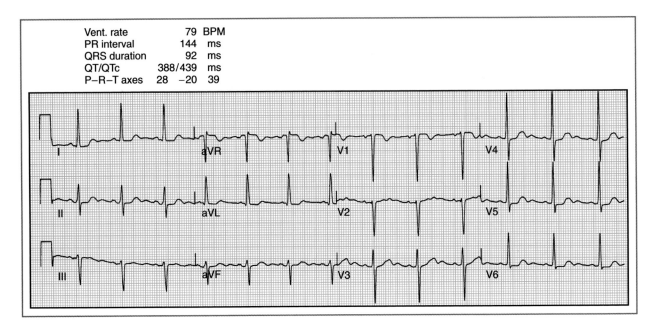

Vent. rate	79	BPM
PR interval	144	ms
QRS duration	92	ms
QT/QTc	388/439	ms
P–R–T axes	28 –20	39

Figure 14–120.

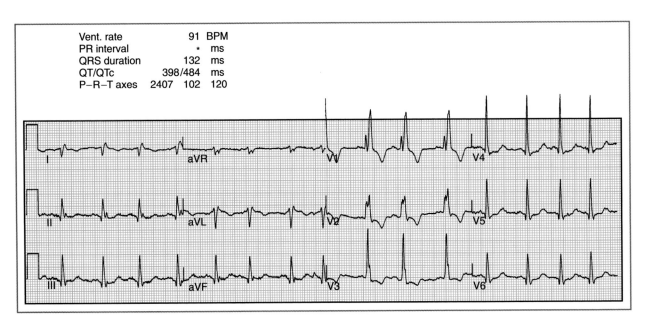

Vent. rate	91	BPM
PR interval	*	ms
QRS duration	132	ms
QT/QTc	398/484	ms
P–R–T axes	2407 102	120

Figure 14–121.

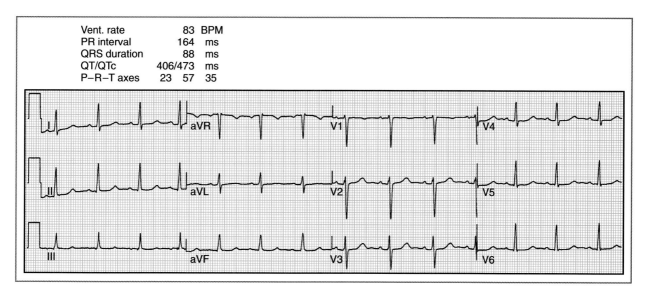

Figure 14–122.

_____

_____

_____

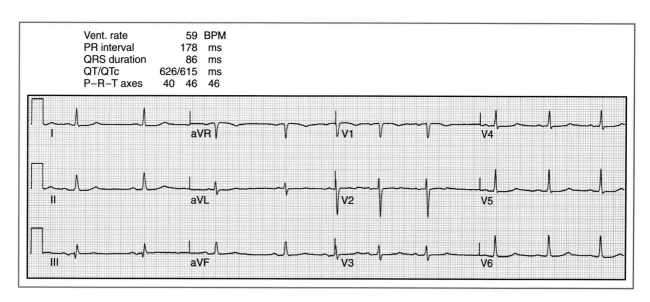

Figure 14–123.

_____

_____

_____

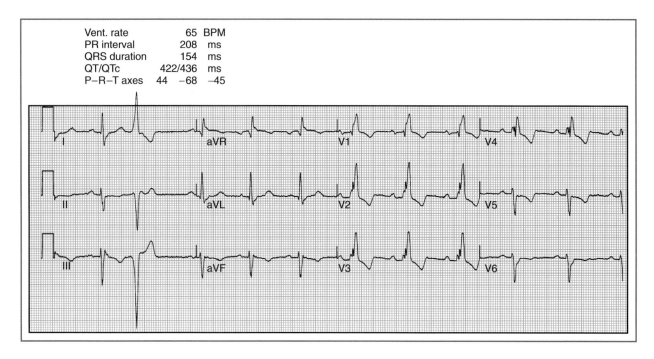

Vent. rate	65	BPM
PR interval	208	ms
QRS duration	154	ms
QT/QTc	422/436	ms
P–R–T axes	44 –68 –45	

Figure 14–124.

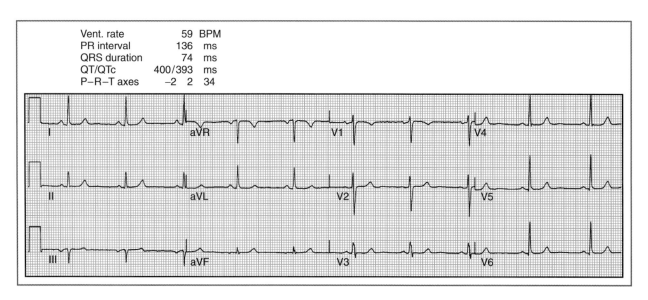

Vent. rate	59	BPM
PR interval	136	ms
QRS duration	74	ms
QT/QTc	400/393	ms
P–R–T axes	–2 2 34	

Figure 14–125.

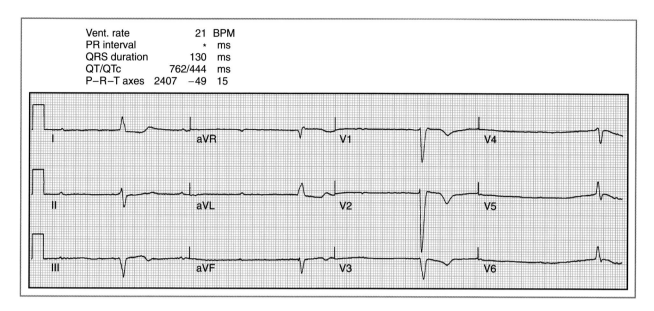

Figure 14–126.

_____
_____
_____

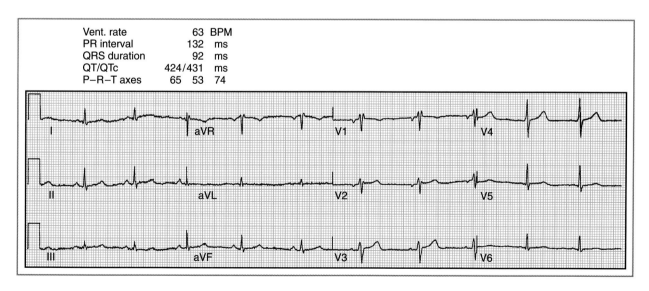

Figure 14–127.

_____
_____
_____

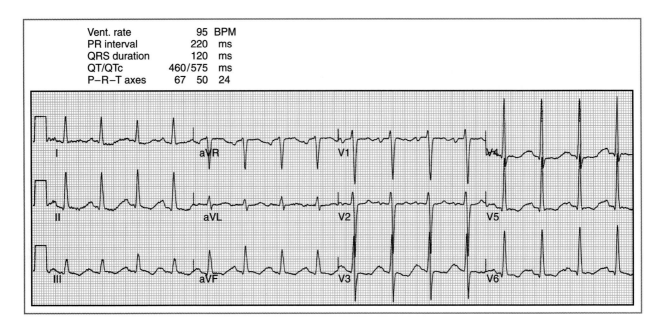

Vent. rate	95	BPM
PR interval	220	ms
QRS duration	120	ms
QT/QTc	460/575	ms
P–R–T axes	67 50 24	

Figure 14–128.

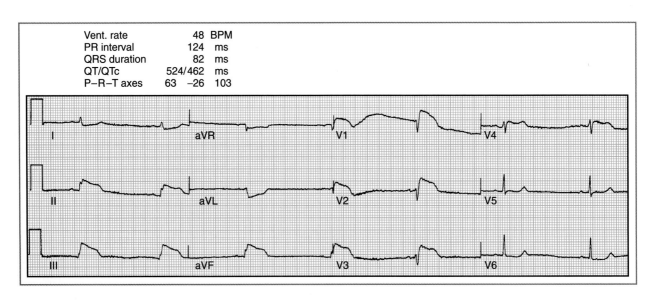

Vent. rate	48	BPM
PR interval	124	ms
QRS duration	82	ms
QT/QTc	524/462	ms
P–R–T axes	63 –26 103	

Figure 14–129.

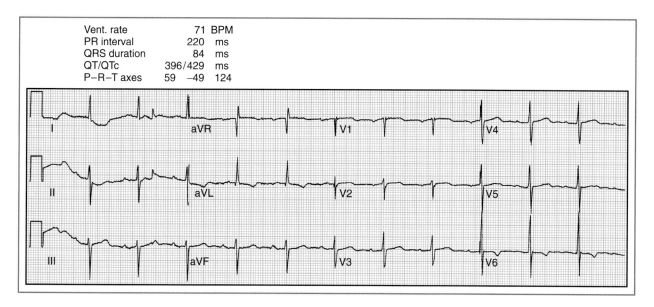

Vent. rate	71	BPM
PR interval	220	ms
QRS duration	84	ms
QT/QTc	396/429	ms
P–R–T axes	59 −49 124	

Figure 14–130.

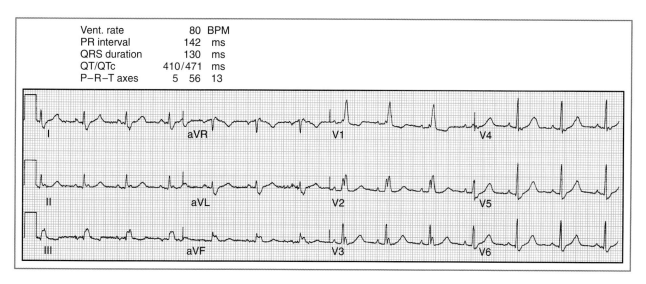

Vent. rate	80	BPM
PR interval	142	ms
QRS duration	130	ms
QT/QTc	410/471	ms
P–R–T axes	5 56 13	

Figure 14–131.

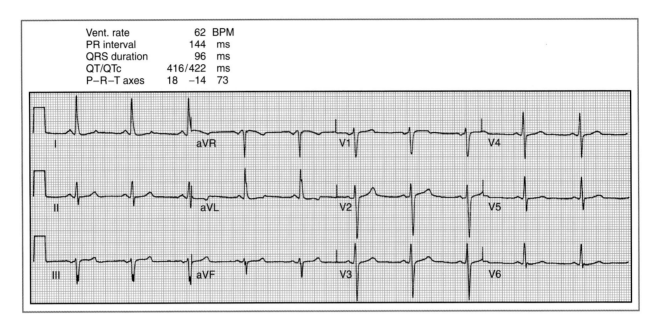

Vent. rate	62	BPM
PR interval	144	ms
QRS duration	96	ms
QT/QTc	416/422	ms
P–R–T axes	18 –14 73	

Figure 14–132.

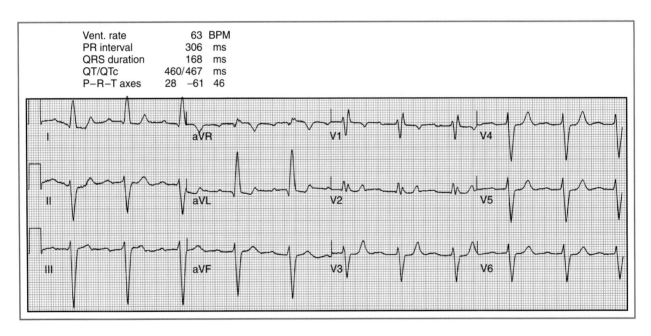

Vent. rate	63	BPM
PR interval	306	ms
QRS duration	168	ms
QT/QTc	460/467	ms
P–R–T axes	28 –61 46	

Figure 14–133.

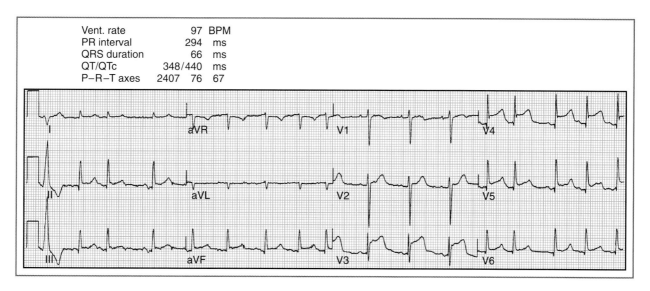

Figure 14–134.

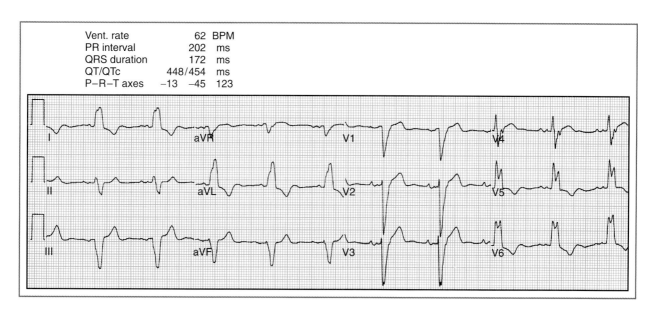

Figure 14–135.

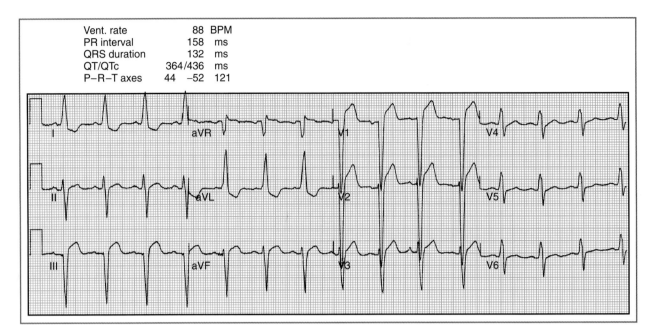

Vent. rate	88	BPM
PR interval	158	ms
QRS duration	132	ms
QT/QTc	364/436	ms
P–R–T axes	44	−52	121

Figure 14–136.

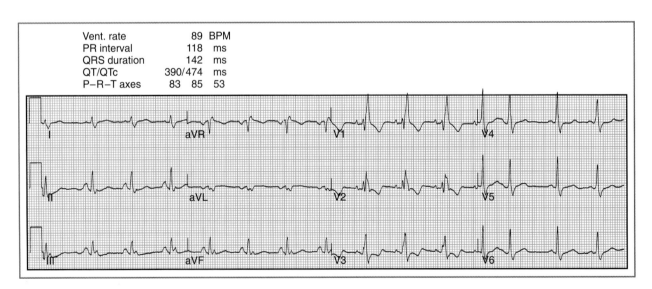

Vent. rate	89	BPM
PR interval	118	ms
QRS duration	142	ms
QT/QTc	390/474	ms
P–R–T axes	83	85	53

Figure 14–137.

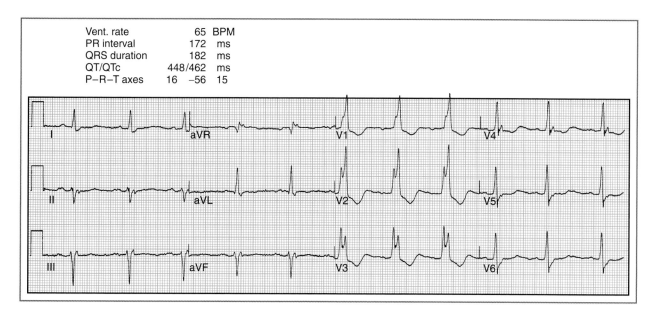

```
Vent. rate        65   BPM
PR interval      172   ms
QRS duration     182   ms
QT/QTc       448/462   ms
P–R–T axes    16  –56  15
```

Figure 14–138.

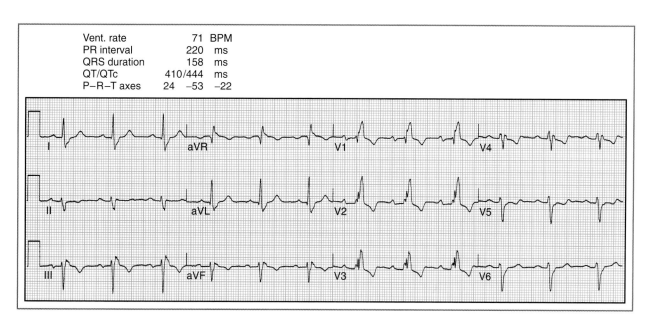

```
Vent. rate        71   BPM
PR interval      220   ms
QRS duration     158   ms
QT/QTc       410/444   ms
P–R–T axes    24  –53  –22
```

Figure 14–139.

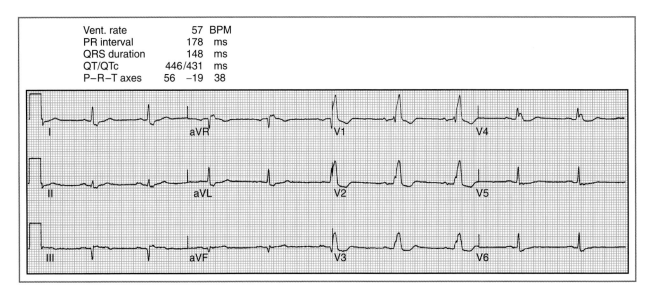

Vent. rate   57   BPM
PR interval   178 ms
QRS duration   148 ms
QT/QTc   446/431 ms
P–R–T axes   56 –19 38

Figure 14–140.

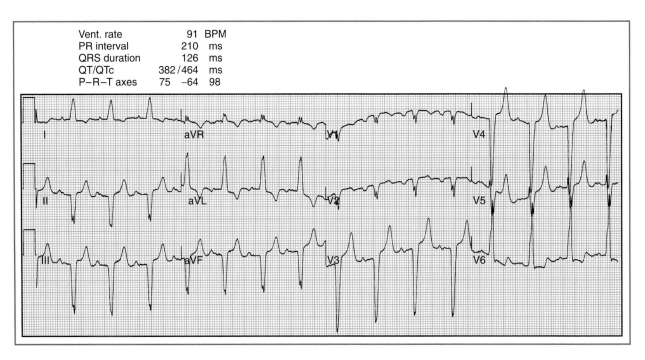

Vent. rate   91   BPM
PR interval   210 ms
QRS duration   126 ms
QT/QTc   382/464   ms
P–R–T axes   75 –64 98

Figure 14–141.

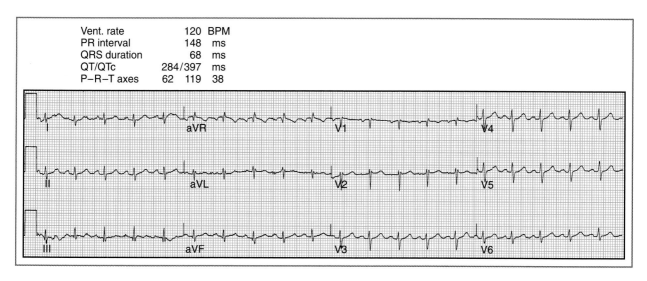

Vent. rate	120	BPM	
PR interval	148	ms	
QRS duration	68	ms	
QT/QTc	284/397	ms	
P–R–T axes	62 119 38		

Figure 14–142.

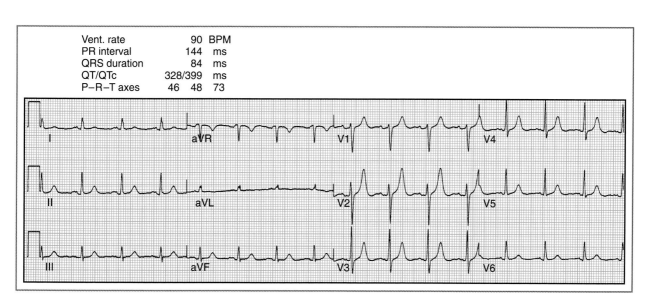

Vent. rate	90	BPM	
PR interval	144	ms	
QRS duration	84	ms	
QT/QTc	328/399	ms	
P–R–T axes	46 48 73		

Figure 14–143.

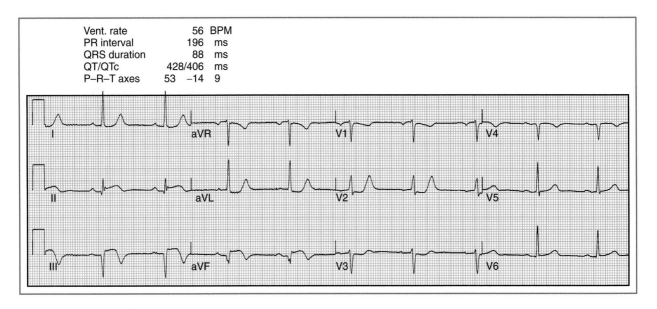

Vent. rate	56	BPM
PR interval	196	ms
QRS duration	88	ms
QT/QTc	428/406	ms
P–R–T axes	53 –14	9

Figure 14–144.

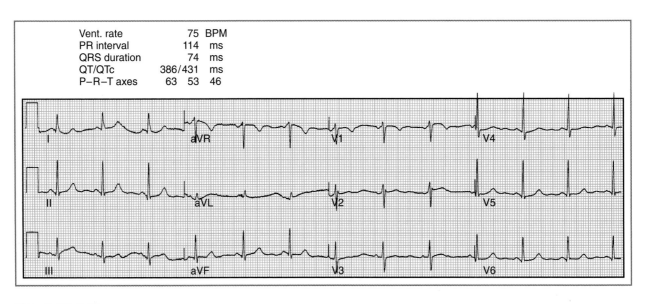

Vent. rate	75	BPM
PR interval	114	ms
QRS duration	74	ms
QT/QTc	386/431	ms
P–R–T axes	63 53	46

Figure 14–145.

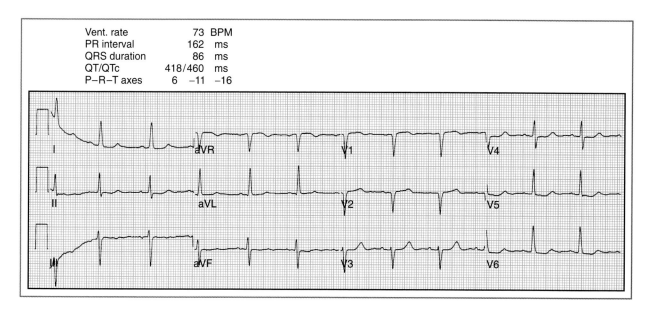

Vent. rate	73	BPM
PR interval	162	ms
QRS duration	86	ms
QT/QTc	418/460	ms
P–R–T axes	6	−11	−16

Figure 14–146.

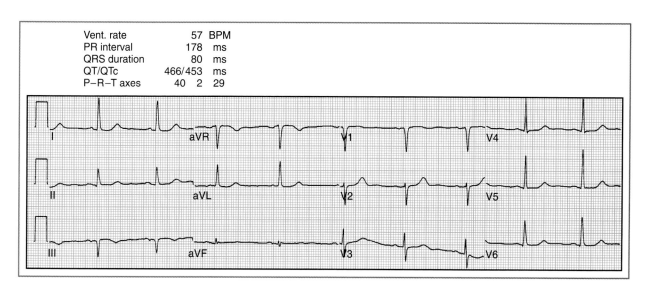

Vent. rate	57	BPM
PR interval	178	ms
QRS duration	80	ms
QT/QTc	466/453	ms
P–R–T axes	40	2	29

Figure 14–147.

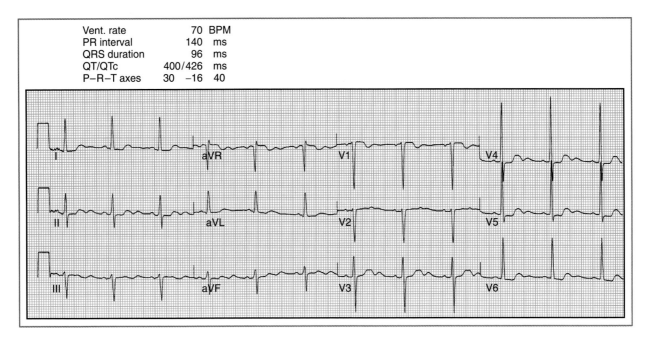

Vent. rate	70	BPM
PR interval	140	ms
QRS duration	96	ms
QT/QTc	400/426	ms
P–R–T axes	30 –16 40	

Figure 14–148.

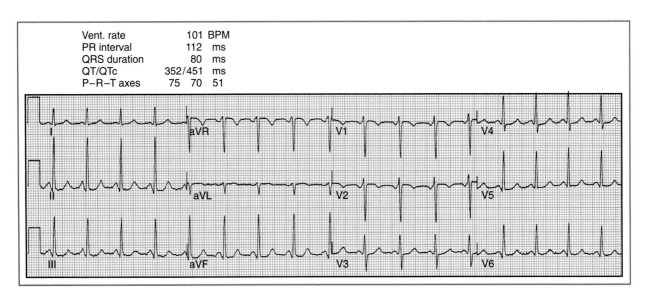

Vent. rate	101	BPM
PR interval	112	ms
QRS duration	80	ms
QT/QTc	352/451	ms
P–R–T axes	75 70 51	

Figure 14–149.

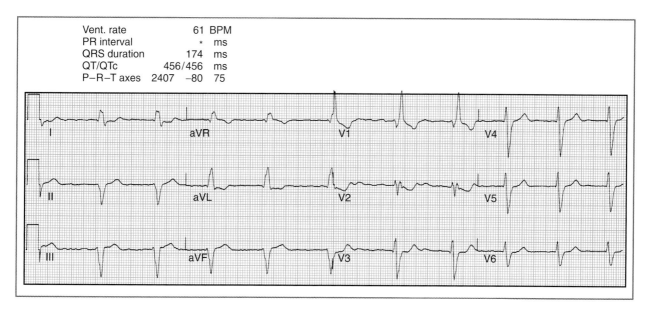

Vent. rate   61   BPM
PR interval   *   ms
QRS duration   174   ms
QT/QTc   456/456   ms
P–R–T axes   2407 –80 75

Figure 14–150.

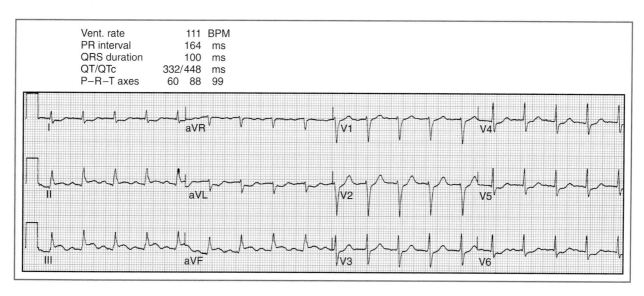

Vent. rate   111   BPM
PR interval   164   ms
QRS duration   100   ms
QT/QTc   332/448   ms
P–R–T axes   60 88 99

Figure 14–151.

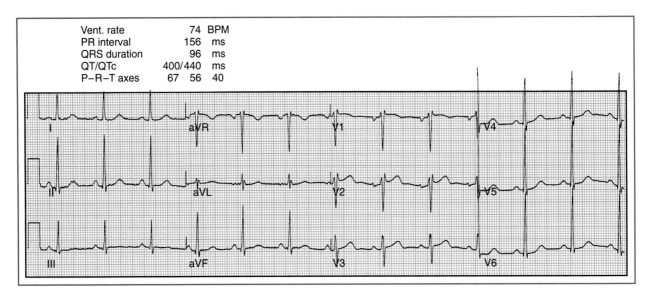

Vent. rate	74	BPM
PR interval	156	ms
QRS duration	96	ms
QT/QTc	400/440	ms
P–R–T axes	67 56 40	

Figure 14–152.

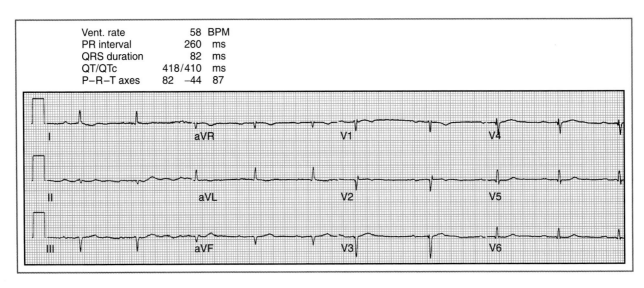

Vent. rate	58	BPM
PR interval	260	ms
QRS duration	82	ms
QT/QTc	418/410	ms
P–R–T axes	82 –44 87	

Figure 14–153.

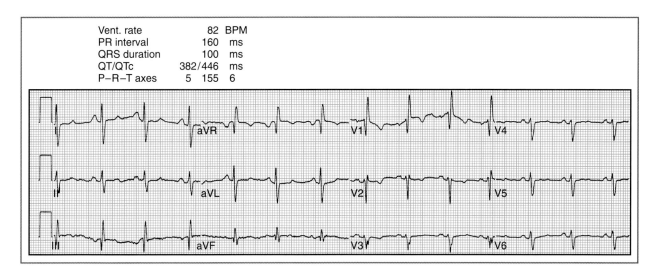

Vent. rate	82	BPM	
PR interval	160	ms	
QRS duration	100	ms	
QT/QTc	382/446	ms	
P–R–T axes	5 155 6		

Figure 14–154.

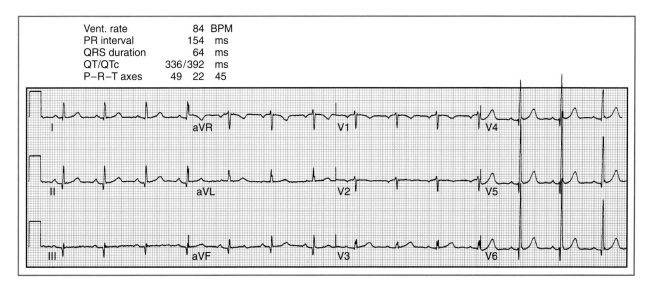

Vent. rate	84	BPM	
PR interval	154	ms	
QRS duration	64	ms	
QT/QTc	336/392	ms	
P–R–T axes	49 22 45		

Figure 14–155.

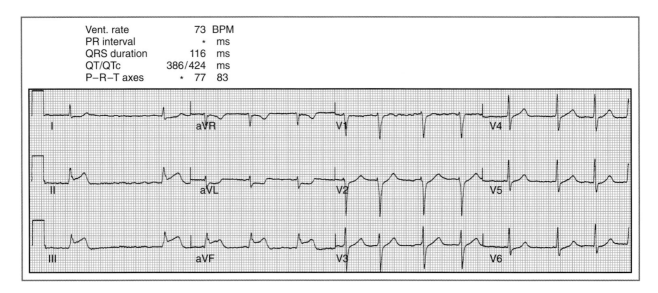

Vent. rate	73	BPM
PR interval	*	ms
QRS duration	116	ms
QT/QTc	386/424	ms
P–R–T axes	* 77	83

Figure 14–156.

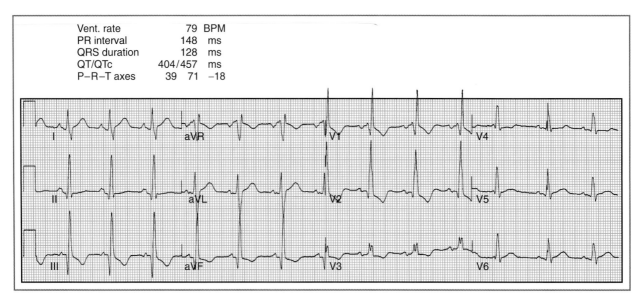

Vent. rate	79	BPM
PR interval	148	ms
QRS duration	128	ms
QT/QTc	404/457	ms
P–R–T axes	39 71	–18

Figure 14–157.

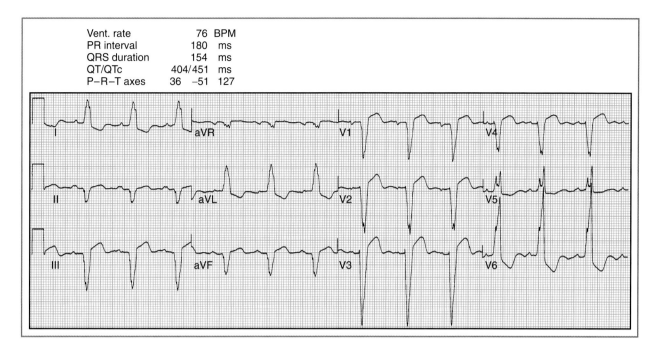

Vent. rate   76 BPM
PR interval   180 ms
QRS duration   154 ms
QT/QTc   404/451 ms
P–R–T axes   36   –51   127

Figure 14–158.

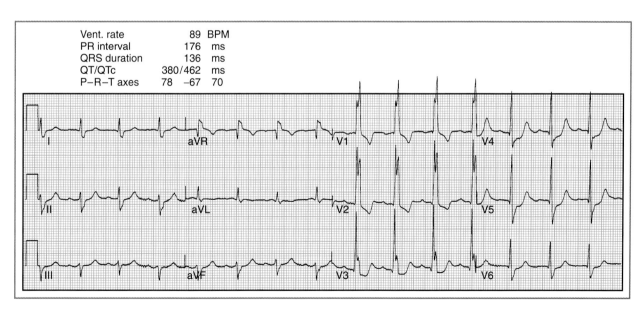

Vent. rate   89 BPM
PR interval   176 ms
QRS duration   136 ms
QT/QTc   380/462 ms
P–R–T axes   78   –67   70

Figure 14–159.

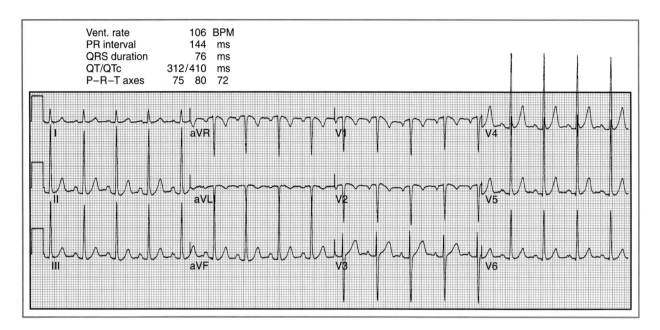

Vent. rate	106	BPM
PR interval	144	ms
QRS duration	76	ms
QT/QTc	312/410	ms
P–R–T axes	75 80 72	

Figure 14–160.

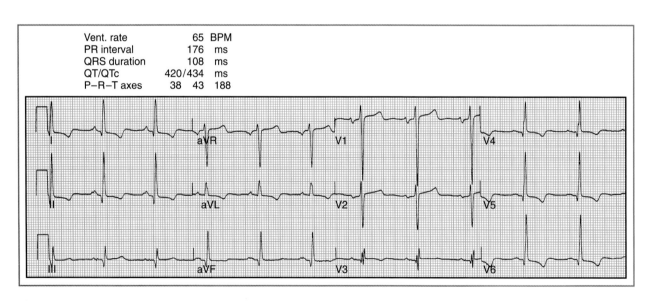

Vent. rate	65	BPM
PR interval	176	ms
QRS duration	108	ms
QT/QTc	420/434	ms
P–R–T axes	38 43 188	

Figure 14–161.

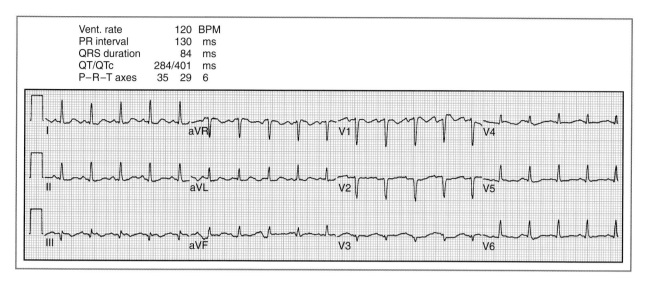

Vent. rate	120	BPM
PR interval	130	ms
QRS duration	84	ms
QT/QTc	284/401	ms
P–R–T axes	35	29 6

Figure 14–162.

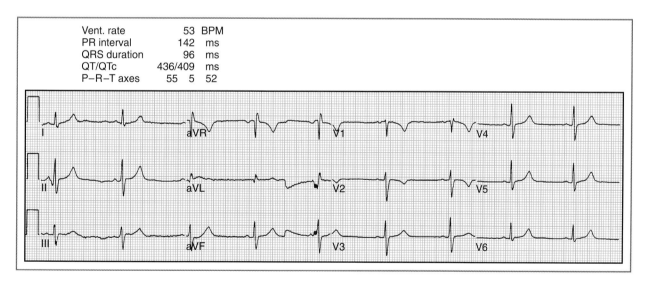

Vent. rate	53	BPM
PR interval	142	ms
QRS duration	96	ms
QT/QTc	436/409	ms
P–R–T axes	55	5 52

Figure 14–163.

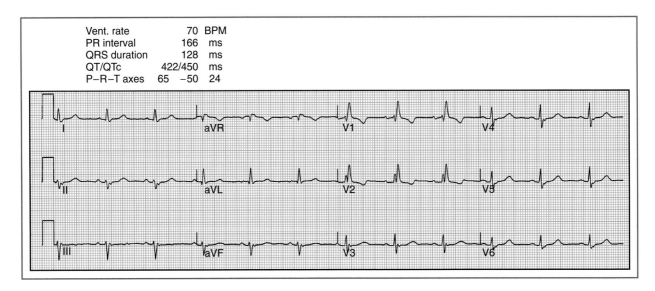

Vent. rate	70	BPM
PR interval	166	ms
QRS duration	128	ms
QT/QTc	422/450	ms
P–R–T axes	65 –50 24	

Figure 14–164.

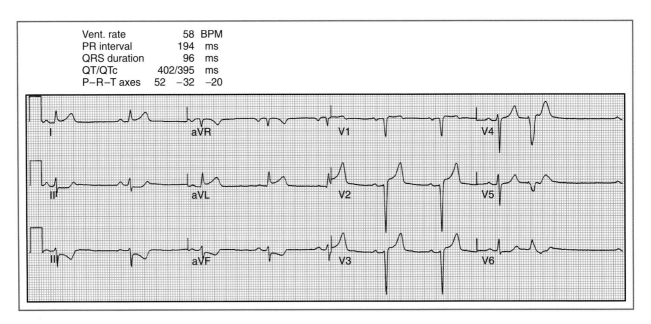

Vent. rate	58	BPM
PR interval	194	ms
QRS duration	96	ms
QT/QTc	402/395	ms
P–R–T axes	52 –32 –20	

Figure 14–165.

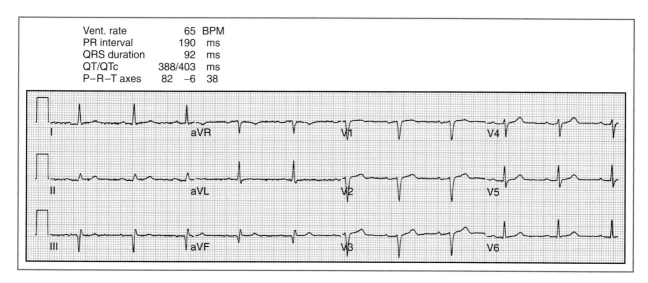

Vent. rate	65	BPM
PR interval	190	ms
QRS duration	92	ms
QT/QTc	388/403	ms
P–R–T axes	82 –6	38

Figure 14–166.

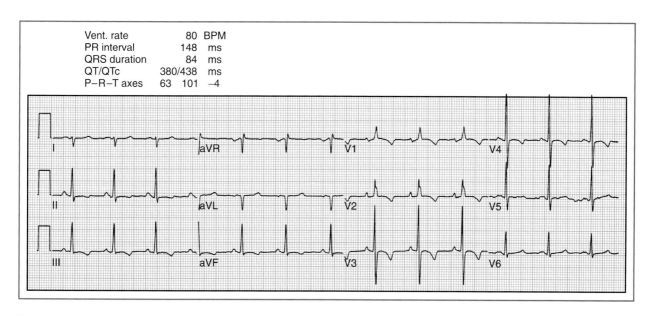

Vent. rate	80	BPM
PR interval	148	ms
QRS duration	84	ms
QT/QTc	380/438	ms
P–R–T axes	63 101	–4

Figure 14–167.

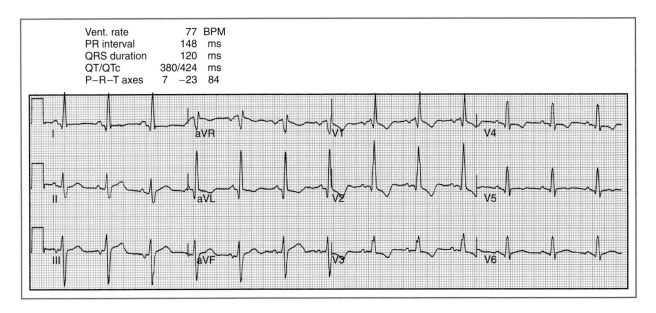

Vent. rate	77	BPM
PR interval	148	ms
QRS duration	120	ms
QT/QTc	380/424	ms
P–R–T axes	7 –23	84

Figure 14–168.

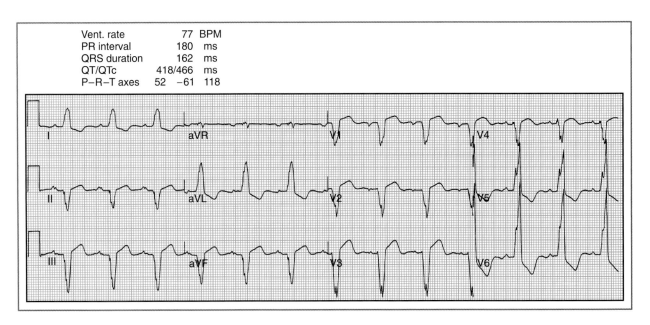

Vent. rate	77	BPM
PR interval	180	ms
QRS duration	162	ms
QT/QTc	418/466	ms
P–R–T axes	52 –61	118

Figure 14–169.

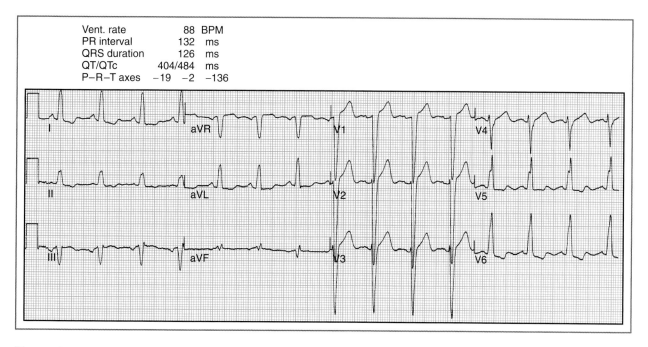

Vent. rate	88	BPM	
PR interval	132	ms	
QRS duration	126	ms	
QT/QTc	404/484	ms	
P–R–T axes	−19 −2 −136		

Figure 14–170.

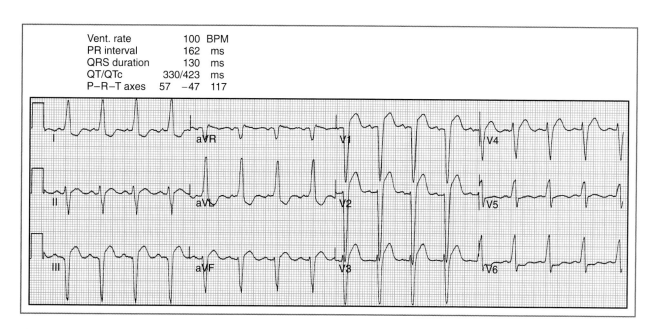

Vent. rate	100	BPM	
PR interval	162	ms	
QRS duration	130	ms	
QT/QTc	330/423	ms	
P–R–T axes	57 −47 117		

Figure 14–171.

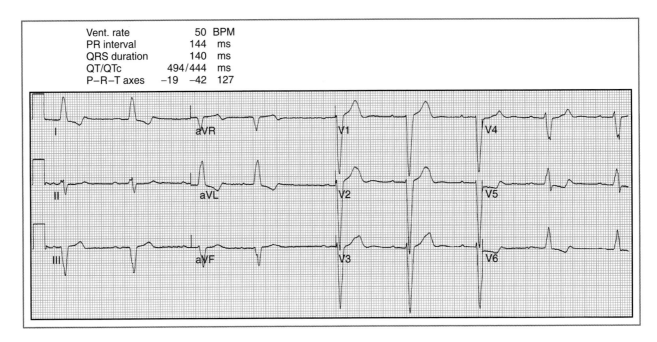

Vent. rate	50	BPM
PR interval	144	ms
QRS duration	140	ms
QT/QTc	494/444	ms
P–R–T axes	−19 −42	127

Figure 14–172.

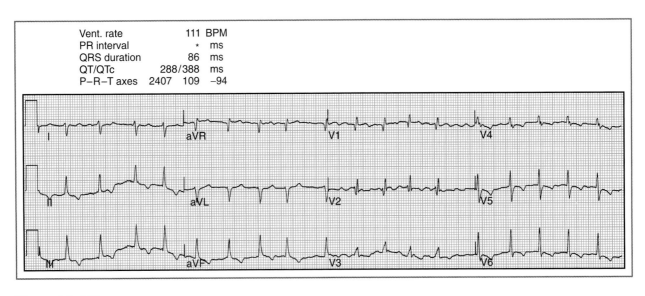

Vent. rate	111	BPM
PR interval	*	ms
QRS duration	86	ms
QT/QTc	288/388	ms
P–R–T axes	2407 109	−94

Figure 14–173.

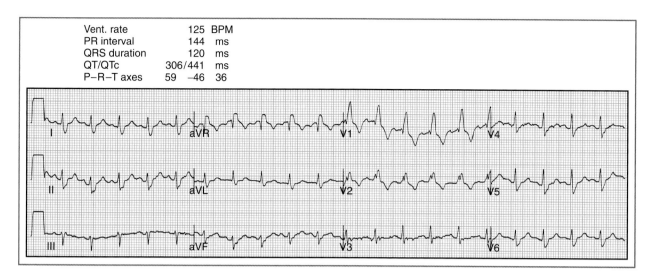

Vent. rate	125	BPM
PR interval	144	ms
QRS duration	120	ms
QT/QTc	306/441	ms
P–R–T axes	59 –46	36

Figure 14–174.

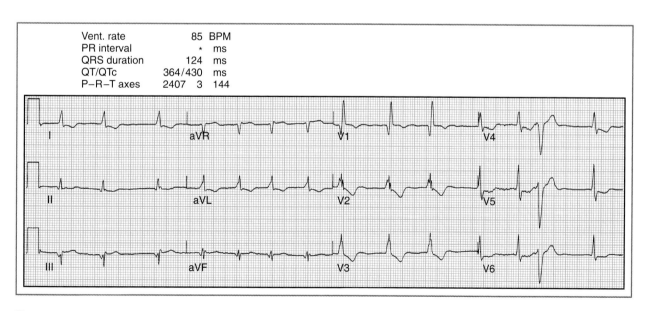

Vent. rate	85	BPM
PR interval	*	ms
QRS duration	124	ms
QT/QTc	364/430	ms
P–R–T axes	2407 3	144

Figure 14–175.

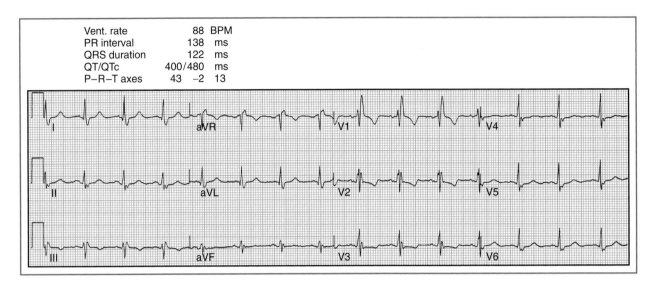

Vent. rate	88	BPM
PR interval	138	ms
QRS duration	122	ms
QT/QTc	400/480	ms
P–R–T axes	43 –2 13	

Figure 14–176.

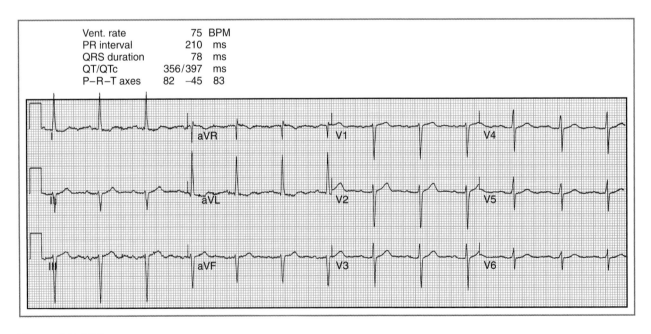

Vent. rate	75	BPM
PR interval	210	ms
QRS duration	78	ms
QT/QTc	356/397	ms
P–R–T axes	82 –45 83	

Figure 14–177.

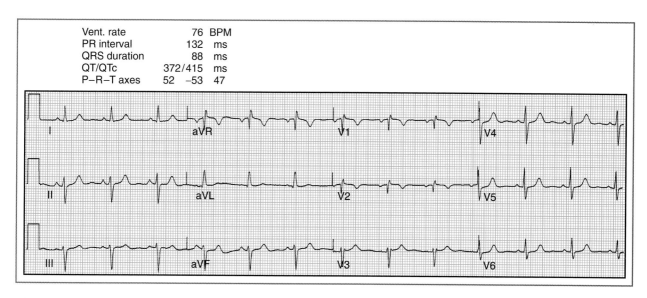

Vent. rate   76   BPM
PR interval   132 ms
QRS duration   88   ms
QT/QTc   372/415   ms
P–R–T axes   52   –53   47

Figure 14–178.

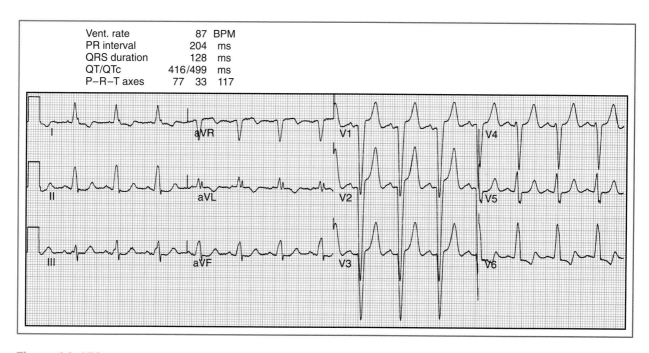

Vent. rate   87   BPM
PR interval   204 ms
QRS duration   128 ms
QT/QTc   416/499   ms
P–R–T axes   77   33   117

Figure 14–179.

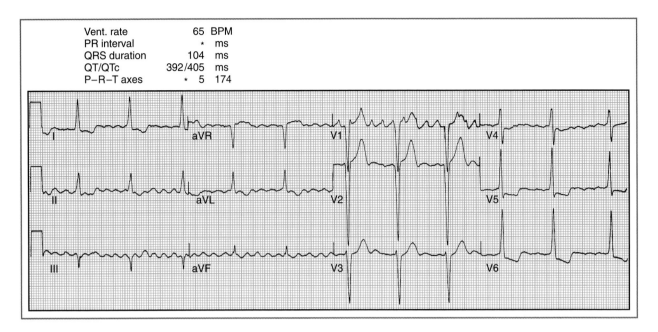

Vent. rate	65	BPM
PR interval	*	ms
QRS duration	104	ms
QT/QTc	392/405	ms
P–R–T axes	* 5	174

Figure 14–180.

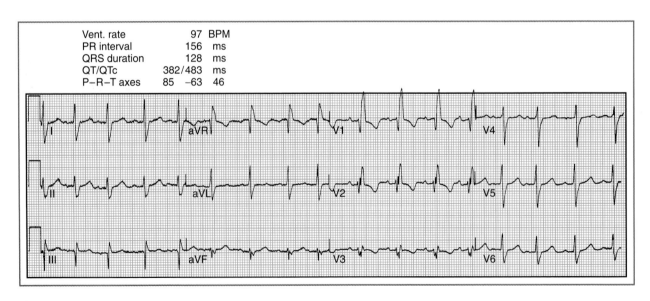

Vent. rate	97	BPM
PR interval	156	ms
QRS duration	128	ms
QT/QTc	382/483	ms
P–R–T axes	85 –63	46

Figure 14–181.

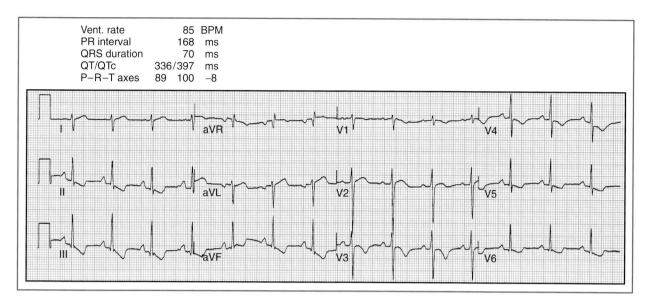

```
Vent. rate          85  BPM
PR interval        168  ms
QRS duration        70  ms
QT/QTc         336/397  ms
P–R–T axes     89  100  –8
```

Figure 14–182.

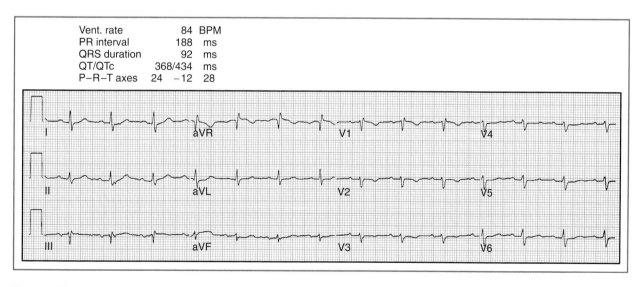

```
Vent. rate          84  BPM
PR interval        188  ms
QRS duration        92  ms
QT/QTc         368/434  ms
P–R–T axes     24  –12  28
```

Figure 14–183.

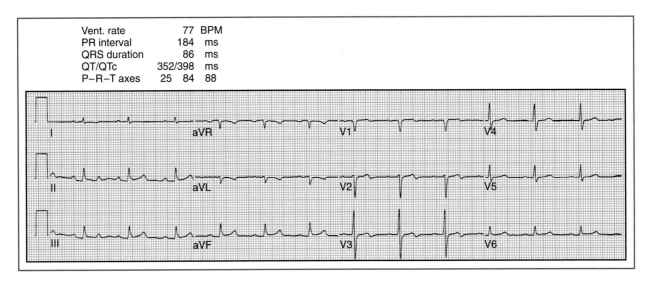

Vent. rate	77	BPM
PR interval	184	ms
QRS duration	86	ms
QT/QTc	352/398	ms
P–R–T axes	25 84	88

Figure 14–184.

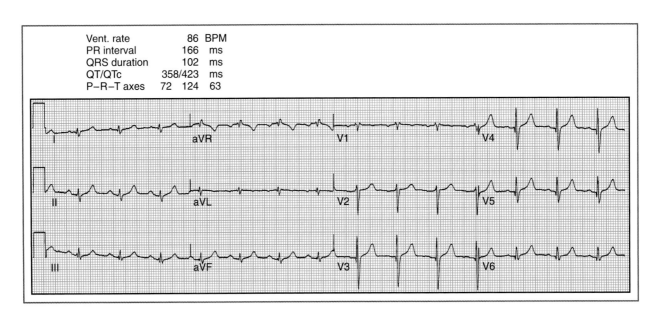

Vent. rate	86	BPM
PR interval	166	ms
QRS duration	102	ms
QT/QTc	358/423	ms
P–R–T axes	72 124	63

Figure 14–185.

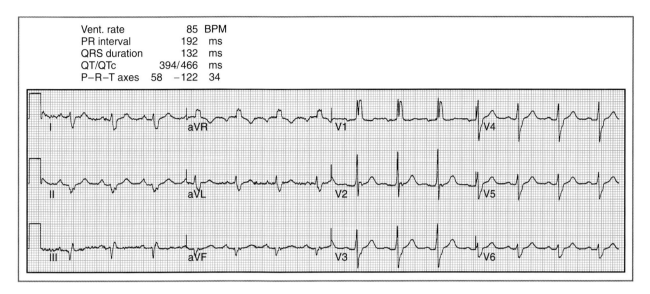

Vent. rate	85	BPM
PR interval	192	ms
QRS duration	132	ms
QT/QTc	394/466	ms
P–R–T axes	58 –122	34

Figure 14–186.

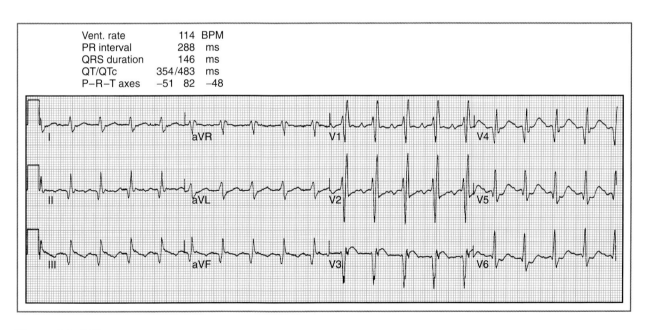

Vent. rate	114	BPM
PR interval	288	ms
QRS duration	146	ms
QT/QTc	354/483	ms
P–R–T axes	–51 82	–48

Figure 14–187.

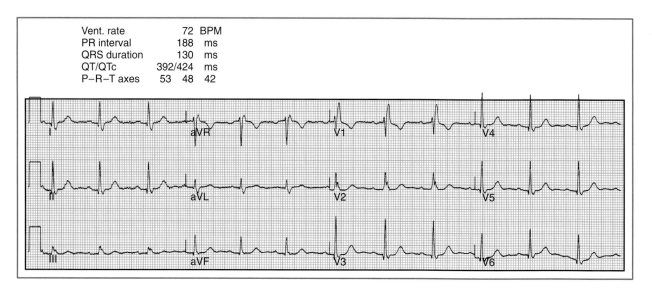

Vent. rate	72	BPM
PR interval	188	ms
QRS duration	130	ms
QT/QTc	392/424	ms
P–R–T axes	53 48 42	

Figure 14–188.

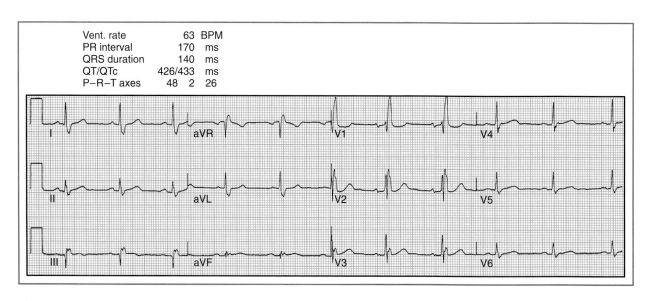

Vent. rate	63	BPM
PR interval	170	ms
QRS duration	140	ms
QT/QTc	426/433	ms
P–R–T axes	48 2 26	

Figure 14–189.

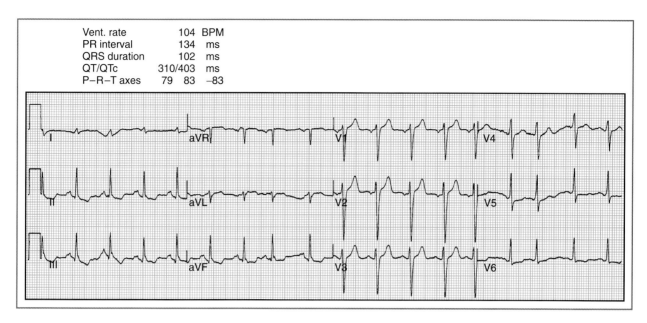

Vent. rate	104	BPM
PR interval	134	ms
QRS duration	102	ms
QT/QTc	310/403	ms
P–R–T axes	79 83	–83

Figure 14–190.

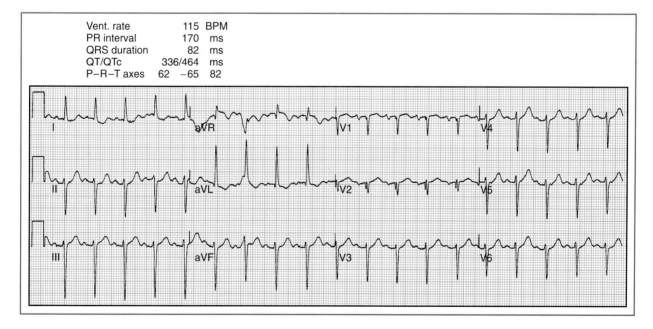

Vent. rate	115	BPM
PR interval	170	ms
QRS duration	82	ms
QT/QTc	336/464	ms
P–R–T axes	62 –65	82

Figure 14–191.

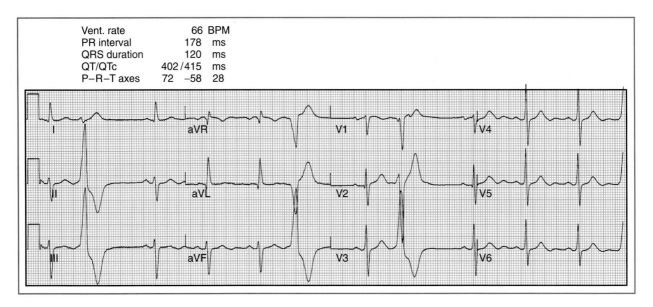

Vent. rate	66	BPM
PR interval	178	ms
QRS duration	120	ms
QT/QTc	402/415	ms
P–R–T axes	72 –58	28

Figure 14–192.

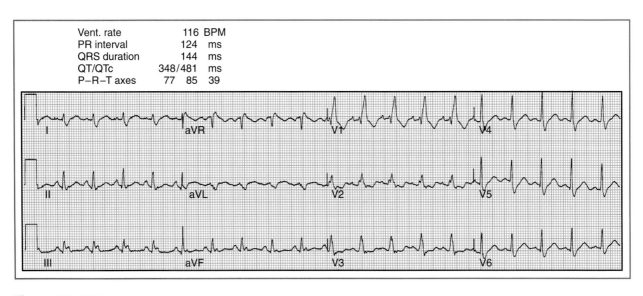

Vent. rate	116	BPM
PR interval	124	ms
QRS duration	144	ms
QT/QTc	348/481	ms
P–R–T axes	77 85	39

Figure 14–193.

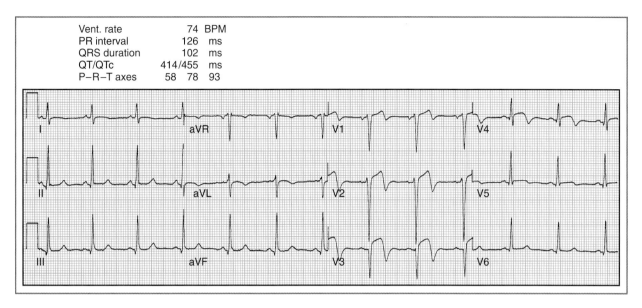

Vent. rate	74	BPM
PR interval	126	ms
QRS duration	102	ms
QT/QTc	414/455	ms
P–R–T axes	58 78 93	

Figure 14–194.

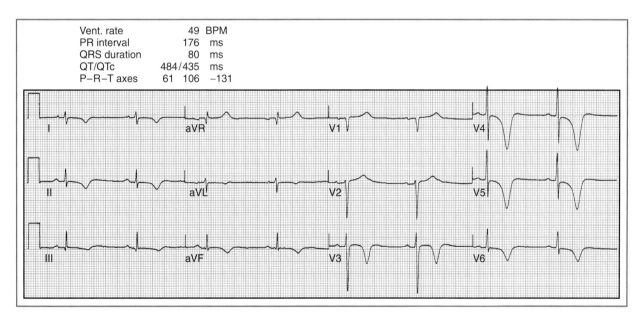

Vent. rate	49	BPM
PR interval	176	ms
QRS duration	80	ms
QT/QTc	484/435	ms
P–R–T axes	61 106 −131	

Figure 14–195.

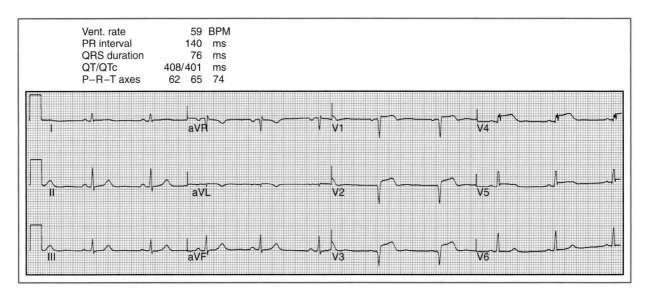

Vent. rate	59 BPM
PR interval	140 ms
QRS duration	76 ms
QT/QTc	408/401 ms
P–R–T axes	62 65 74

Figure 14–196.

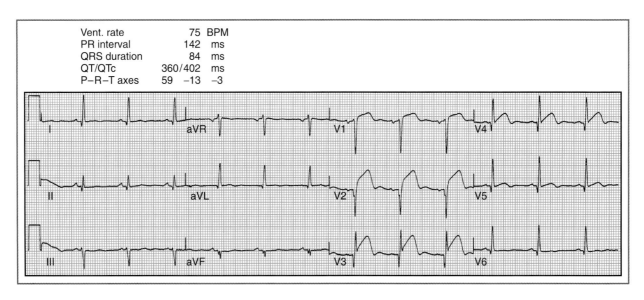

Vent. rate	75 BPM
PR interval	142 ms
QRS duration	84 ms
QT/QTc	360/402 ms
P–R–T axes	59 −13 −3

Figure 14–197.

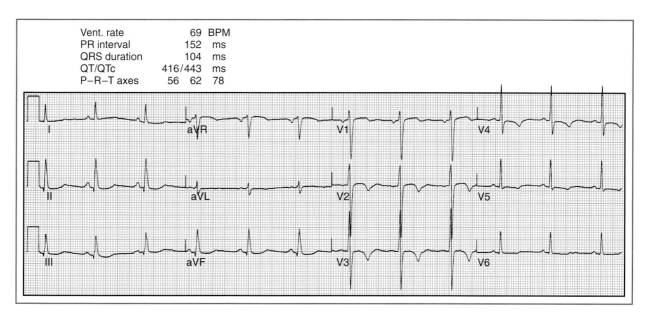

Vent. rate   69 BPM
PR interval   152 ms
QRS duration   104 ms
QT/QTc   416/443 ms
P–R–T axes   56 62 78

Figure 14–198.

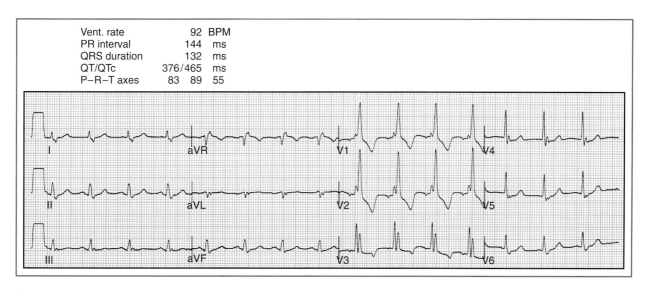

Vent. rate   92 BPM
PR interval   144 ms
QRS duration   132 ms
QT/QTc   376/465 ms
P–R–T axes   83 89 55

Figure 14–199.

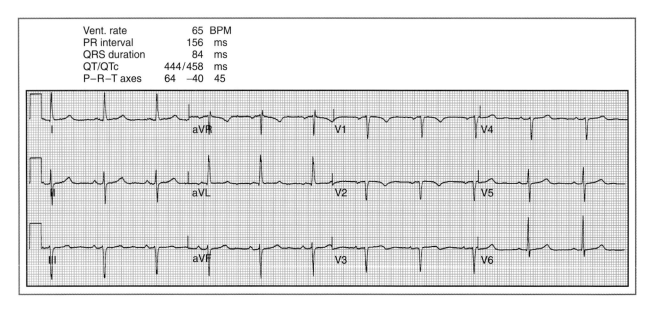

Vent. rate	65	BPM
PR interval	156	ms
QRS duration	84	ms
QT/QTc	444/458	ms
P–R–T axes	64 –40 45	

Figure 14–200.

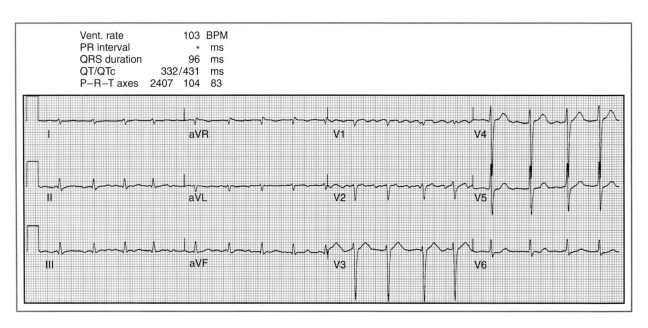

Vent. rate	103	BPM
PR interval	*	ms
QRS duration	96	ms
QT/QTc	332/431	ms
P–R–T axes	2407 104 83	

Figure 14–201.

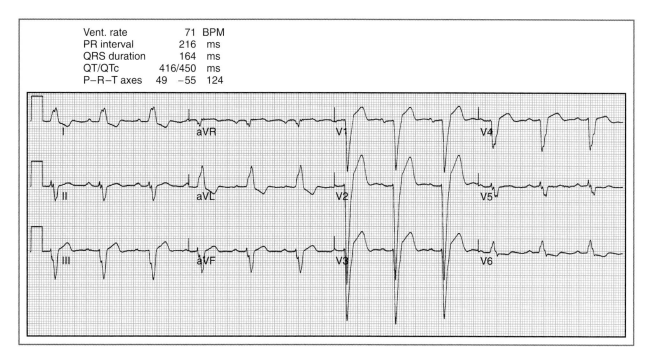

Vent. rate	71	BPM
PR interval	216	ms
QRS duration	164	ms
QT/QTc	416/450	ms
P–R–T axes	49	–55	124

Figure 14–202.

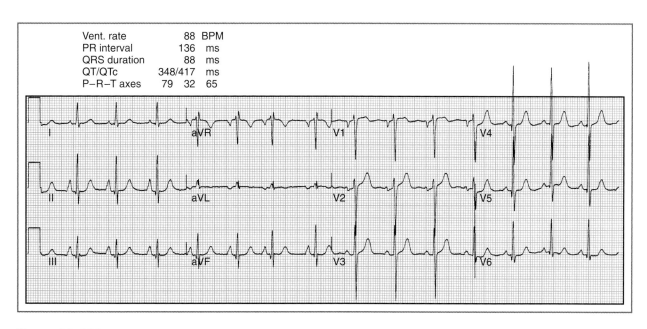

Vent. rate	88	BPM
PR interval	136	ms
QRS duration	88	ms
QT/QTc	348/417	ms
P–R–T axes	79	32	65

Figure 14–203.

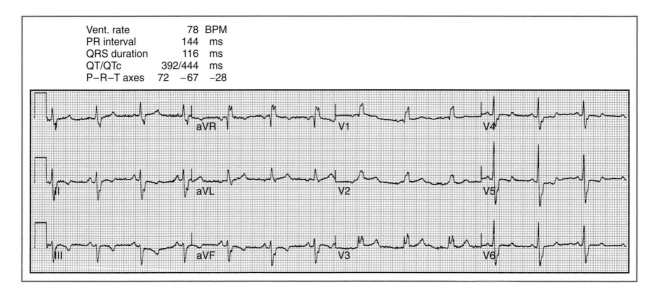

Vent. rate	78	BPM
PR interval	144	ms
QRS duration	116	ms
QT/QTc	392/444	ms
P–R–T axes	72 –67 –28	

Figure 14–204.

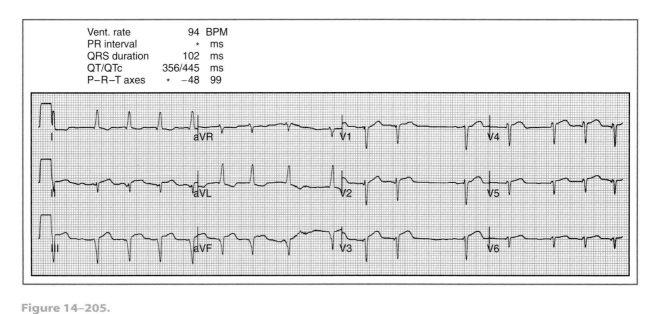

Vent. rate	94	BPM
PR interval	*	ms
QRS duration	102	ms
QT/QTc	356/445	ms
P–R–T axes	* –48 99	

Figure 14–205.

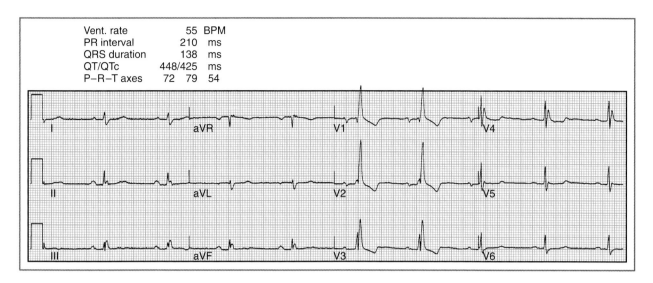

Vent. rate 55 BPM
PR interval 210 ms
QRS duration 138 ms
QT/QTc 448/425 ms
P–R–T axes 72 79 54

Figure 14–206.

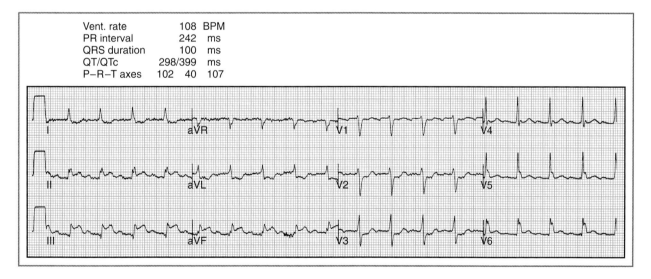

Vent. rate 108 BPM
PR interval 242 ms
QRS duration 100 ms
QT/QTc 298/399 ms
P–R–T axes 102 40 107

Figure 14–207.

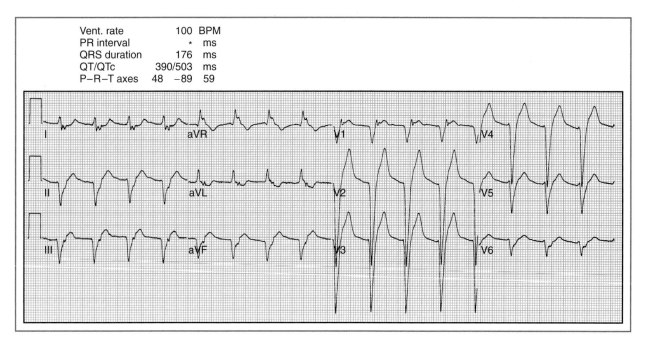

Vent. rate	100	BPM
PR interval	*	ms
QRS duration	176	ms
QT/QTc	390/503	ms
P–R–T axes	48	–89	59

Figure 14–208.

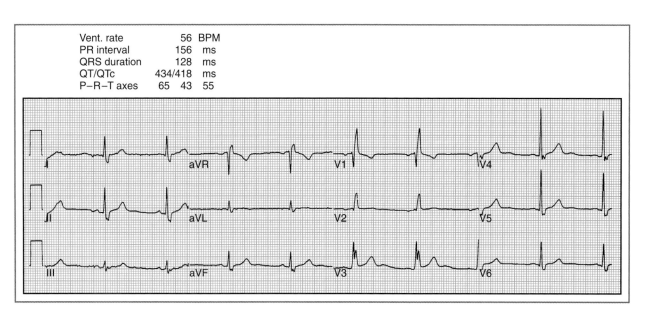

Vent. rate	56	BPM
PR interval	156	ms
QRS duration	128	ms
QT/QTc	434/418	ms
P–R–T axes	65	43	55

Figure 14–209.

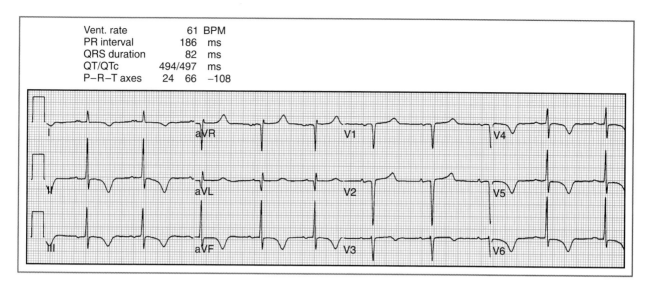

Figure 14–210.

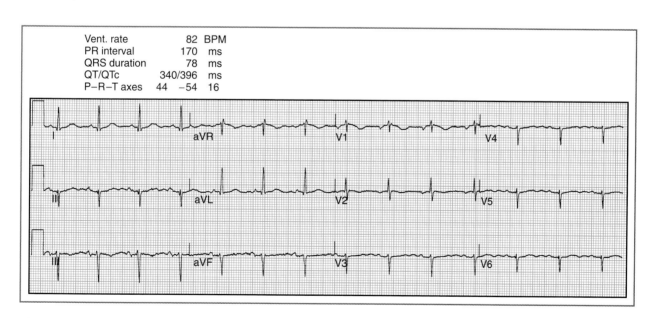

Figure 14–211.

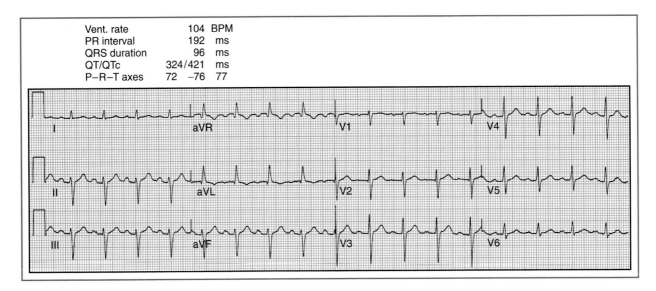

Vent. rate	104	BPM
PR interval	192	ms
QRS duration	96	ms
QT/QTc	324/421	ms
P–R–T axes	72 –76	77

Figure 14–212.

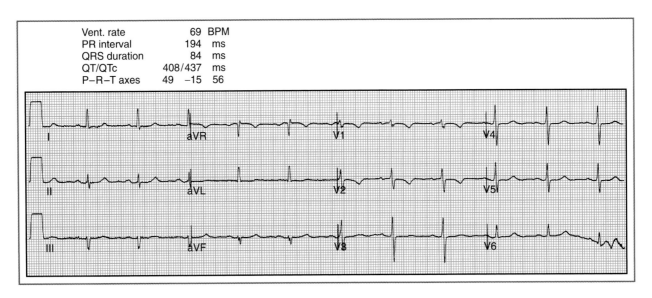

Vent. rate	69	BPM
PR interval	194	ms
QRS duration	84	ms
QT/QTc	408/437	ms
P–R–T axes	49 –15	56

Figure 14–213.

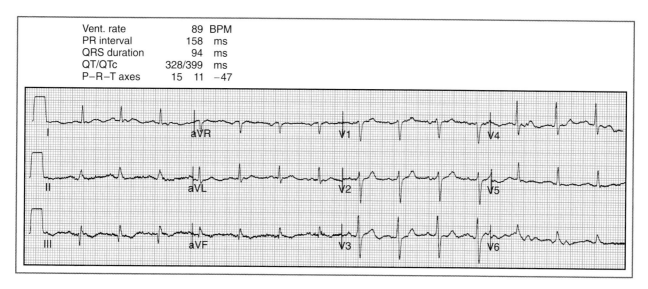

Figure 14–214.

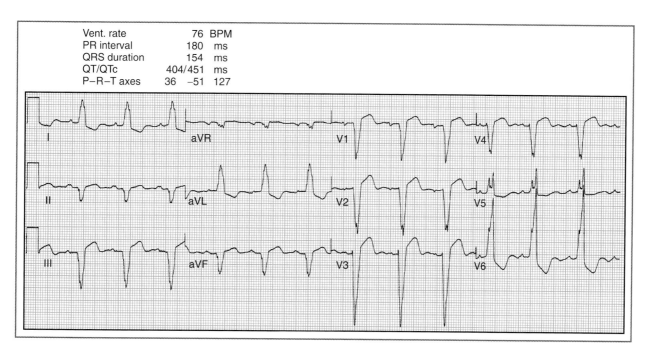

Figure 14–215.

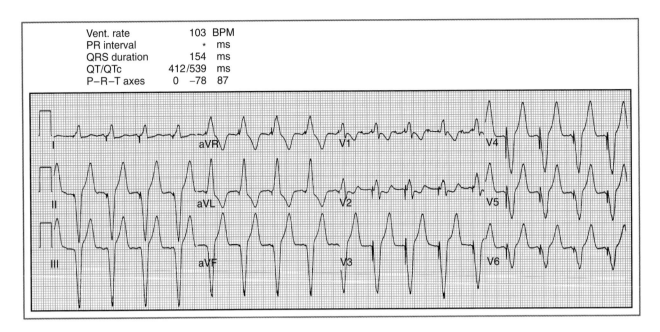

Vent. rate	103	BPM
PR interval	*	ms
QRS duration	154	ms
QT/QTc	412/539	ms
P–R–T axes	0 –78 87	

Figure 14–216.

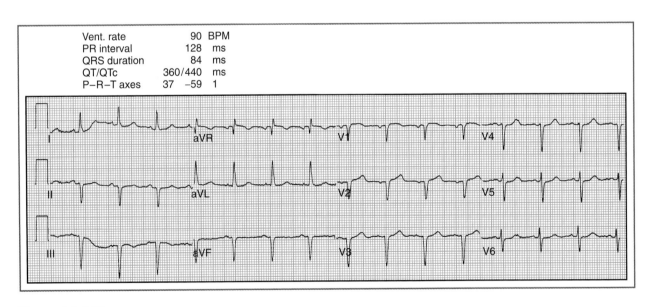

Vent. rate	90	BPM
PR interval	128	ms
QRS duration	84	ms
QT/QTc	360/440	ms
P–R–T axes	37 –59 1	

Figure 14–217.

Vent. rate	77	BPM
PR interval	168	ms
QRS duration	146	ms
QT/QTc	408/461	ms
P–R–T axes	34 0 41	

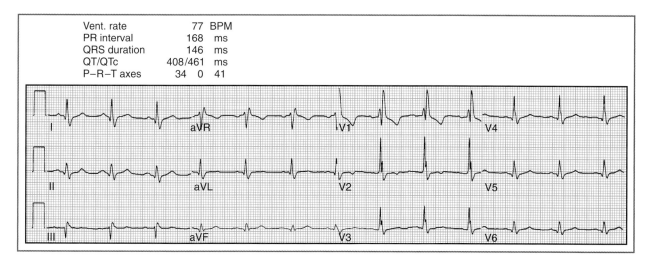

Figure 14–218.

Vent. rate	68	BPM
PR interval	172	ms
QRS duration	94	ms
QT/QTc	418/444	ms
P–R–T axes	71 –65 79	

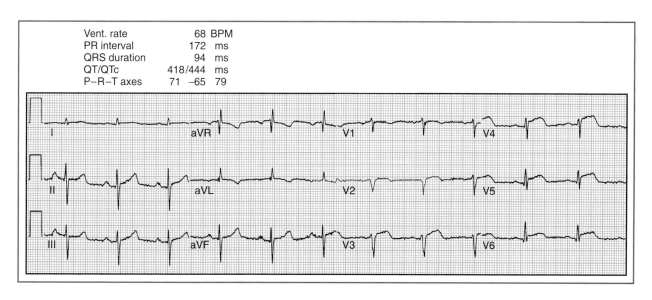

Figure 14–219.

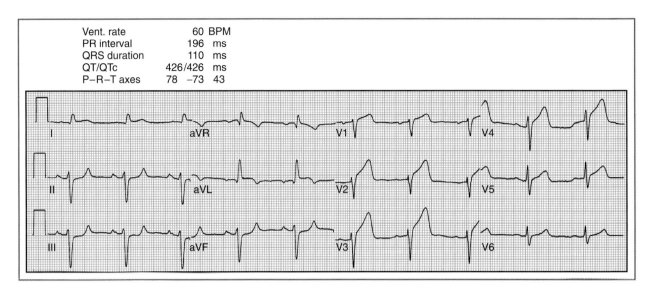

```
Vent. rate          60 BPM
PR interval        196 ms
QRS duration       110 ms
QT/QTc         426/426 ms
P–R–T axes      78  –73  43
```

Figure 14–220.

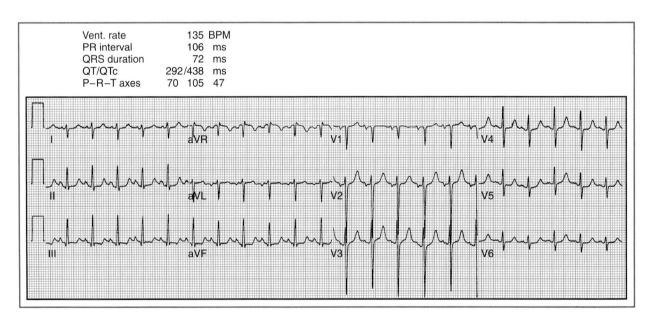

```
Vent. rate         135 BPM
PR interval        106 ms
QRS duration        72 ms
QT/QTc         292/438 ms
P–R–T axes      70  105  47
```

Figure 14–221.

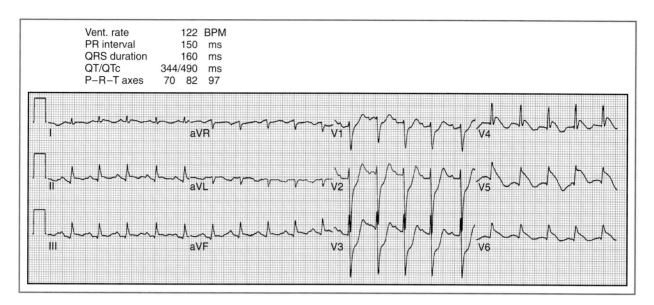

Vent. rate	122	BPM
PR interval	150	ms
QRS duration	160	ms
QT/QTc	344/490	ms
P–R–T axes	70 82 97	

Figure 14–222.

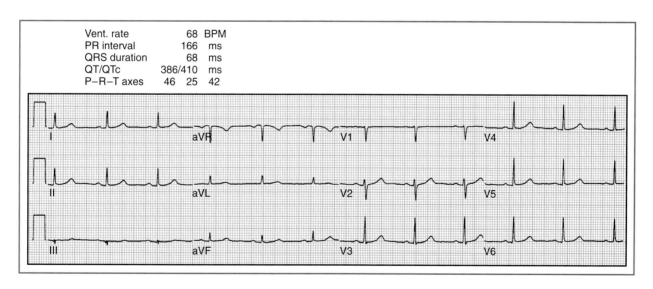

Vent. rate	68	BPM
PR interval	166	ms
QRS duration	68	ms
QT/QTc	386/410	ms
P–R–T axes	46 25 42	

Figure 14–223.

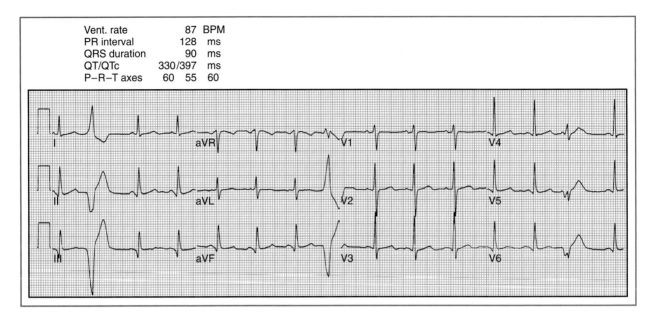

Vent. rate   87   BPM
PR interval   128   ms
QRS duration   90   ms
QT/QTc   330/397   ms
P–R–T axes   60 55 60

Figure 14–224.

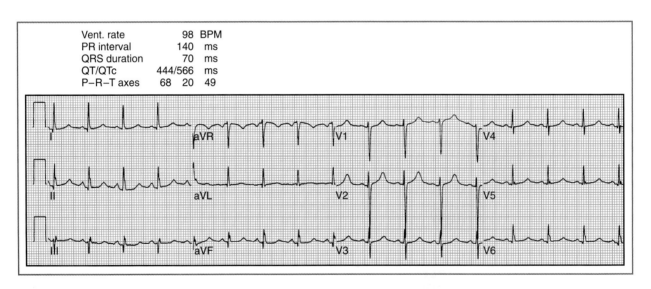

Vent. rate   98   BPM
PR interval   140   ms
QRS duration   70   ms
QT/QTc   444/566   ms
P–R–T axes   68 20 49

Figure 14–225.

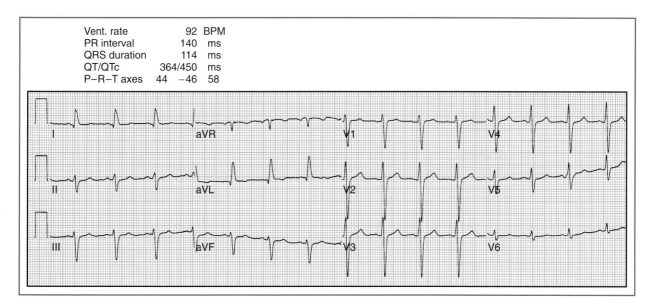

Vent. rate	92	BPM
PR interval	140	ms
QRS duration	114	ms
QT/QTc	364/450	ms
P–R–T axes	44 –46	58

Figure 14–226.

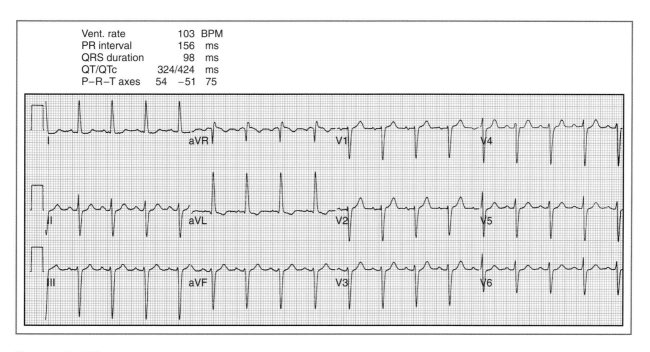

Vent. rate	103	BPM
PR interval	156	ms
QRS duration	98	ms
QT/QTc	324/424	ms
P–R–T axes	54 –51	75

Figure 14–227.

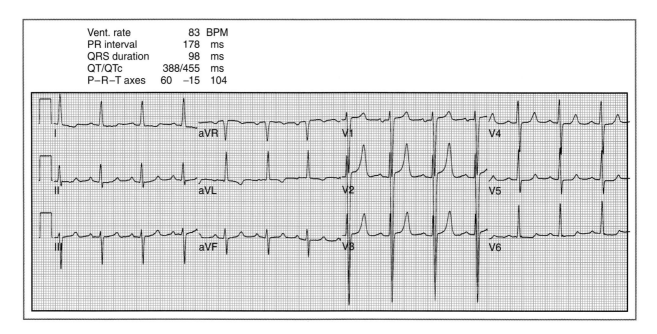

Vent. rate	83	BPM
PR interval	178	ms
QRS duration	98	ms
QT/QTc	388/455	ms
P–R–T axes	60 –15	104

Figure 14–228.

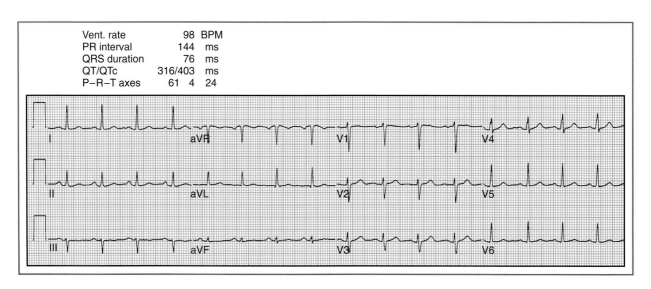

Vent. rate	98	BPM
PR interval	144	ms
QRS duration	76	ms
QT/QTc	316/403	ms
P–R–T axes	61 4	24

Figure 14–229.

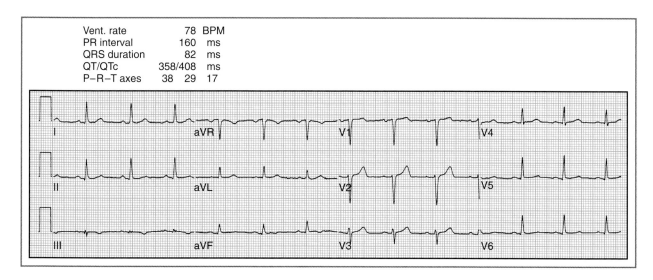

Figure 14–230.

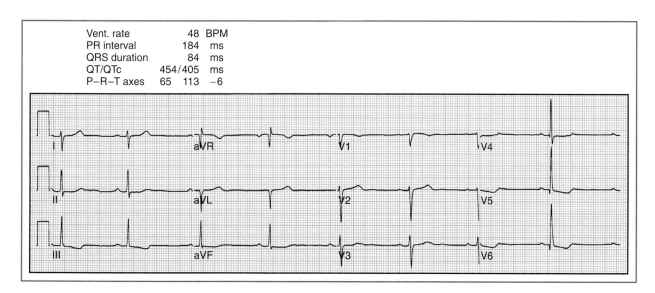

Figure 14–231.

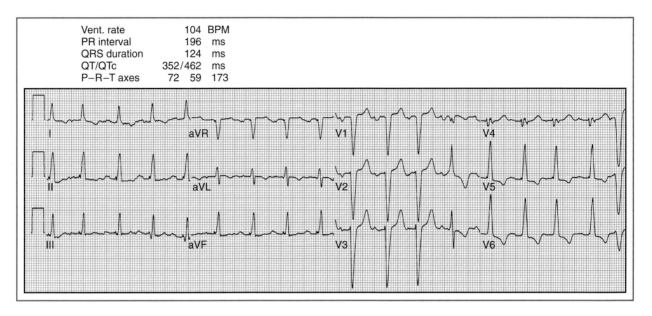

Vent. rate	104	BPM
PR interval	196	ms
QRS duration	124	ms
QT/QTc	352/462	ms
P–R–T axes	72	59 173

Figure 14–232.

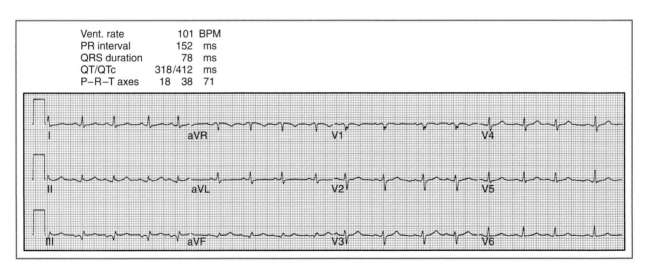

Vent. rate	101	BPM
PR interval	152	ms
QRS duration	78	ms
QT/QTc	318/412	ms
P–R–T axes	18	38 71

Figure 14–233.

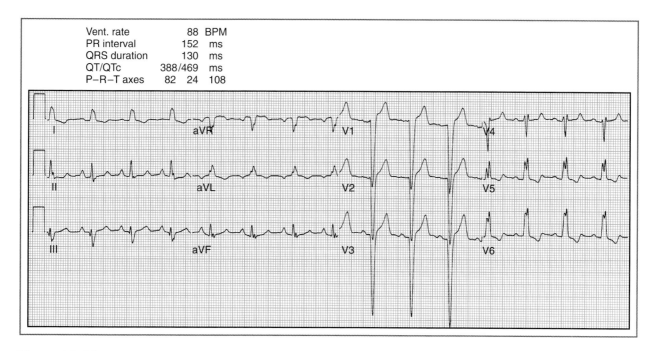

Vent. rate	88	BPM
PR interval	152	ms
QRS duration	130	ms
QT/QTc	388/469	ms
P–R–T axes	82 24	108

Figure 14–234.

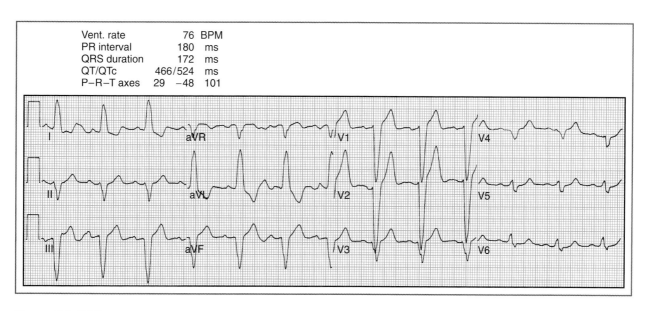

Vent. rate	76	BPM
PR interval	180	ms
QRS duration	172	ms
QT/QTc	466/524	ms
P–R–T axes	29 –48	101

Figure 14–235.

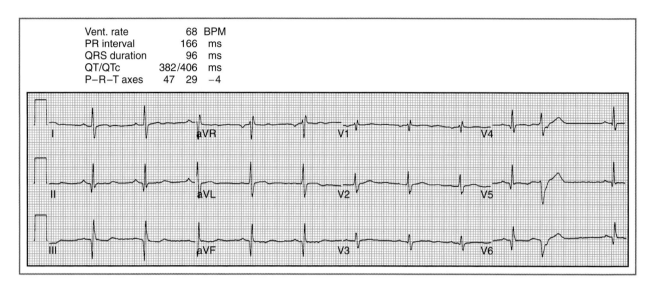

Vent. rate	68 BPM
PR interval	166 ms
QRS duration	96 ms
QT/QTc	382/406 ms
P–R–T axes	47 29 −4

Figure 14–236.

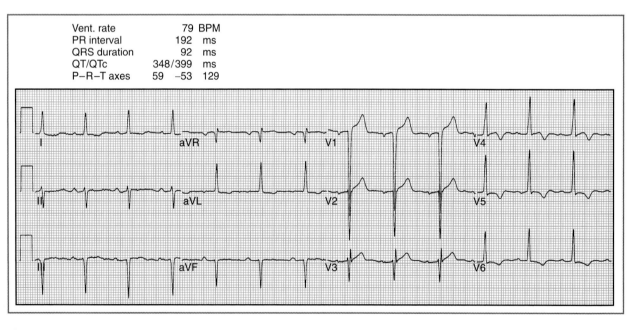

Vent. rate	79 BPM
PR interval	192 ms
QRS duration	92 ms
QT/QTc	348/399 ms
P–R–T axes	59 −53 129

Figure 14–237.

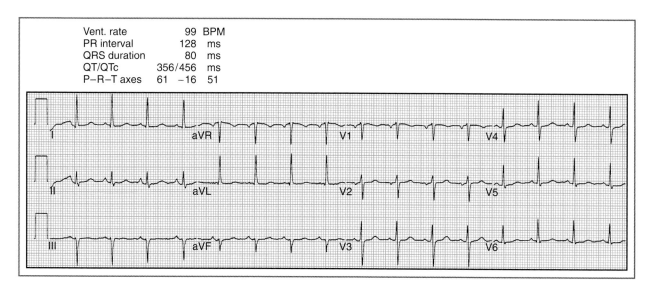

Vent. rate   99   BPM
PR interval   128   ms
QRS duration   80   ms
QT/QTc   356/456 ms
P–R–T axes   61   –16   51

Figure 14–238.

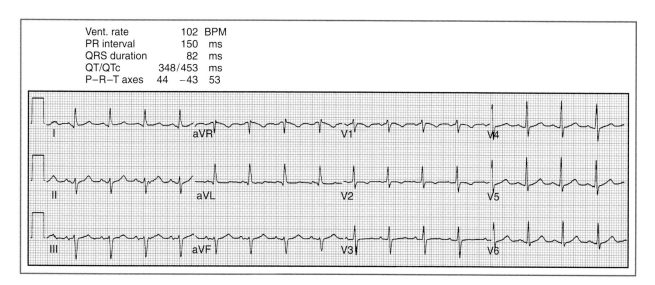

Vent. rate   102   BPM
PR interval   150   ms
QRS duration   82   ms
QT/QTc   348/453 ms
P–R–T axes   44   –43   53

Figure 14–239.

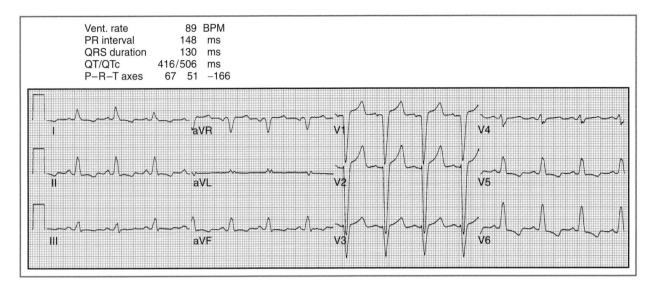

Vent. rate	89	BPM
PR interval	148	ms
QRS duration	130	ms
QT/QTc	416/506	ms
P–R–T axes	67 51	–166

Figure 14–240.

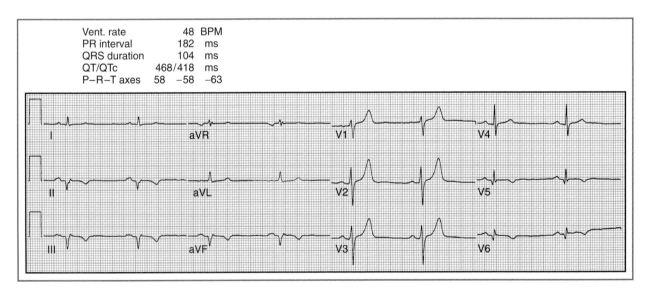

Vent. rate	48	BPM
PR interval	182	ms
QRS duration	104	ms
QT/QTc	468/418	ms
P–R–T axes	58 –58	–63

Figure 14–241.

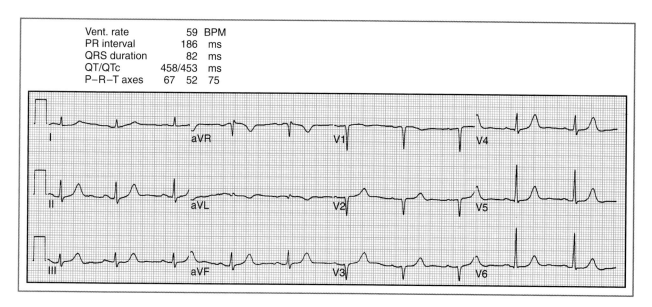

Figure 14–242.

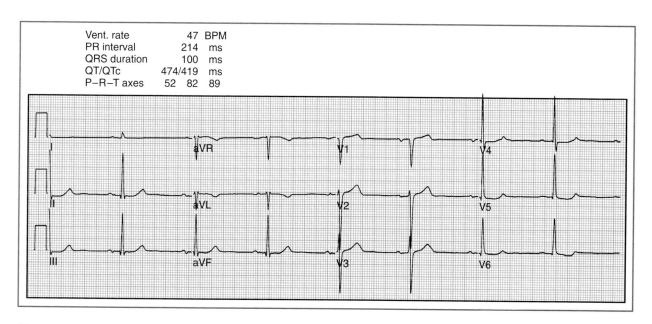

Figure 14–243.

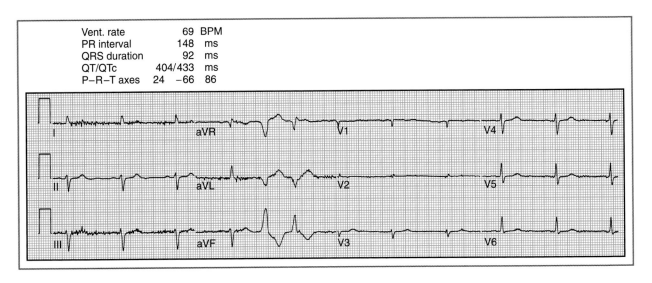

Vent. rate	69	BPM
PR interval	148	ms
QRS duration	92	ms
QT/QTc	404/433	ms
P–R–T axes	24 –66	86

Figure 14–244.

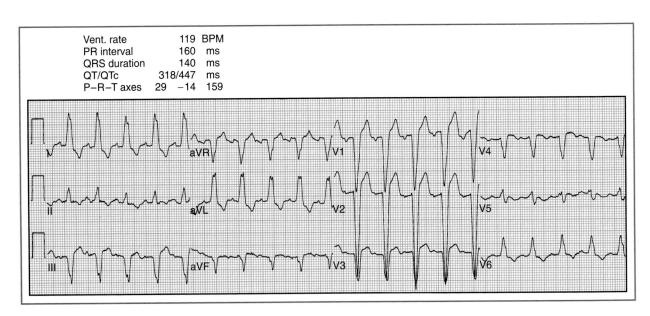

Vent. rate	119	BPM
PR interval	160	ms
QRS duration	140	ms
QT/QTc	318/447	ms
P–R–T axes	29 –14	159

Figure 14–245.

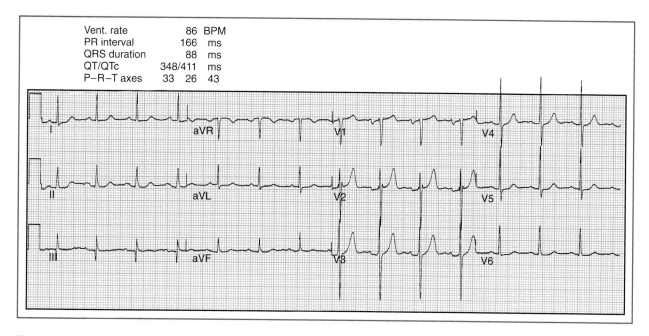

Vent. rate   86   BPM
PR interval   166   ms
QRS duration   88   ms
QT/QTc   348/411   ms
P–R–T axes   33   26   43

Figure 14–246.

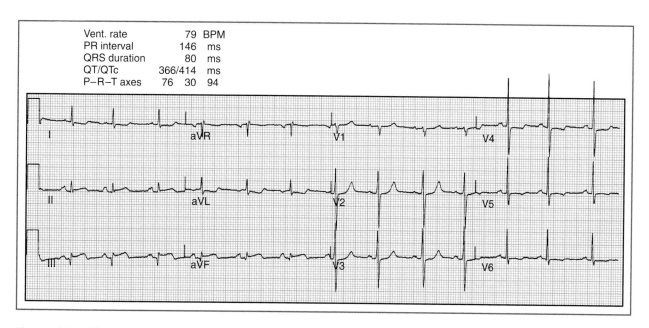

Vent. rate   79   BPM
PR interval   146   ms
QRS duration   80   ms
QT/QTc   366/414   ms
P–R–T axes   76   30   94

Figure 14–247.

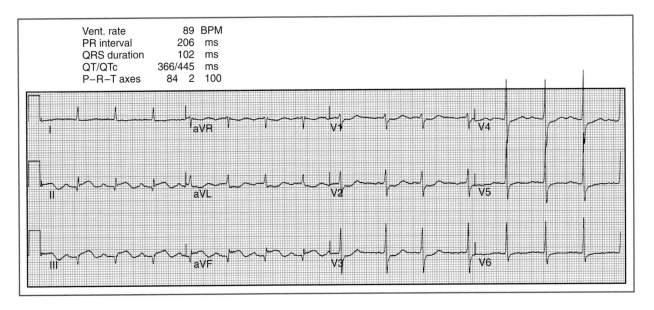

Vent. rate 89 BPM
PR interval 206 ms
QRS duration 102 ms
QT/QTc 366/445 ms
P–R–T axes 84 2 100

Figure 14–248.

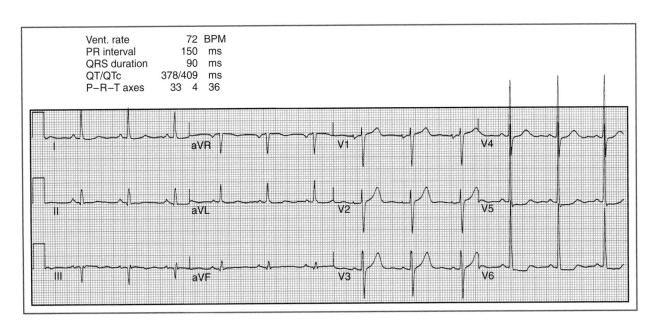

Vent. rate 72 BPM
PR interval 150 ms
QRS duration 90 ms
QT/QTc 378/409 ms
P–R–T axes 33 4 36

Figure 14–249.

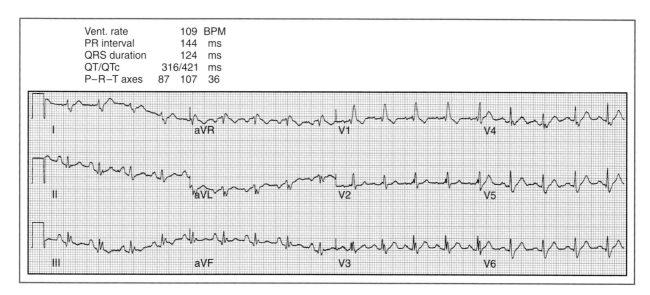

Vent. rate	109	BPM
PR interval	144	ms
QRS duration	124	ms
QT/QTc	316/421	ms
P–R–T axes	87 107 36	

Figure 14–250.

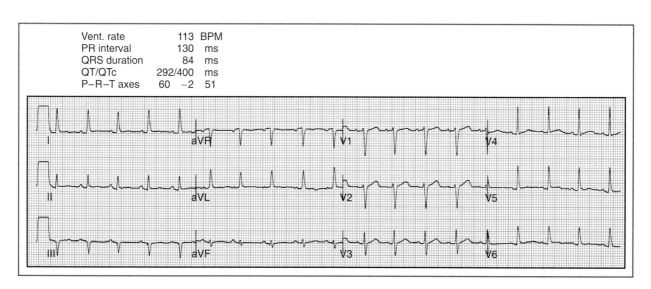

Vent. rate	113	BPM
PR interval	130	ms
QRS duration	84	ms
QT/QTc	292/400	ms
P–R–T axes	60 –2 51	

Figure 14–251.

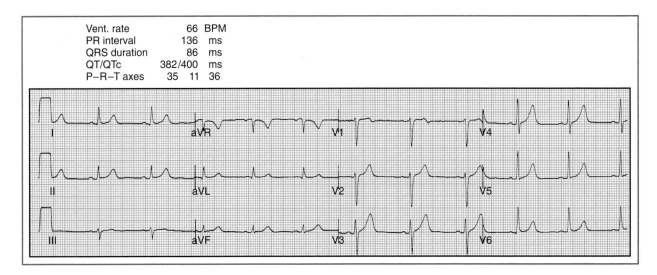

Vent. rate	66	BPM
PR interval	136	ms
QRS duration	86	ms
QT/QTc	382/400	ms
P–R–T axes	35	11	36

Figure 14–252.

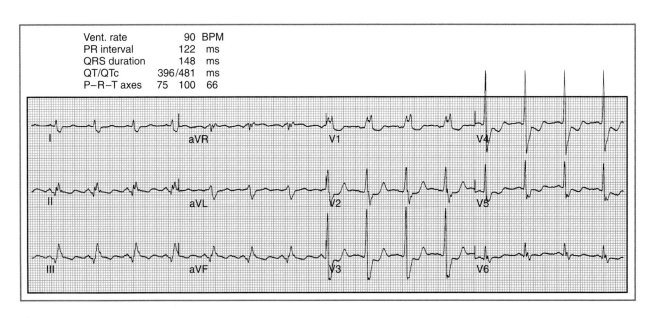

Vent. rate	90	BPM
PR interval	122	ms
QRS duration	148	ms
QT/QTc	396/481	ms
P–R–T axes	75	100	66

Figure 14–253.

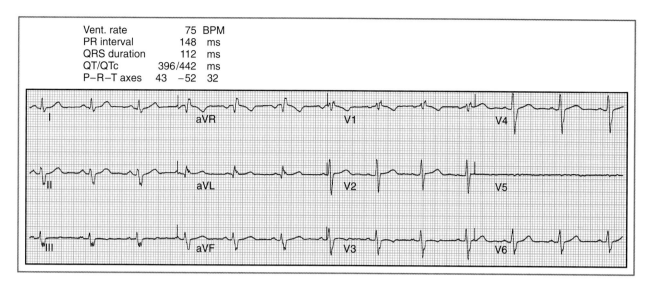

Figure 14–254.

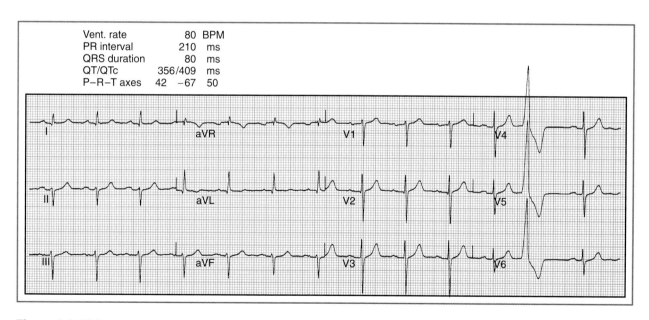

Figure 14–255.

Vent. rate	64	BPM
PR interval	158	ms
QRS duration	80	ms
QT/QTc	368/374	ms
P–R–T axes	36 –19	2

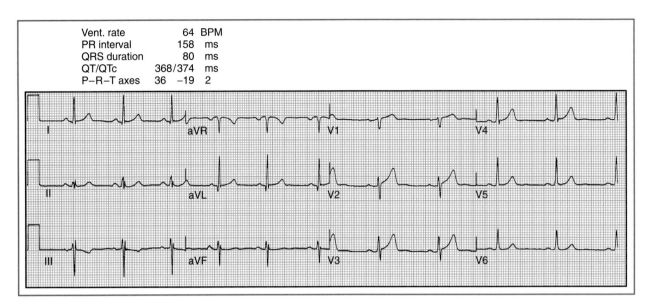

Figure 14–256.

Vent. rate	147	BPM
PR interval	*	ms
QRS duration	122	ms
QT/QTc	304/471	ms
P–R–T axes	2407 160	28

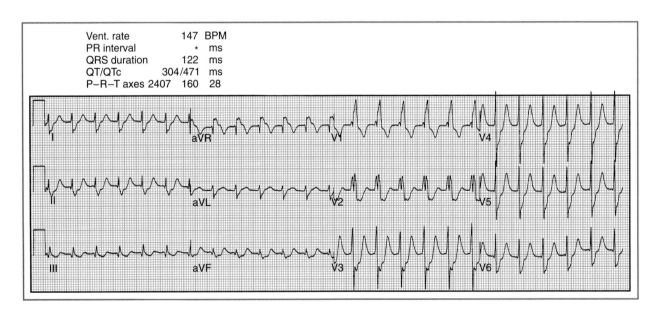

Figure 14–257.

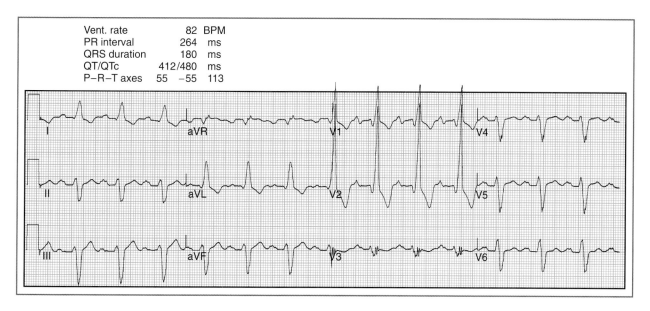

Vent. rate	82	BPM
PR interval	264	ms
QRS duration	180	ms
QT/QTc	412/480	ms
P–R–T axes	55 –55	113

Figure 14–258.

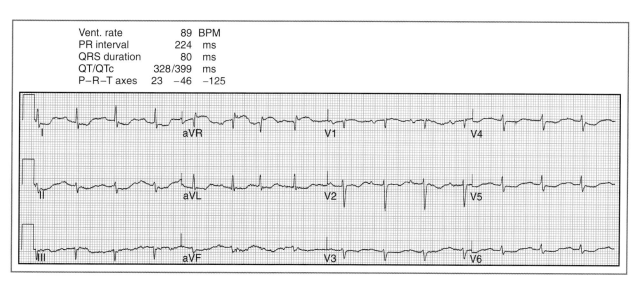

Vent. rate	89	BPM
PR interval	224	ms
QRS duration	80	ms
QT/QTc	328/399	ms
P–R–T axes	23 –46	–125

Figure 14–259.

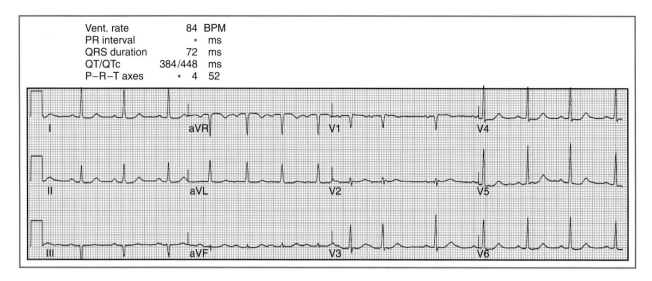

Vent. rate	84	BPM
PR interval	*	ms
QRS duration	72	ms
QT/QTc	384/448	ms
P–R–T axes	* 4	52

Figure 14–260.

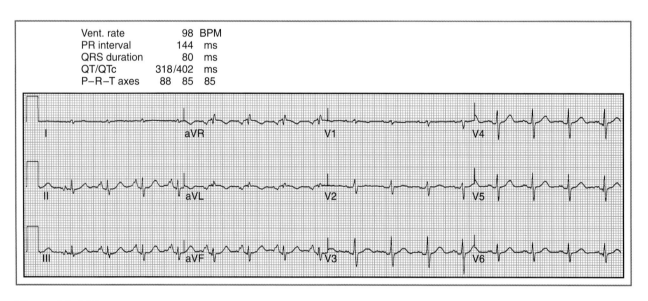

Vent. rate	98	BPM
PR interval	144	ms
QRS duration	80	ms
QT/QTc	318/402	ms
P–R–T axes	88 85	85

Figure 14–261.

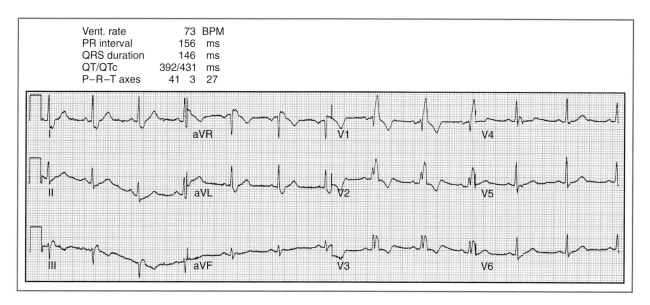

Vent. rate	73	BPM
PR interval	156	ms
QRS duration	146	ms
QT/QTc	392/431	ms
P–R–T axes	41 3 27	

Figure 14–262.

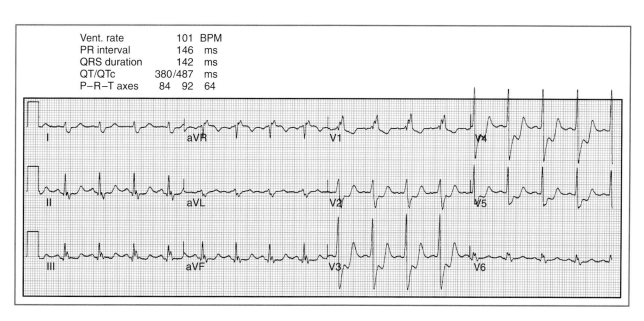

Vent. rate	101	BPM
PR interval	146	ms
QRS duration	142	ms
QT/QTc	380/487	ms
P–R–T axes	84 92 64	

Figure 14–263.

Vent. rate	133	BPM
PR interval	*	ms
QRS duration	72	ms
QT/QTc	292/433	ms
P–R–T axes	* 47	84

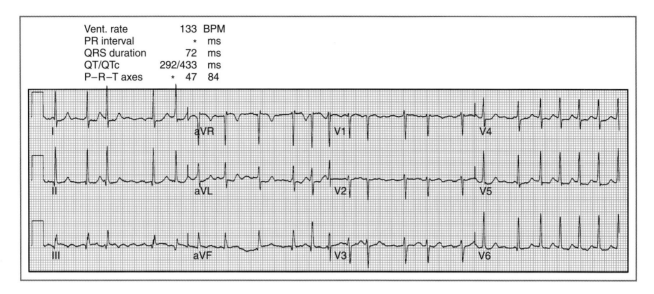

Figure 14–264.

Vent. rate	66	BPM
PR interval	162	ms
QRS duration	102	ms
QT/QTc	414/427	ms
P–R–T axes	74 –77	–104

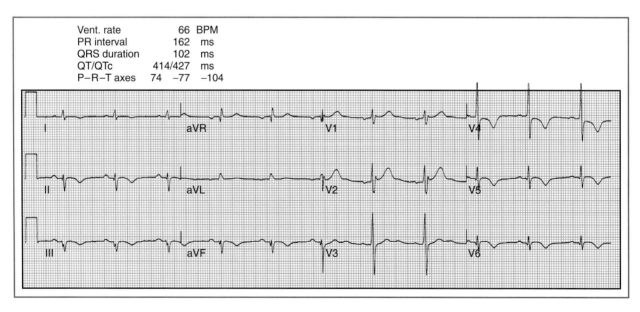

Figure 14–265.

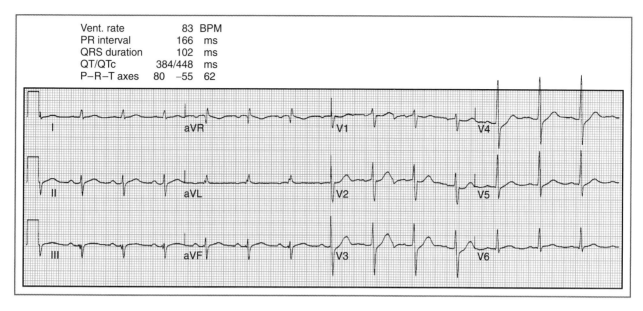

Vent. rate	83	BPM
PR interval	166	ms
QRS duration	102	ms
QT/QTc	384/448	ms
P–R–T axes	80 –55	62

Figure 14–266.

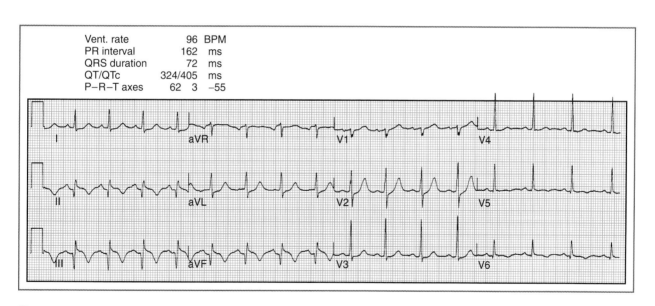

Vent. rate	96	BPM
PR interval	162	ms
QRS duration	72	ms
QT/QTc	324/405	ms
P–R–T axes	62 3	–55

Figure 14–267.

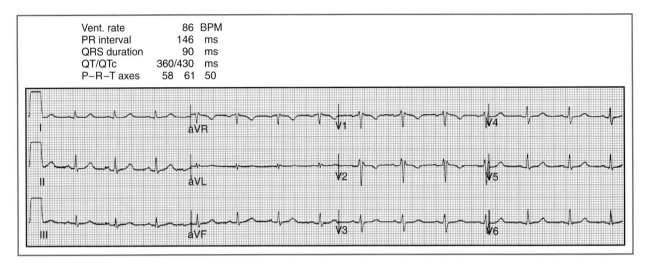

Vent. rate	86	BPM
PR interval	146	ms
QRS duration	90	ms
QT/QTc	360/430	ms
P–R–T axes	58 61 50	

Figure 14–268.

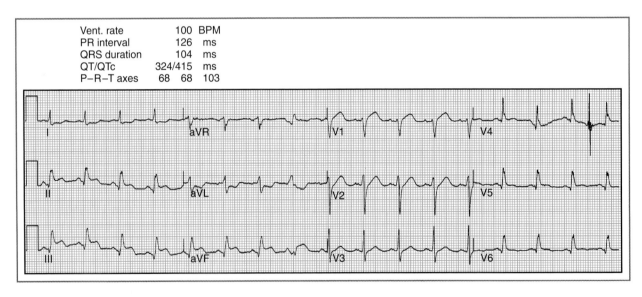

Vent. rate	100	BPM
PR interval	126	ms
QRS duration	104	ms
QT/QTc	324/415	ms
P–R–T axes	68 68 103	

Figure 14–269.

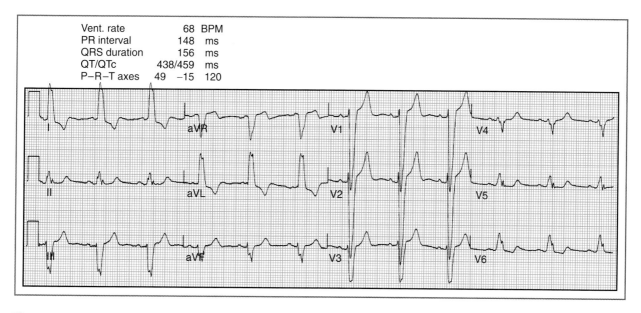

Figure 14-270.

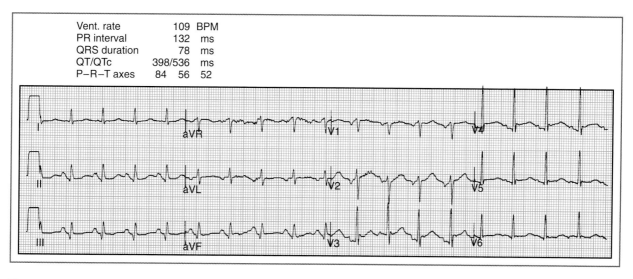

Figure 14-271.

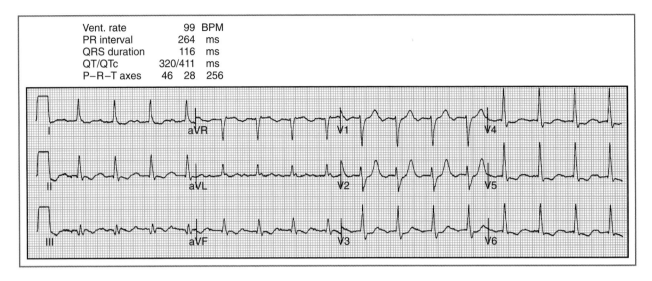

Vent. rate	99	BPM
PR interval	264	ms
QRS duration	116	ms
QT/QTc	320/411	ms
P–R–T axes	46 28 256	

Figure 14–272.

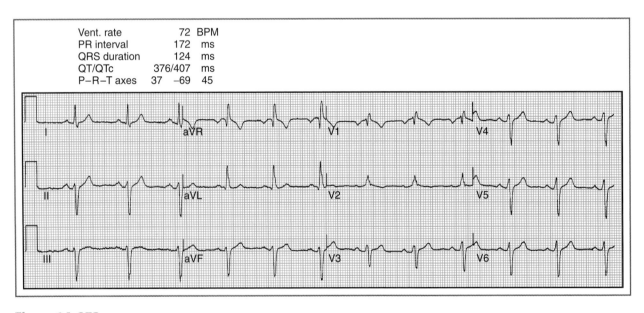

Vent. rate	72	BPM
PR interval	172	ms
QRS duration	124	ms
QT/QTc	376/407	ms
P–R–T axes	37 −69 45	

Figure 14–273.

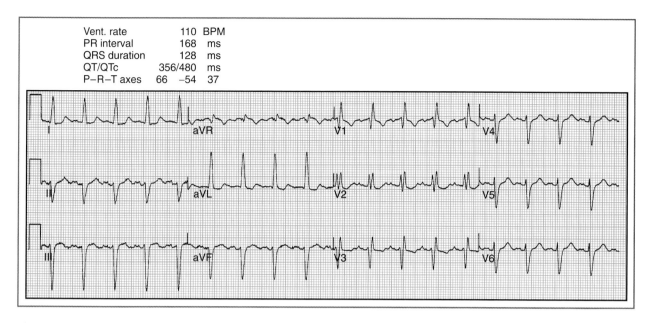

Vent. rate	110	BPM
PR interval	168	ms
QRS duration	128	ms
QT/QTc	356/480	ms
P–R–T axes	66 –54	37

Figure 14–274.

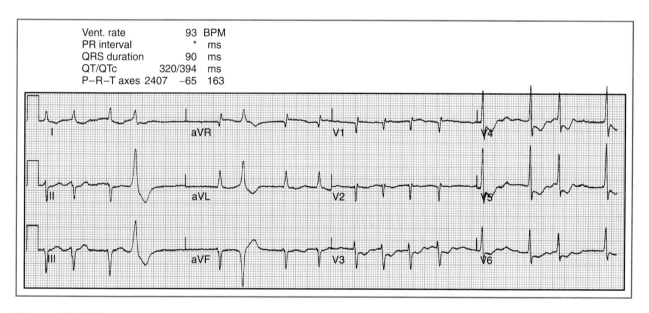

Vent. rate	93	BPM
PR interval	*	ms
QRS duration	90	ms
QT/QTc	320/394	ms
P–R–T axes	2407 –65	163

Figure 14–275.

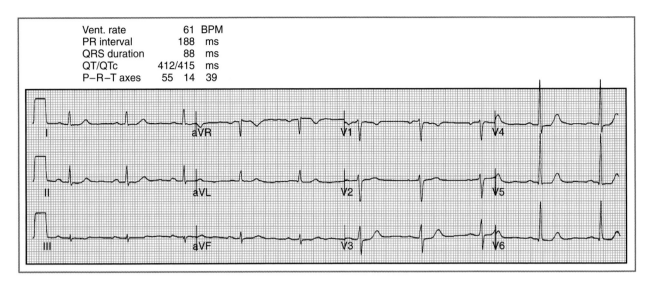

Vent. rate	61 BPM
PR interval	188 ms
QRS duration	88 ms
QT/QTc	412/415 ms
P–R–T axes	55 14 39

Figure 14–276.

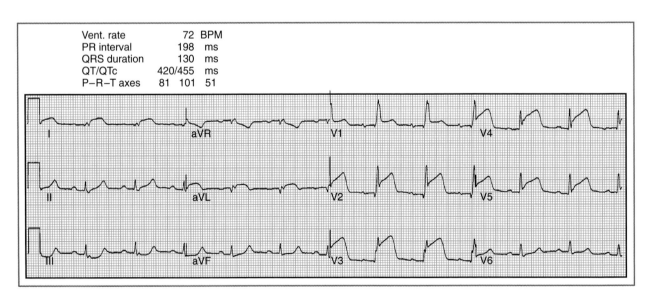

Vent. rate	72 BPM
PR interval	198 ms
QRS duration	130 ms
QT/QTc	420/455 ms
P–R–T axes	81 101 51

Figure 14–277.

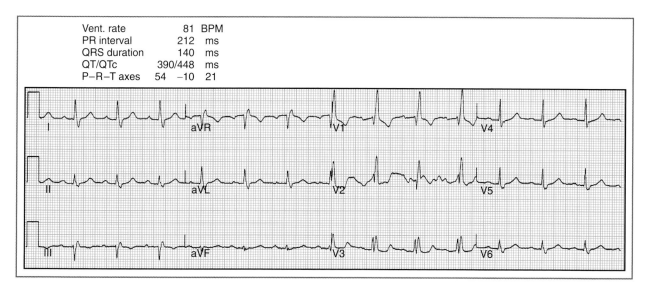

Vent. rate	81	BPM
PR interval	212	ms
QRS duration	140	ms
QT/QTc	390/448	ms
P–R–T axes	54 –10	21

Figure 14–278.

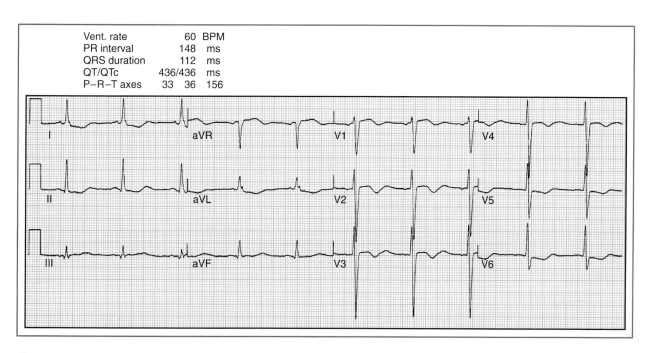

Vent. rate	60	BPM
PR interval	148	ms
QRS duration	112	ms
QT/QTc	436/436	ms
P–R–T axes	33 36	156

Figure 14–279.

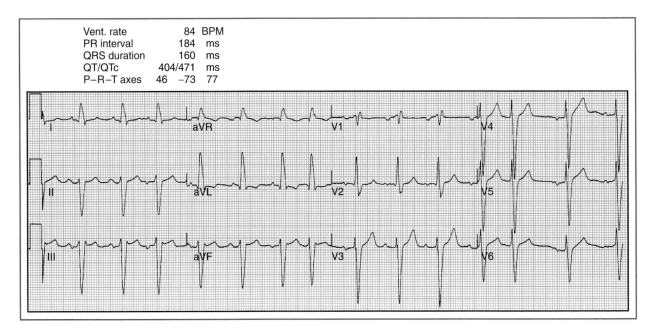

Vent. rate	84	BPM
PR interval	184	ms
QRS duration	160	ms
QT/QTc	404/471	ms
P–R–T axes	46	–73	77

Figure 14–280.

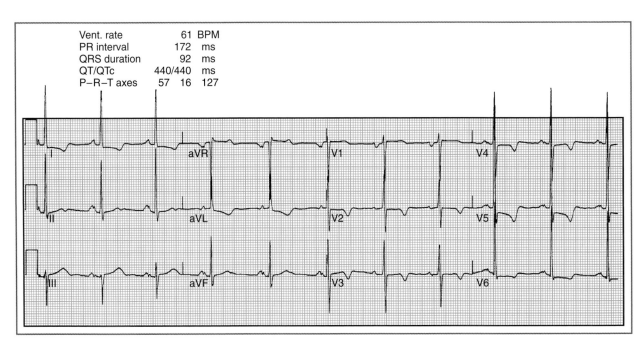

Vent. rate	61	BPM
PR interval	172	ms
QRS duration	92	ms
QT/QTc	440/440	ms
P–R–T axes	57	16	127

Figure 14–281.

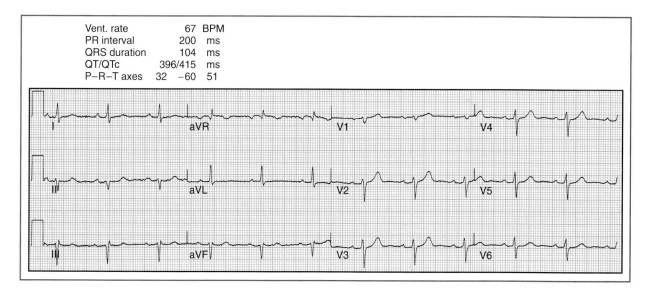

```
Vent. rate        67  BPM
PR interval       200 ms
QRS duration      104 ms
QT/QTc        396/415 ms
P–R–T axes    32  –60  51
```

Figure 14–282.

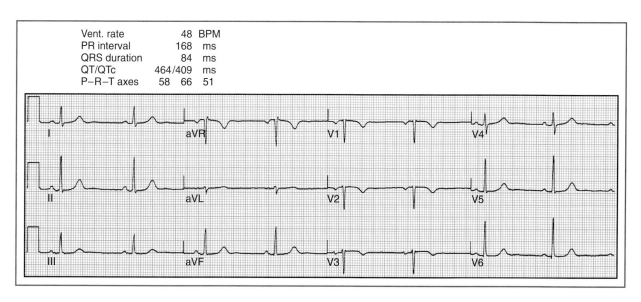

```
Vent. rate         48  BPM
PR interval        168 ms
QRS duration        84 ms
QT/QTc         464/409 ms
P–R–T axes     58   66  51
```

Figure 14–283.

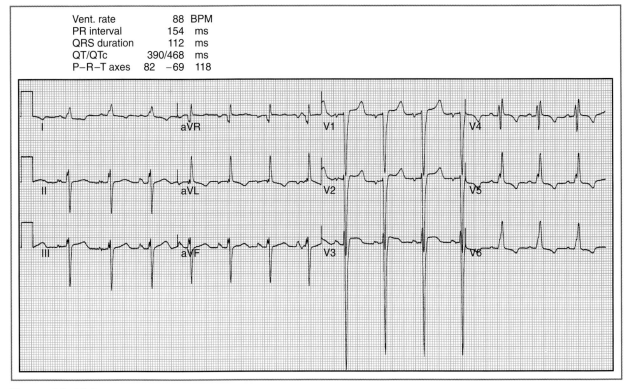

Vent. rate	88	BPM
PR interval	154	ms
QRS duration	112	ms
QT/QTc	390/468	ms
P–R–T axes	82 –69	118

Figure 14–284.

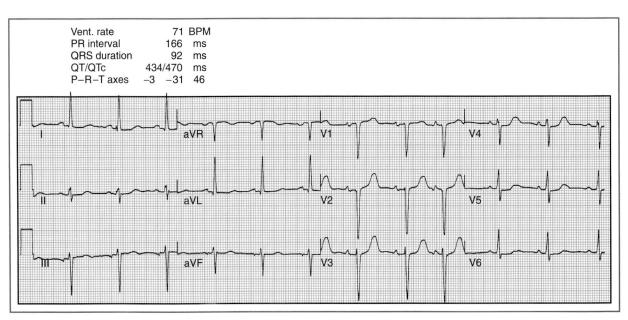

Vent. rate	71	BPM
PR interval	166	ms
QRS duration	92	ms
QT/QTc	434/470	ms
P–R–T axes	–3 –31	46

Figure 14–285.

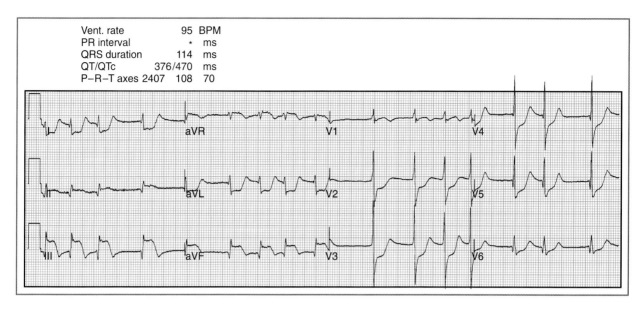

```
Vent. rate          95  BPM
PR interval          *  ms
QRS duration       114  ms
QT/QTc         376/470  ms
P–R–T axes 2407   108   70
```

Figure 14–286.

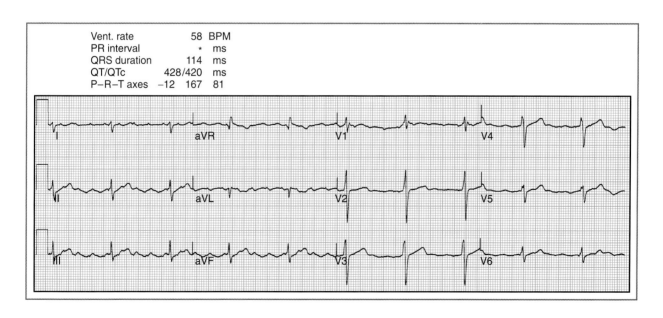

```
Vent. rate          58  BPM
PR interval          *  ms
QRS duration       114  ms
QT/QTc         428/420  ms
P–R–T axes   –12   167   81
```

Figure 14–287.

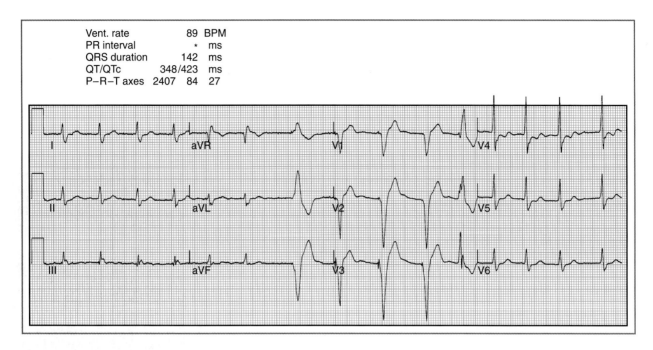

Vent. rate	89	BPM	
PR interval	*	ms	
QRS duration	142	ms	
QT/QTc	348/423	ms	
P–R–T axes	2407	84	27

Figure 14–288.

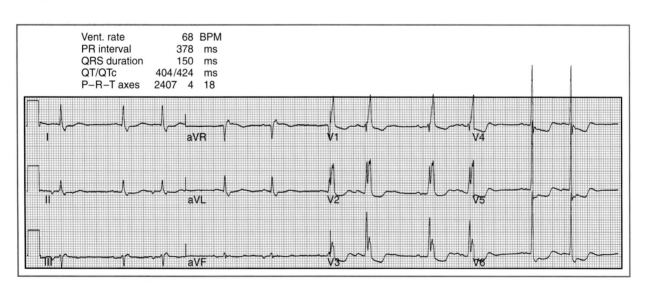

Vent. rate	68	BPM	
PR interval	378	ms	
QRS duration	150	ms	
QT/QTc	404/424	ms	
P–R–T axes	2407	4	18

Figure 14–289.

Vent. rate	65	BPM
PR interval	156	ms
QRS duration	158	ms
QT/QTc	428/442	ms
P–R–T axes	72 –65	62

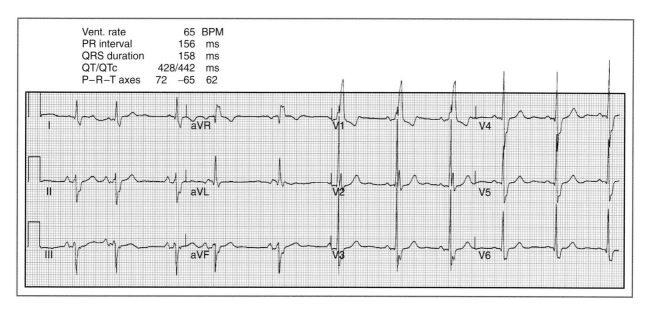

Figure 14–290.

Vent. rate	89	BPM
PR interval	152	ms
QRS duration	156	ms
QT/QTc	394/479	ms
P–R–T axes	63 –62	39

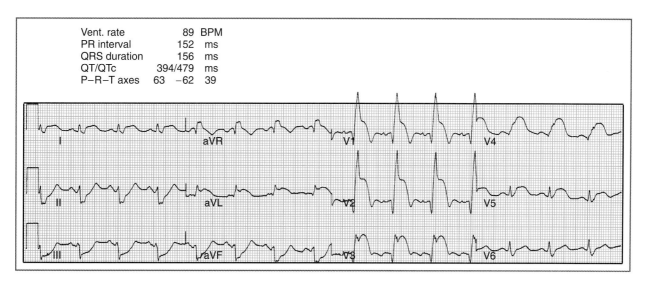

Figure 14–291.

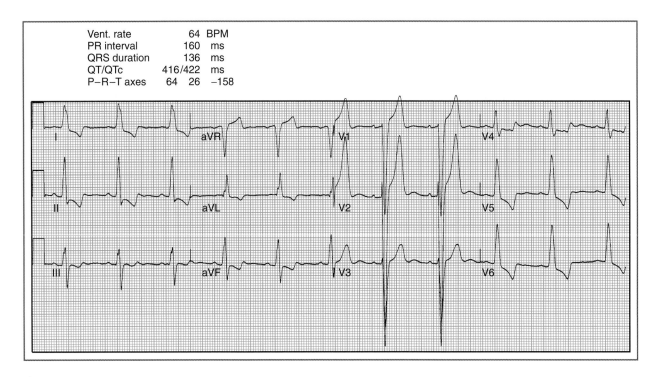

Vent. rate	64 BPM
PR interval	160 ms
QRS duration	136 ms
QT/QTc	416/422 ms
P–R–T axes	64 26 –158

Figure 14–292.

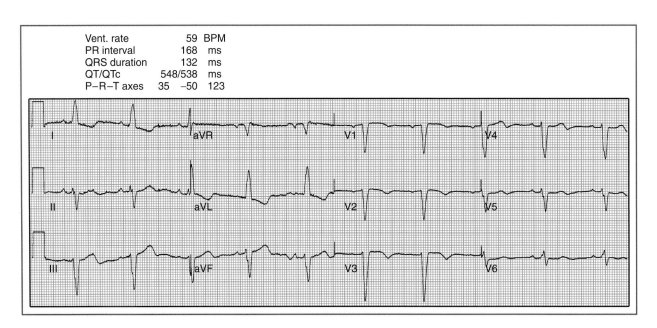

Vent. rate	59 BPM
PR interval	168 ms
QRS duration	132 ms
QT/QTc	548/538 ms
P–R–T axes	35 –50 123

Figure 14–293.

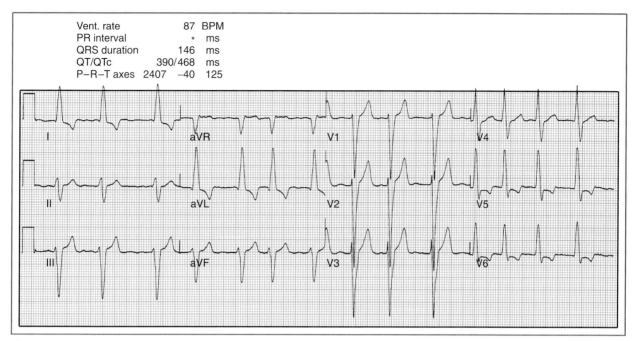

Vent. rate   87   BPM
PR interval   *   ms
QRS duration   146   ms
QT/QTc   390/468   ms
P–R–T axes   2407   –40   125

Figure 14–294.

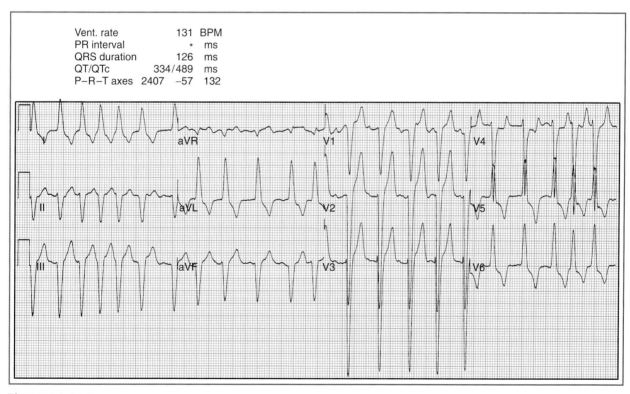

Vent. rate   131   BPM
PR interval   *   ms
QRS duration   126   ms
QT/QTc   334/489   ms
P–R–T axes   2407   –57   132

Figure 14–295.

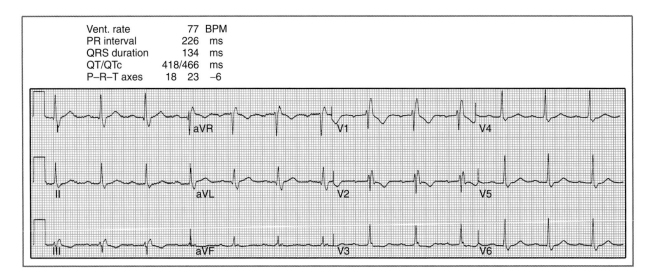

Vent. rate	77	BPM
PR interval	226	ms
QRS duration	134	ms
QT/QTc	418/466	ms
P–R–T axes	18 23 –6	

Figure 14–296.

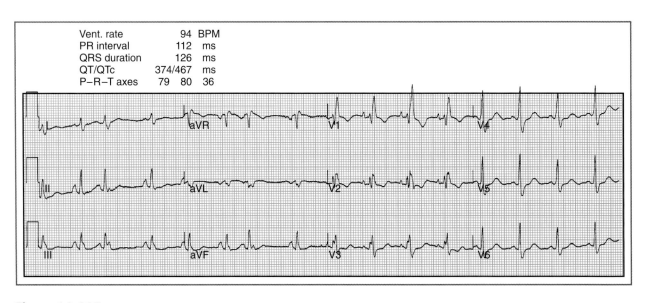

Vent. rate	94	BPM
PR interval	112	ms
QRS duration	126	ms
QT/QTc	374/467	ms
P–R–T axes	79 80 36	

Figure 14–297.

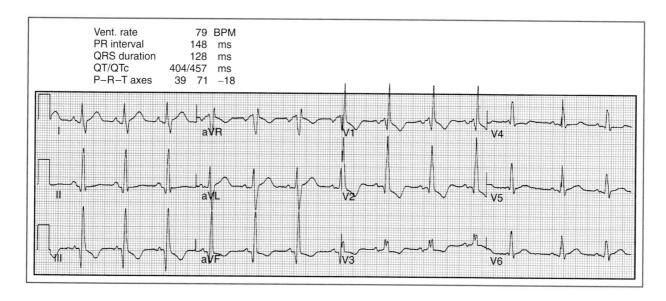

Vent. rate	79	BPM
PR interval	148	ms
QRS duration	128	ms
QT/QTc	404/457	ms
P–R–T axes	39 71	–18

Figure 14–298.

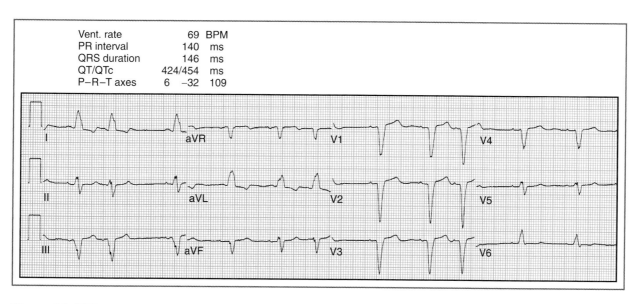

Vent. rate	69	BPM
PR interval	140	ms
QRS duration	146	ms
QT/QTc	424/454	ms
P–R–T axes	6 –32	109

Figure 14–299.

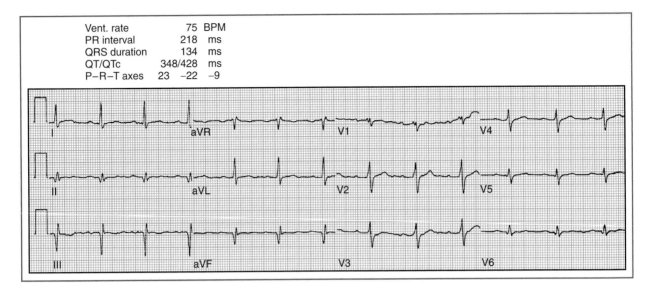

Vent. rate	75	BPM
PR interval	218	ms
QRS duration	134	ms
QT/QTc	348/428	ms
P–R–T axes	23 –22 –9	

Figure 14–300.

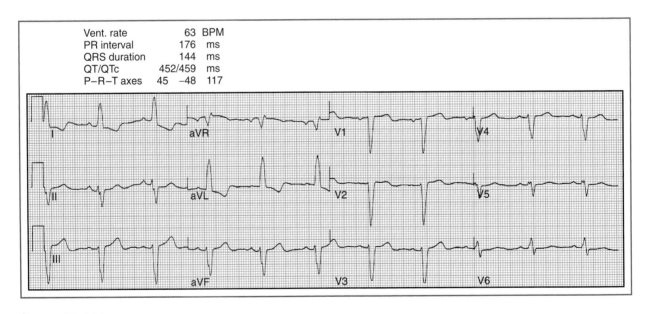

Vent. rate	63	BPM
PR interval	176	ms
QRS duration	144	ms
QT/QTc	452/459	ms
P–R–T axes	45 –48 117	

Figure 14–301.

ANSWER KEY

CHAPTER 3

Figure 3–10
Lead I: ↑
Lead II: ↓
Lead III: ↓
R axis: -46
Axis: Pathological left
Hemiblock: Anterior

Figure 3–11
Lead I: ↑
Lead II: ↑
Lead III: ↑
R axis: 48
Axis: Normal
Hemiblock:

Figure 3–12
Lead I: ↑
Lead II: half-way
Lead III: ↓
R axis: -31
Axis: Physiological left
Hemiblock:

Figure 3–13
Lead I: ↓
Lead II: ↑
Lead III: ↑
R axis: 106
Axis: Right
Hemiblock: Posterior

Figure 3–14
Lead I: ↑
Lead II: ↑
Lead III: ↑
R axis: 69
Axis: Normal
Hemiblock:

Figure 3–15
Lead I: ↑
Lead II: ↑
Lead III: ↓
R axis: -15
Axis: Physiological left
Hemiblock:

Figure 3–16
Lead I: ↑
Lead II: ↑
Lead III: ↓
R axis: -11
Axis: Physiological left
Hemiblock:

Figure 3–17
Lead I: ↑
Lead II: ↓
Lead III: ↓
R axis: -75
Axis: Pathological left
Hemiblock: Anterior

Figure 3–18
Lead I: ↑
Lead II: ↓
Lead III: ↓
R axis: -46
Axis: Pathological left
Hemiblock: Anterior

Figure 3–19
Lead I: ↓
Lead II: ↑
Lead III: ↑
R axis: 100
Axis: Right
Hemiblock: Posterior

Figure 3–20
Lead I: ↑
Lead II: ↓
Lead III: ↓
R axis: -67
Axis: Pathological left
Hemiblock: Anterior

CHAPTER 4

Figure 4–8
QRS Duration: 136.
Bundle Branch Block: left.

Figure 4–9
QRS Duration: 186.
Bundle Branch Block: right.

Figure 4–10
QRS Duration: 118.
Bundle Branch Block: not long enough.

Figure 4–11
QRS Duration: 136.
Bundle Branch Block: left.

Figure 4–12
QRS Duration: 144.
Bundle Branch Block: right.

Figure 4–13
QRS Duration: 138.
Bundle Branch Block: right.

Figure 4–14
QRS Duration: 184.
Bundle Branch Block: left.

Figure 4–15
QRS Duration: 128.
Bundle Branch Block: right.

Figure 4–16
QRS Duration: 152.
Bundle Branch Block: left.

Figure 4–17
QRS Duration: 146.
Bundle Branch Block: right.

Figure 4–18
QRS Duration: 144.
Bundle Branch Block: left.

Figure 4–19
QRS Duration: 150.
Bundle Branch Block: left.

CHAPTER 5

Figure 5–5
Lead I: ↑
Lead II: ↓
Lead III: ↓
R Axis: -79
Axis: Path left
Hemiblock: Anterior
QRS Width? 164
BBB? Right
BFB? Yes
Risk for: Complete heart block? Yes
           Sudden cardiac death? Yes
           Hemodynamic compromise? No

Figure 5–6
Lead I: ↓
Lead II: ↓
Lead III: ↑
R Axis: 145
Axis: Right
Hemiblock: Posterior
QRS Width? 216
BBB? Right
BFB? Yes
Risk for: Complete heart block? Yes
           Sudden cardiac death? Yes
           Hemodynamic compromise? Yes

Figure 5–7
Lead I: ↓
Lead II: ↓
Lead III: ↑
R Axis: 147
Axis: Right
Hemiblock: Posterior
QRS Width? 150
BBB? Right
BFB? Yes
Risk for: Complete heart block? Yes
           Sudden cardiac death? Yes
           Hemodynamic compromise? No

Figure 5–8
Lead I: ↑
Lead II: ↓
Lead III: ↓
R Axis: -46
Axis: Path left
Hemiblock: Anterior
QRS Width? 100
BBB? No
BFB? No
Risk for: Complete heart block? No
           Sudden cardiac death? Yes
           Hemodynamic compromise? No

Figure 5–9
Lead I: ↑
Lead II: ↑
Lead III: ↑
R Axis: 35
Axis: Normal
Hemiblock: No
QRS Width? 136
BBB? Right
BFB? No
Risk for: Complete heart block? No
           Sudden cardiac death? Yes
           Hemodynamic compromise? No

Figure 5–10
Lead I: ↑
Lead II: ↓
Lead III: ↓
R Axis: -66
Axis: Path left

Hemiblock: Anterior
QRS Width? 144
BBB? Left
BFB? Yes
Risk for: Complete heart block? Yes
           Sudden cardiac death? Yes
           Hemodynamic compromise? No

Figure 5–11
Lead I: ↓
Lead II: half
Lead III: ↑
R Axis: 132
Axis: Right
Hemiblock: Posterior
QRS Width? 132
BBB? Right
BFB? Yes
Risk for: Complete heart block? Yes
           Sudden cardiac death? Yes
           Hemodynamic compromise? No

Figure 5–12
Lead I: ↑
Lead II: ↓
Lead III: ↓
R Axis: -85
Axis: Path left
Hemiblock: Anterior
QRS Width? 164
BBB? Right
BFB? Yes
Risk for: Complete heart block? Yes
           Sudden cardiac death? Yes
           Hemodynamic compromise? No

Figure 5–13
Lead I: ↑
Lead II: ↓
Lead III: ↓
R Axis: -65
Axis: Path left
Hemiblock: Anterior
QRS Width? 128
BBB? Right
BFB? Yes
Risk for: Complete heart block? Yes
           Sudden cardiac death? Yes
           Hemodynamic compromise? No

Figure 5–14
Lead I: ↑
Lead II: ↓
Lead III: ↓
R Axis: -82
Axis: Path left
Hemiblock: Anterior
QRS Width? 196
BBB? Right
BFB? Yes
Risk for: Complete heart block? Yes
           Sudden cardiac death? Yes
           Hemodynamic compromise? Yes

Figure 5–15
Lead I: ↑
Lead II: ↓
Lead III: ↓
R Axis: -52
Axis: Path left
Hemiblock: Anterior
QRS Width? 140
BBB? Right
BFB? Yes
Risk for: Complete heart block? Yes
          Sudden cardiac death? Yes
          Hemodynamic compromise? No

Figure 5–16
Lead I: ↑
Lead II: ↓
Lead III: ↓
R Axis: -71
Axis: Path left
Hemiblock: Anterior
QRS Width? 144
BBB? Right
BFB? Yes
Risk for: Complete heart block? Yes
          Sudden cardiac death? Yes
          Hemodynamic compromise? No

Figure 5–17
Lead I: ↑
Lead II: ↑
Lead III: ↑
R Axis: 38
Axis: Normal
Hemiblock: None
QRS Width? 124
BBB? Left
BFB? Yes
Risk for: Complete heart block? Yes
          Sudden cardiac death? Yes
          Hemodynamic compromise? No

Figure 5–18
Lead I: ↑
Lead II: ↑
Lead III: ↑
R Axis: 55
Axis: Normal
Hemiblock: None
QRS Width? 124
BBB? Right
BFB? No
Risk for: Complete heart block? No
          Sudden cardiac death? Yes
          Hemodynamic compromise? No

Figure 5–19
Lead I: ↑
Lead II: ↑
Lead III: ↓
R Axis: 1
Axis: Normal/physiologic left
Hemiblock: No

QRS Width? 166
BBB? Left
BFB? Yes
Risk for: Complete heart block? Yes
          Sudden cardiac death? Yes
          Hemodynamic compromise? No

CHAPTER 6

Figure 6–16: Ventricular tachycardia.

1. First criterion of ERAD has not been met.
2. Morphology in V1: Negative deflection, no diagnostic criteria.
3. QRS morphology in V6: Lead V6 is a negatively deflected complex, indicating ventricular tachycardia.

Figure 6–17: Ventricular tachycardia.

1. Extreme right-axis deviation suggests VT, but Lead V1 is negative.
2. Morphology in V1: Because V1 is negative deflection, the R wave is > 40 ms wide, indicating VT.
3. Morphology in V6: Lead V6 is clearly a negative deflection, indicating ventricular tachycardia.

Figure 6–18: Ventricular tachycardia.

1. Extreme right-axis deviation suggests VT, but Lead V1 is negatively deflected. Criterion has not been fully met.
2. QRS morphology in V1: Uncertain, nondiagnostic.
3. Negative deflection in Lead V6 makes this VT.

Figure 6–19: Wide complex tachycardia.

1. First criterion of ERAD has not been met.
2. QRS morphology in V1: Upright deflection; "little mountain/big mountain" shape is of no help. In this criterion, "big mountain" first would be VT.
3. QRS morphology in V6: Lead V6 clearly demonstrates a negative deflection, indicating ventricular tachycardia.

Figure 6–20: Ventricular tachycardia.

1. Pathological left axis: First criterion of ERAD has not been met.
2. QRS morphology in V1: Complex is upright in Lead V1 but has no recognizable pattern that indicates VT.
3. QRS morphology in V6: A negative deflection here indicates ventricular tachycardia.
4. An indicator of AV dissociation exists here. Note in the AV lead that there appears to be a break in the arrhythmia for two normally conducted capture beats.

Figure 6–21: Ventricular tachycardia.

1. First criterion of ERAD has not been met.
2. QRS morphology in V1: Upright, monomorphic peak indicates VT.
3. QRS morphology in V6: A negative deflection indicates VT.

Figure 6–22: Ventricular tachycardia.

1. First criterion of ERAD has not been met.
2. QRS morphology in V1: Upright, monomorphic peak indicates VT.
3. QRS morphology in V6: A negative deflection indicates VT.

CHAPTER 8

Figure 8–8
T wave inversion: aVL, V4, V5, V6

Figure 8–9
ST elevation: V2, V3
ST depression: II, aVF
T wave inversion: V4, V5, V6, I, aVL

Figure 8–10
ST elevation: II, III, aVF, V5, V6
ST depression: I, aVL, aVR, V1, V2, V3, V4

Figure 8–11
ST elevation: II, III, aVF, V5, V6
ST depression: aVL, aVR, V1, V2, V3
Pathological Q waves: III, aVF

Figure 8–12
ST elevation: V1, V2, V3, V4, V5
ST depression: III, aVF
Pathological Q waves: V1, V2, V3

Figure 8–13
ST elevation: V1, V2, V3, V4, V5, V6, aVL
ST depression: II, III, aVF
Pathological Q waves: V1, V2, V3, V4, V5

Figure 8–14
ST elevation: II, III, aVF, V5, V6
ST depression: I, aVL
Pathological Q waves: III

Figure 8–15
ST elevation: II, III, aVF
ST depression: aVF, V1, V2, V3, V4
Pathological Q waves: II, III, aVF

Figure 8–16
ST elevation: V1, V2, V3, V4, V5
Pathological Q waves: V1, V2, V3, V4

Figure 8–17
ST elevation: II, III, aVF
ST depression: I, aVL, V2, V4, V5
Pathological Q waves: III

CHAPTER 9

Figure 9–4
Location: Anteroseptal
Rationale: Elevation in V1–V4. Reciprocal depression in III, aVF.

Figure 9–5
Location: Anteroseptal
Rationale: ST elevation in V1-V3. Recip. in II, II, aVF.

Figure 9–6
Location: Lateral
Rationale: ST elevation in I and aVL. ST depression in V5, V6, II, III, aVF.

Figure 9–7
Location: Inferior
Rationale: ST elevation in II, III, aVF. Recip. in I and aVL.

Figure 9–8
Location: Inferior
Rationale: ST elevation in II, III, aVF. Recip. in aVL.

Figure 9–9
Location: Inferior
Rationale: Elevation in II, III, aVF. Reciprocal in I, aVF.

Figure 9–10
Location: Anteroseptal
Rationale: ST elevation in V2–V5. Reciprocal in III, aVF.

Figure 9–11
Location: Inferior
Rationale: ST elevation in II, III, aVF. Recip. in I, aVL.

Figure 9–12
Location: Inferolateral
Rationale: ST elevation in II, III, aVF, V5–V6. Recip. I, aVL.

CHAPTER 10

Figure 10–5
ST elevation: II, III, aVF, V4R, V8, V9
ST depression: I, aVL, aVR, V1, V2, V3
Pathological Q waves: II, III, aVF, V8, V9
Location: Inferior/posterior right ventricle
Rationale: Reciprocal depression

Figure 10–6
ST elevation: II, III, aVF
ST depression: I, aVL, V2, V3
Location: Inferior
Rationale: Reciprocal changes

Figure 10–7
Location: None

Figure 10–8
Location: None

Figure 10–9
ST elevation: II, III, aVF, V8, V9
ST depression: I, aVL, V1, V2, V3
Location: Inferior/posterior
Rationale: Reciprocal changes

Figure 10–10
Location: None

CHAPTER 11

Figure 11–8
Q waves in lateral leads? No
R wave regression? No
S wave notching? Yes, V3, V4
ST segment elevation in upright complexes? No
ST depression in V1, V2, or V3? No
ST elevation ≥5 mm in negative complexes? No
Score on calculator: 0

Figure 11–9
Q waves in lateral leads? No
R wave regression? No
S wave notching? Yes, V4, V5
ST segment elevation in upright complexes? No
ST depression in V1, V2, or V3? No
ST elevation ≥5 mm in negative complexes? Yes, V2
Score on calculator: 2—50%

Figure 11–10
Q waves in lateral leads? No
R wave regression? No
S wave notching? No
ST segment elevation in upright complexes? No
ST depression in V1, V2, or V3? No
ST elevation ≥5 mm in negative complexes? No
Score on calculator: 0

Figure 11–11
Q waves in lateral leads? No
R wave regression? No
S wave notching? No
ST segment elevation in upright complexes? Yes, II
ST depression in V1, V2, or V3? Yes, V3
ST elevation ≥5 mm in negative complexes? No
Score on calculator: 8—92%

Figure 11–12
Q waves in lateral leads? No
R wave regression? Yes, V1–V4

S wave notching? No
ST segment elevation in upright complexes? No
ST depression in V1, V2, or V3? No
ST elevation ≥5 mm in negative complexes? Yes, V3
Score on calculator: 2—50%

CHAPTER 12

Figure 12–8
LVH with strain. Rule of 35.

Figure 12–9
LVH with strain. Rule of 35.

Figure 12–10
LVH with biatrial enlargement. Rule of 35.

Figure 12–11
LAE.

Figure 12–12
LVH with strain.

Figure 12–13
None.

Figure 12–14
LVH (Lead aVL >11 mm)

Figure 12–15
LVH with strain. Rule of 35.

Figure 12–16
LVH with strain and LAE. Rule of 35.

Figure 12–17
LVH with strain and LAE. Rule of 35.

CHAPTER 14

Figure 14–2
Atrial fibrillation, right-axis deviation, posterior hemiblock, right bundle branch block.

Figure 14–3
Sinus bradycardia, right bundle branch block.

Figure 14–4
Sinus tachycardia with PVCs, right-axis deviation, posterior hemiblock.

Figure 14–5
SVT with aberrancy, right-axis deviation, posterior hemi-
    block, right bundle branch block.

Figure 14–6
Junctional escape rhythm, inferior MI.

Figure 14–7
Sinus rhythm with first-degree block, pathological left axis,
    left bundle branch block, late S wave notching in V3 and
    V4, ST elevation 5 mm in V2.

Figure 14–8
Atrial fibrillation with PVCs, right-axis deviation, posterior
    hemiblock, right bundle branch block.

Figure 14–9
Sinus tachycardia, left atrial enlargement.

Figure 14–10
Sinus rhythm with PVCs, inferolateral ischemia, biatrial
    enlargement.

Figure 14–11
Normal sinus rhythm, pathological left axis, anterior
    hemiblock.

Figure 14–12
Normal sinus rhythm, pathological left axis, anterior
    hemiblock, septal infarct (old).

Figure 14–13
Sinus bradycardia, right bundle branch block.

Figure 14–14
Atrial fibrillation, pathological left axis, anterior hemiblock,
    right bundle branch block, inferior MI.

Figure 14–15
Sinus tachycardia, pathological left axis, anterior hemiblock,
    left ventricular hypertrophy, left atrial enlargement.

Figure 14–16
Normal sinus rhythm, pathological left axis, anterior hemi-
    block, anteroseptal infarct (old).

Figure 14–17
Normal sinus rhythm, left ventricular hypertrophy with
    strain, biatrial enlargement.

Figure 14–18
Normal sinus rhythm, digitalis effect (V6), prolonged QT.

Figure 14–19
Sinus bradycardia, right bundle branch block, left atrial
    enlargement.

Figure 14–20
Normal sinus rhythm, pathological left axis, anterior hemi-
    block, right bundle branch block.

Figure 14–21
Normal sinus rhythm, inferolateral MI.

Figure 14–22
Normal sinus rhythm, left bundle branch block, prolonged
    QT.

Figure 14–23
Normal sinus rhythm, pathological left-axis deviation, left
    bundle branch block.

Figure 14–24
Normal sinus rhythm.

Figure 14–25
Normal sinus rhythm.

Figure 14–26
Normal sinus rhythm, pathological left-axis deviation, ante-
    rior hemiblock.

Figure 14–27
Normal sinus rhythm, first-degree block, pathological left
    axis, anterior hemiblock, left ventricular hypertrophy
    with strain, left atrial enlargement.

Figure 14–28
Normal sinus rhythm, pathological left-axis deviation, ante-
    rior hemiblock.

Figure 14–29
Normal sinus rhythm, left ventricular hypertrophy with strain.

Figure 14–30
Normal sinus rhythm, anteroseptal MI.

Figure 14–31
Normal sinus rhythm.

Figure 14–32
Sinus bradycardia, right bundle branch block.

Figure 14–33
Normal sinus rhythm, lateral ischemia.

Figure 14–34
Normal sinus rhythm.

Figure 14–35
Normal sinus rhythm with PVCs, left ventricular hypertrophy.

Figure 14–36
Normal sinus rhythm with first-degree block, anteroseptal MI, left atrial enlargement.

Figure 14–37
Normal sinus rhythm, right bundle branch block.

Figure 14–38
Atrial fibrillation with RVR, left bundle branch block, prolonged QT.

Figure 14–39
Junctional rhythm, right bundle branch block, anterior ischemia.

Figure 14–40
Sinus tachycardia, left bundle branch block, prolonged QT.

Figure 14–41
Atrial fibrillation, physiological left axis, prolonged QT Interval.

Figure 14–42
Sinus bradycardia, right bundle branch block.

Figure 14–43
Sinus rhythm with first-degree block, pathological left axis, anterior hemiblock, left ventricular hypertrophy with strain.

Figure 14–44
Sinus rhythm with first-degree block and PVCs, pathological left axis, anterior hemiblock, anterior MI, prolonged QT.

Figure 14–45
Normal sinus rhythm, pathological left axis, anterior hemiblock, septal infarct (old).

Figure 14–46
Normal sinus rhythm.

Figure 14–47
Normal sinus rhythm, right atrial enlargement, left ventricular hypertrophy.

Figure 14–48
Normal sinus rhythm with first-degree block, pathological left axis, anterior hemiblock, left ventricular hypertrophy with strain, left atrial enlargement.

Figure 14–49
Normal sinus rhythm, pathological left axis, anterior hemiblock.

Figure 14–50
Normal sinus rhythm, left bundle branch block.

Figure 14–51
Normal sinus rhythm, left bundle branch block.

Figure 14–52
Sinus bradycardia, lateral infarction.

Figure 14–53
Atrial fibrillation, pathological left axis, left bundle branch block.

Figure 14–54
Normal sinus rhythm, left bundle branch block.

Figure 14–55
Normal sinus rhythm, left atrial enlargement.

Figure 14–56
Normal sinus rhythm.

Figure 14–57
Normal sinus rhythm, pathological left axis, left bundle branch block, prolonged QT.

Figure 14–58
Normal sinus rhythm, pathological left axis, left bundle branch block.

Figure 14–59
Normal sinus rhythm, pathological left axis, anterior hemiblock, right bundle branch block.

Figure 14–60
Normal sinus rhythm with first-degree block, lateral ischemia.

Figure 14–61
Normal sinus rhythm, left bundle branch block.

Figure 14–62
Normal sinus rhythm.

Figure 14–63
Normal sinus rhythm, pathological left axis, anterior hemiblock.

Figure 14–64
Normal sinus rhythm, acute inferior MI.

Figure 14–65
Normal sinus rhythm, acute lateral infarction, prolonged
QT.

Figure 14–66
Normal sinus rhythm with first-degree block and PVCs,
acute inferior MI.

Figure 14–67
Sinus bradycardia, early repolarization.

Figure 14–68
Sinus bradycardia, right-axis deviation, posterior hemiblock,
acute inferolateral MI.

Figure 14–69
Normal sinus rhythm.

Figure 14–70
Normal sinus rhythm, right-axis deviation, posterior
hemiblock, acute inferior lateral MI.

Figure 14–71
Normal sinus rhythm, left bundle branch block, R-wave
regression (V1–V4), prolonged QT.

Figure 14–72
Normal sinus rhythm, right-axis deviation, posterior hemiblock, right bundle branch block.

Figure 14–73
Normal sinus rhythm, pathological left axis, anterior hemiblock.

Figure 14–74
Normal sinus rhythm with first-degree block, pathological
left axis, anterior hemiblock.

Figure 14–75
Normal sinus rhythm with first-degree block, PVCs, pathological left axis, anterior hemiblock, right bundle branch
block, anteroseptal ischemia.

Figure 14–76
Sinus tachycardia, pathological left axis, anterior hemiblock.

Figure 14–77
Normal sinus rhythm, left atrial enlargement.

Figure 14–78
Normal sinus rhythm.

Figure 14–79
Sinus tachycardia, right-axis posterior hemiblock, acute
inferior MI.

Figure 14–80
Normal sinus rhythm, anterolateral MI, left atrial enlargement.

Figure 14–81
Normal sinus rhythm, acute inferior MI.

Figure 14–82
Second-degree type I, pathological left axis, left bundle
branch block.

Figure 14–83
Sinus bradycardia, right bundle branch block.

Figure 14–84
Sinus bradycardia, right bundle branch block.

Figure 14–85
Normal sinus rhythm, right bundle branch block.

Figure 14–86
Sinus bradycardia with first-degree heart block, pathological
left axis, anterior hemiblock.

Figure 14–87
Normal sinus rhythm, pathological left axis, anterior
hemiblock.

Figure 14–88
Normal sinus rhythm, pathological left axis, anterior hemiblock, left ventricular hypertrophy with strain, left atrial
enlargement.

Figure 14–89
Sinus tachycardia, left bundle branch block, ST elevation
>5 mm in Lead V3.

Figure 14–90
Normal sinus rhythm, left bundle branch block.

Figure 14–91
Normal sinus rhythm, left ventricular hypertrophy with strain.

Figure 14–92
Normal sinus rhythm with PVC, biatrial enlargement.

Figure 14–93
Normal sinus rhythm, left ventricular hypertrophy, biatrial
enlargement.

Figure 14–94
Normal sinus rhythm.

Figure 14–95
Normal sinus rhythm with PAC's, right axis, posterior hemi-block, right bundle branch block, bifascicular block.

Figure 14–96
Atrial fibrillation with PVCs, right-axis deviation, posterior hemiblock, left ventricular hypertrophy with strain.

Figure 14–97
Sinus tachycardia, left bundle branch block.

Figure 14–98
Normal sinus rhythm, left bundle branch block.

Figure 14–99
Sinus tachycardia, right atrial enlargement.

Figure 14–100
Sinus tachycardia, pathological left axis, anterior hemi-block.

Figure 14–101
Sinus tachycardia, left ventricular hypertrophy, left atrial enlargement.

Figure 14–102
Sinus rhythm a junctional escape, right bundle branch block, left atrial enlargement.

Figure 14–103
Normal sinus rhythm with first-degree block, right-axis de-viation, posterior hemiblock, right bundle branch block, prolonged QT.

Figure 14–104
Sinus arrhythmia, pathological left axis, anterior hemi-block.

Figure 14–105
Sinus bradycardia, pathological left axis, anterior hemi-block, anteroseptal infarct (old).

Figure 14–106
Sinus bradycardia, pathological left axis, anterior hemi-block, right bundle branch block.

Figure 14–107
Normal sinus rhythm, right bundle branch block, prolonged QT.

Figure 14–108
Normal sinus rhythm, left ventricular hypertrophy with strain, left atrial enlargement.

Figure 14–109
Atrial fibrillation, acute inferior MI.

Figure 14–110
Normal sinus rhythm.

Figure 14–111
Normal sinus rhythm, inferior infarct (old).

Figure 14–112
Normal sinus rhythm, pathological left axis, left bundle branch block.

Figure 14–113
Normal sinus rhythm, right bundle branch block.

Figure 14–114
Normal sinus rhythm, pathological left axis, anterior hemi-block, right bundle branch block.

Figure 14–115
Atrial fibrillation with RVR, acute inferior infarction.

Figure 14–116
Normal sinus rhythm, subendocardial injury.

Figure 14–117
Sinus tachycardia with a PVC, right bundle branch block, prolonged QT.

Figure 14–118
Sinus tachycardia, right bundle branch block.

Figure 14–119
Sinus tachycardia with first-degree block, pathological left axis, anterior hemiblock, right bundle branch block.

Figure 14–120
Normal sinus rhythm, possible hypokalemia, U waves in V3–V6.

Figure 14–121
Atrial fibrillation, right-axis posterior hemiblock, right bun-dle branch block, anterior ischemia.

Figure 14–122
Normal sinus rhythm.

Figure 14–123
Sinus bradycardia, prolonged QT.

Figure 14–124
Normal sinus rhythm with PVCs, pathological left axis, anterior hemiblock, right bundle branch block.

Figure 14–125
Sinus bradycardia.

Figure 14–126
Complete heart block with ventricular escape.

Figure 14–127
Normal sinus rhythm, left atrial enlargement.

Figure 14–128
Normal sinus rhythm with a first-degree block, left ventricular hypertrophy with strain, left atrial enlargement.

Figure 14–129
Sinus bradycardia, anteroseptal MI, inferior MI.

Figure 14–130
Normal sinus rhythm with first-degree block, pathological left axis, anterior hemiblock, lateral ischemia.

Figure 14–131
Normal sinus rhythm, right bundle branch block.

Figure 14–132
Normal sinus rhythm.

Figure 14–133
Normal sinus rhythm with first-degree block, pathological left axis, anterior hemiblock, right bundle branch block.

Figure 14–134
Normal sinus rhythm with first-degree block and PACs, anterolateral infarction, acute pericarditis, concave ST elevation in all leads.

Figure 14–135
Normal sinus rhythm with first-degree block, pathological left axis, left bundle branch block.

Figure 14–136
Normal sinus rhythm, pathological left axis, left bundle branch block.

Figure 14–137
Normal sinus rhythm with PACs, right bundle branch block, right atrial enlargement.

Figure 14–138
Normal sinus rhythm, pathological left axis, anterior hemiblock, right bundle branch block, anterior ischemia.

Figure 14–139
Normal sinus rhythm with first-degree block, pathological left axis, anterior hemiblock, right bundle branch block, anteroseptal ischemia.

Figure 14–140
Sinus bradycardia, right bundle branch block.

Figure 14–141
Normal sinus rhythm with first-degree bock, pathological left axis, left bundle branch block, hyperkalemia.

Figure 14–142
Sinus tachycardia, right-axis, posterior hemiblock.

Figure 14–143
Normal sinus rhythm, hyperkalemia.

Figure 14–144
Sinus bradycardia, acute inferior MI.

Figure 14–145
Normal sinus rhythm.

Figure 14–146
Normal sinus rhythm, septal infarct (old).

Figure 14–147
Sinus bradycardia.

Figure 14–148
Normal sinus rhythm, left ventricular hypertrophy with strain, hypokalemia, U waves present.

Figure 14–149
Sinus tachycardia, right atrial enlargement, short PR interval.

Figure 14–150
Atrial fibrillation, pathological left axis, anterior hemiblock, right bundle branch block.

Figure 14–151
Sinus tachycardia, acute inferior MI.

Figure 14–152
Normal sinus rhythm, left ventricular hypertrophy, left atrial enlargement.

Figure 14–153
Sinus bradycardia with first-degree block, pathological left
   axis, anterior hemiblock.

Figure 14–154
Normal sinus rhythm, right-axis deviation, posterior hemiblock. Voltage criteria for right ventricular hypertrophy.

Figure 14–155
Normal sinus rhythm.

Figure 14–156
Atrial fibrillation, acute inferior MI.

Figure 14–157
Normal sinus rhythm, right bundle branch block.

Figure 14–158
Normal sinus rhythm, pathological left axis, left bundle
   branch block.

Figure 14–159
Normal sinus rhythm, pathological left axis, anterior hemiblock, right bundle branch block.

Figure 14–160
Sinus tachycardia, left ventricular hypertrophy, left atrial
   enlargement.

Figure 14–161
Normal sinus rhythm, left ventricular hypertrophy with
   strain, left atrial enlargement.

Figure 14–162
Sinus tachycardia.

Figure 14–163
Sinus bradycardia.

Figure 14–164
Normal sinus rhythm, pathological left axis, anterior hemiblock, right bundle branch block.

Figure 14–165
Sinus bradycardia with PVC, acute anteroseptal MI.

Figure 14–166
Normal sinus rhythm.

Figure 14–167
Normal sinus rhythm, right-axis deviation, posterior hemiblock, consider right ventricular hypertrophy.

Figure 14–168
Normal sinus rhythm, left ventricular hypertrophy with strain.

Figure 14–169
Normal sinus rhythm, pathological left axis, left bundle
   branch block.

Figure 14–170
Normal sinus rhythm, left-bundle branch block.

Figure 14–171
Normal sinus rhythm, pathological left axis, left bundle
   branch block.

Figure 14–172
Sinus bradycardia, pathological left axis, left bundle branch
   block.

Figure 14–173
Atrial fibrillation with RVR, right-axis posterior hemiblock,
   anterolateral ischemia.

Figure 14–174
Sinus tachycardia, pathological left axis, anterior hemiblock,
   right bundle branch block.

Figure 14–175
Atrial fibrillation with PVCs, right bundle branch block, lateral ischemia.

Figure 14–176
Normal sinus rhythm, right bundle branch block.

Figure 14–177
Normal sinus rhythm with first-degree block, pathological
   left axis, anterior hemiblock, left ventricular hypertrophy.

Figure 14–178
Normal sinus rhythm, pathological left axis, anterior hemiblock.

Figure 14–179
Normal sinus rhythm, left bundle branch block, hyperkalemia.

Figure 14–180
Atrial flutter, left ventricular hypertrophy with strain.

Figure 14–181
Normal sinus rhythm, pathological left axis, anterior hemiblock, right bundle branch block.

Figure 14–182
Normal sinus rhythm, right-axis deviation, posterior hemiblock, right atrial enlargement, consider pulmonary
   embolism (S1-Q3–T3).

Figure 14–183
Normal sinus rhythm.

Figure 14–184
Normal sinus rhythm.

Figure 14–185
Normal sinus rhythm, right-axis deviation, posterior hemiblock.

Figure 14–186
Normal sinus rhythm, right-axis deviation, posterior hemiblock, right bundle branch block.

Figure 14–187
Sinus tachycardia with first-degree block, right bundle branch block.

Figure 14–188
Normal sinus rhythm, right bundle branch block.

Figure 14–189
Normal sinus rhythm, right bundle branch block.

Figure 14–190
Sinus tachycardia with PAC, left atrial enlargement.

Figure 14–191
Sinus tachycardia, pathological left axis, anterior hemiblock, left ventricular hypertrophy with strain.

Figure 14–192
Normal sinus rhythm with PVCs, pathological left axis, anterior hemiblock.

Figure 14–193
Sinus tachycardia, right bundle branch block.

Figure 14–194
Normal sinus rhythm, acute anterior MI, Wellen's Warning in V2 and V3.

Figure 14–195
Sinus bradycardia, right-axis posterior hemiblock, anterolateral ischemia.

Figure 14–196
Sinus bradycardia, acute anteroseptal infarction.

Figure 14–197
Normal sinus rhythm, acute anteroseptal MI.

Figure 14–198
Normal sinus rhythm, anterolateral ischemia.

Figure 14–199
Normal sinus rhythm, right bundle branch block.

Figure 14–200
Normal sinus rhythm, pathological left axis, anterior hemiblock.

Figure 14–201
Atrial fibrillation with RVR, right-axis posterior hemiblock.

Figure 14–202
Normal sinus rhythm with first-degree block, pathological left axis, left bundle branch block, late S wave notching in V4 and V5, ST elevation = 5 mm in V2.

Figure 14–203
Normal sinus rhythm, left ventricular hypertrophy with strain, biatrial enlargement.

Figure 14–204
Normal sinus rhythm, pathological left axis, anterior hemiblock.

Figure 14–205
Atrial fibrillation, pathological left axis, anterior hemiblock.

Figure 14–206
Sinus bradycardia with first-degree block, right bundle branch block, left atrial enlargement.

Figure 14–207
Sinus tachycardia with first-degree block, acute inferior MI.

Figure 14–208
Accelerated idioventricular rhythm.

Figure 14–209
Sinus bradycardia, right bundle branch block.

Figure 14–210
Normal sinus rhythm, inferior ischemia, anterolateral ischemia.

Figure 14–211
Normal sinus rhythm, pathological left axis, anterior hemiblock, left atrial enlargement.

Figure 14–212
Sinus tachycardia, pathological left axis, anterior hemiblock.

Figure 14–213
Normal sinus rhythm.

Figure 14–214
Normal sinus rhythm.

Figure 14–215
Normal sinus rhythm, pathological left axis, left bundle branch block.

Figure 14–216
AV sequential paced rhythm.

Figure 14–217
Normal sinus rhythm, pathological left axis, anterior hemiblock, anteroseptal infarct (probably old).

Figure 14–218
Normal sinus rhythm, right bundle branch block.

Figure 14–219
Normal sinus rhythm, pathological left axis, anterior hemiblock, acute anterolateral MI.

Figure 14–220
Normal sinus rhythm, pathological left axis, anterior hemiblock, acute anteroseptal MI.

Figure 14–221
Sinus tachycardia, right-axis posterior hemiblock.

Figure 14–222
Sinus tachycardia, left bundle branch block (AMI), Q waves in aVL and V5, ST elevation in V5, ST depression in V2 (score of 8 on calculator).

Figure 14–223
Normal sinus rhythm.

Figure 14–224
Normal sinus rhythm with PVCs.

Figure 14–225
Normal sinus rhythm, prolonged QT.

Figure 14–226
Normal sinus rhythm, pathological left axis, anterior hemiblock.

Figure 14–227
Sinus tachycardia, pathological left axis, anterior hemiblock, left ventricular hypertrophy with strain.

Figure 14–228
Normal sinus rhythm, left ventricular hypertrophy, hyperkalemia.

Figure 14–229
Normal sinus rhythm.

Figure 14–230
Normal sinus rhythm.

Figure 14–231
Sinus bradycardia, right-axis deviation, posterior hemiblock, inferior lateral ischemia.

Figure 14–232
Sinus tachycardia, left bundle branch block, left atrial enlargement.

Figure 14–233
Sinus arrhythmia.

Figure 14–234
Normal sinus rhythm, left bundle branch block, right atrial enlargement.

Figure 14–235
Normal sinus rhythm, pathological left axis, left bundle branch block.

Figure 14–236
Normal sinus rhythm with PVC.

Figure 14–237
Normal sinus rhythm, pathological left axis, anterior hemiblock, left ventricular hypertrophy with strain, left atrial enlargement.

Figure 14–238
Normal sinus rhythm, biatrial enlargement.

Figure 14–239
Sinus tachycardia, pathological left axis, anterior hemiblock.

Figure 14–240
Normal sinus rhythm, left bundle branch block, prolonged QT.

Figure 14–241
Sinus bradycardia, pathological left axis, anterior hemiblock.

Figure 14–242
Sinus bradycardia, old septal infarct, left atrial enlargement.

Figure 14–243
Sinus bradycardia with first-degree block.

Figure 14–244
Normal sinus rhythm with a couplet of PVCs, pathological left axis, anterior hemiblock.

Figure 14–245
Sinus tachycardia, left bundle branch block.

Figure 14–246
Normal sinus rhythm, left atrial enlargement.

Figure 14–247
Normal sinus rhythm, acute inferior MI.

Figure 14–248
Sinus arrhythmia, acute inferior infarction.

Figure 14–249
Normal sinus rhythm, left ventricular hypertrophy with strain, left atrial enlargement.

Figure 14–250
Sinus tachycardia, right-axis deviation, posterior hemiblock, right bundle branch block.

Figure 14–251
Sinus tachycardia.

Figure 14–252
Normal sinus rhythm.

Figure 14–253
Normal sinus rhythm, right-axis deviation, posterior hemiblock, right bundle branch block, anterolateral ischemia.

Figure 14–254
Normal sinus rhythm, pathological left axis, anterior hemiblock.

Figure 14–255
Normal sinus rhythm with first-degree block and PVCs, pathological left axis, anterior hemiblock.

Figure 14–256
Normal sinus rhythm, left ventricular hypertrophy, left atrial enlargement.

Figure 14–257
Superventricular tachycardia with aberrancy, right-axis deviation, posterior hemiblock, right bundle branch block.

Figure 14–258
Sinus rhythm with first-degree block, pathological left axis, anterior hemiblock, right bundle branch block, prolonged QT.

Figure 14–259
Sinus rhythm with first-degree block, pathological left axis, anterior hemiblock, inferior subendocardial injury.

Figure 14–260
Sinus rhythm with PACs, digitalis effect (Leads I, V5, and V6).

Figure 14–261
Normal sinus rhythm, right atrial enlargement.

Figure 14–262
Normal sinus rhythm, right bundle branch block, left atrial enlargement.

Figure 14–263
Sinus tachycardia, right bundle branch block, anterolateral ischemia.

Figure 14–264
Atrial fibrillation with RVR.

Figure 14–265
Normal sinus rhythm, pathological left axis, anterior hemiblock, inferolateral ischemia.

Figure 14–266
Normal sinus rhythm, pathological left axis, anterior hemiblock.

Figure 14–267
Normal sinus rhythm, acute inferior infarction.

Figure 14–268
Normal sinus rhythm.

Figure 14–269
Normal sinus rhythm with PVCs, acute inferior infarction.

Figure 14–270
Normal sinus rhythm, left bundle branch block.

Figure 14–271
Sinus tachycardia, left atrial enlargement.

Figure 14–272
Normal sinus rhythm with first-degree block, left atrial enlargement, inferolateral ischemia.

Figure 14–273
Normal sinus rhythm, pathological left axis, anterior hemiblock, right bundle branch block.

Figure 14–274
Sinus tachycardia, pathological left axis, anterior hemiblock, right bundle branch block.

Figure 14–275
Atrial fibrillation with multifocal PVCs, anterolateral subendocardial injury.

Figure 14–276
Normal sinus rhythm, digitalis effect (Leads V6 and V5).

Figure 14–277
Normal sinus rhythm, right-axis deviation, posterior hemiblock, right bundle branch block, acute anteroseptal MI with lateral extension.

Figure 14–278
Normal sinus rhythm with first-degree block, right bundle branch block.

Figure 14–279
Normal sinus rhythm, anterolateral ischemia.

Figure 14–280
Normal sinus rhythm with PACs, pathological left axis, anterior hemiblock, right bundle branch block.

Figure 14–281
Normal sinus rhythm, left ventricular hypertrophy with strain, biatrial enlargement.

Figure 14–282
Normal sinus rhythm, pathological left axis, anterior hemiblock.

Figure 14–283
Sinus bradycardia, anterior ischemia, left atrial enlargement.

Figure 14–284
Normal sinus rhythm, pathological left axis, anterior hemiblock, left ventricular hypertrophy with strain.

Figure 14–285
Normal sinus rhythm.

Figure 14–286
Atrial fibrillation, acute inferior MI.

Figure 14–287
Atrial flutter, right-axis deviation, posterior hemiblock, consider right ventricular hypertrophy.

Figure 14–288
Atrial fibrillation with paced rhythm.

Figure 14–289
Sinus rhythm with first-degree block and PACs, right bundle branch block, anterolateral ischemia.

Figure 14–290
Sinus arrhythmia, pathological left axis, anterior hemiblock, right bundle branch block.

Figure 14–291
Normal sinus rhythm, pathological left axis, anterior hemiblock, right bundle branch block, acute anteroseptal MI with lateral extension.

Figure 14–292
Normal sinus rhythm, left bundle branch block, hyperkalemia.

Figure 14–293
Sinus bradycardia, pathological left axis, left bundle branch block.

Figure 14–294
Atrial fibrillation, pathological left axis, left bundle branch
  block.

Figure 14–295
Atrial fibrillation with RVR, pathological left axis,
  left bundle branch block.

Figure 14–296
Normal sinus rhythm with first-degree block, right bundle
  branch block.

Figure 14–297
Normal sinus rhythm with PVCs, right bundle branch block,
  right atrial enlargement.

Figure 14–298
Normal sinus rhythm, right bundle branch block.

Figure 14–299
Sinus rhythm with PACs, left bundle branch block.

Figure 14–300
Normal sinus rhythm with first-degree block.

Figure 14–301
Normal sinus rhythm, pathological left axis, left bundle
  branch block.

ECG INDEX

How to use this index: Look at the alphabetized list below for a particular ECG characteristic you wish to study. When you find that characteristic, listed beside it are all the figure numbers (in Chapter 14 only) in which that characteristic appears.

A

accelerated idioventricular rhythm, 14-208
anterior MI, 14-44, 14-194
anterolateral MI, 14-80, 14-219, 14-134
anterolateral subendocardial injury, 14-275
anteroseptal MI, 14-16, 14-30, 14-36, 14-105, 14-129, 14-154, 14-196, 14-197, 14-217, 14-220, 14-277, 14-291
atrial enlargement, 14-9, 14-15, 14-19, 14-27, 14-36, 14-47, 14-48, 14-55, 14-77, 14-80, 14-88, 14-99, 14-101, 14-102, 14-108, 14-127, 14-128, 14-137, 14-149, 14-152, 14-160, 14-161, 14-182, 14-190, 14-206, 14-211, 14-232, 14-234, 14-237, 14-242, 14-246, 14-249, 14-256, 14-261, 14-262, 14-271, 14-272, 14-283, 14-297
atrial fibrillation, 14-2, 14-8, 14-14, 14-38, 14-41, 14-53, 14-95, 14-96, 14-109, 14-115, 14-121, 14-150, 14-156, 14-173, 14-175, 14-201, 14-205, 14-264, 14-275, 14-286, 14-288, 14-294, 14-295
atrial flutter, 14-180, 14-287
AV sequential paced rhythm, 14-216

B

biatrial enlargement, 14-10, 14-17, 14-92, 14-93, 14-203, 14-238, 14-281
bundle branch block, left, 14-7, 14-22, 14-23, 14-38, 14-40, 14-50, 14-51, 14-53, 14-54, 14-57, 14-58, 14-61, 14-71, 14-82, 14-89, 14-90, 14-97, 14-98, 14-112, 14-135, 14-136, 14-141, 14-158, 14-169, 14-170, 14-171, 14-172, 14-179, 14-202, 14-215, 14-222, 14-232, 14-234, 14-235, 14-240, 14-245, 14-270, 14-292, 14-293, 14-294, 14-295, 14-299, 14-301
bundle branch block, right, 14-2, 14-3, 14-5, 14-8, 14-13, 14-14, 14-19, 14-20, 14-32, 14-37, 14-39, 14-41, 14-42, 14-59, 14-72, 14-75, 14-83, 14-84, 14-85, 14-95, 14-102, 14-103, 14-106, 14-107, 14-113, 14-114, 14-117, 14-118, 14-119, 14-121, 14-124, 14-131, 14-133, 14-137, 14-138, 14-139, 14-140, 14-150, 14-157, 14-159, 14-164, 14-174, 14-175, 14-176, 14-181, 14-186, 14-187, 14-188, 14-189, 14-193, 14-199, 14-206, 14-209, 14-218, 14-250, 14-253, 14-257, 14-258, 14-262, 14-263, 14-273, 14-274, 14-277, 14-278, 14-280, 14-289, 14-290, 14-291, 14-296, 14-297, 14-298

D

digitalis effect, 14-18, 14-260, 14-276

F

first-degree block, 14-7, 14-24, 14-27, 14-43, 14-44, 14-48, 14-60, 14-66, 14-74, 14-75, 14-103, 14-119, 14-128, 14-130, 14-133, 14-134, 14-135, 14-139, 14-141, 14-153, 14-177, 14-187, 14-202, 14-206, 14-207, 14-243, 14-255, 14-258, 14-259, 14-272, 14-278, 14-289, 14-296, 14-300

H

heart block, complete, with ventricular escape, 14-126
hemiblock, anterior, 14-11, 14-12, 14-14, 14-15, 14-16, 14-20, 14-26, 14-27, 14-28, 14-43, 14-44, 14-45, 14-48, 14-49, 14-59, 14-63, 14-68, 14-73, 14-74, 14-75, 14-76, 14-86, 14-87, 14-88, 14-100, 14-104, 14-105, 14-106, 14-114, 14-119, 14-124, 14-130, 14-133, 14-138, 14-139, 14-150, 14-153, 14-159, 14-164, 14-174, 14-177, 14-178, 14-181, 14-191, 14-192, 14-200, 14-204, 14-205, 14-211, 14-212, 14-217, 14-219, 14-220, 14-226, 14-227, 14-237, 14-239, 14-241, 14-244, 14-254, 14-255, 14-258, 14-259, 14-265, 14-266, 14-273, 14-274, 14-280, 14-282, 14-284, 14-290, 14-291
hemiblock, posterior, 14-2, 14-4, 14-5, 14-8, 14-70, 14-72, 14-79, 14-96, 14-103, 14-121, 14-142, 14-154, 14-167, 14-173, 14-182, 14-185, 14-186, 14-195, 14-201, 14-221, 14-231, 14-250, 14-253, 14-257, 14-277, 14-287
hyperkalemia, 14-141, 14-143, 14-179, 14-228, 14-292
hypokalemia, possible, 14-120, 14-148

I

idioventricular rhythm, accelerated, 14-208
inferior MI, 14-6, 14-14, 14-64, 14-66, 14-70, 14-79, 14-81, 14-109, 14-111, 14-115, 14-129, 14-144, 14-151, 14-156, 14-207, 14-247, 14-248, 14-267, 14-269, 14-286
inferior subendocardial injury, 14-259
inferolateral MI, 14-21, 14-68, 14-70
ischemia, myocardial, 14-10, 14-33, 14-39, 14-60, 14-75, 14-95, 14-121, 14-130, 14-138, 14-139, 14-173, 14-175, 14-195, 14-198, 14-210, 14-231, 14-253, 14-263, 14-265, 14-272, 14-279, 14-283, 14-289

J

junctional escape rhythm, 14-6
junctional rhythm, 14-39

L

lateral infarction, 14-52, 14-65

Subject Index